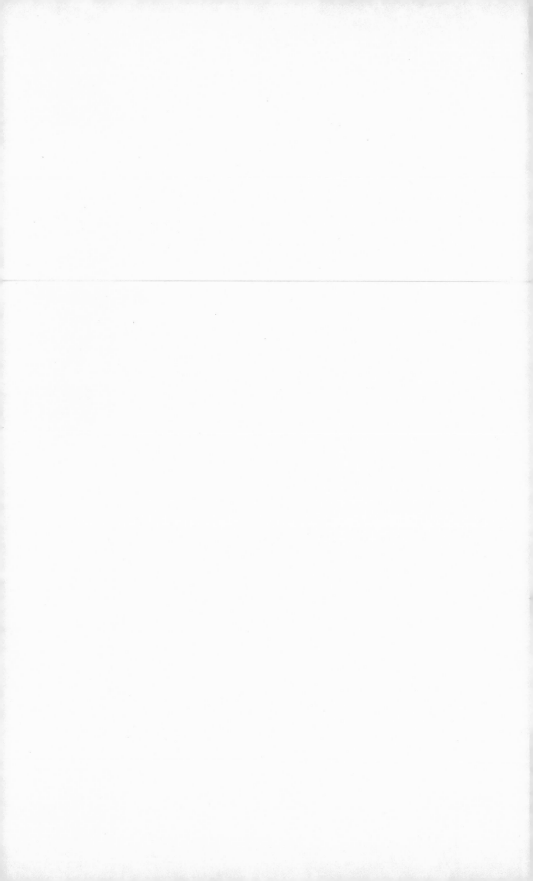

EXTREMES

EXTREMES

Surviving the World's
Harshest Environments

Nick Middleton

Thomas Dunne Books
St. Martin's Press ✻ New York

THOMAS DUNNE BOOKS.
An imprint of St. Martin's Press.

Library of Congress Cataloging-in-Publication Data

www.stmartins.com

ISBN 0-312-34266-7
EAN 978-0312-34266-1

First published in Great Britain under the title
Surviving Extremes: Ice, Jungle, Sand and Swamp
by Channel Four Books an imprint of Pan Macmillan Ltd.

First U.S. Edition: June 2005

10 9 8 7 6 5 4 3 2 1

Contents

Acknowledgements

This book and the accompanying television series could not have been produced without a great deal of effort from a large number of people. Most of these people live in the extreme places visited and appear in these pages. I am very grateful to them all for contributing their time, expertise and assistance so generously.

I would also like to thank the following people:

In Greenland: Rikke Hoegh Olesen, Mads Ole Kristiansen, Mark Soldinger, Guy Pugh, John Quinn, Ian Watts and Simon Tindall.

In Congo: Annaelle Loembe, Patrick Boudjan, Crickette Sanz, Bryan Curran, Fiona Maisels, Louis Sarno, Andrew Palmer, Jacky Houdret, Patrick Boland and Olly Wietzel.

In Niger: Laila Almoghaman Mohamed, Boubacar Hassan, Ramadane Adji Weddey, Mohamed Ixa, Teresa Griffiths, Jonathan Partridge, Paul Paragon, Adrian O'Toole and Dudu Douglas-Hamilton.

In Papua: Akai Chairuddin, Bob Palege, Jack Cox, Father Niko, John Cutts, Will Anderson, Ali Kazimi and Lenny Whitehall.

In Britain: Lorraine Desai, Doreen Montgomery, Mark Carwardine, Margot Eardley, Gordon Faith, Sarah MacDonald and Dusty Miller.

At Keo Films: Zam Baring, Katherine Perry, Claire Hamilton, Ben Roy, Jon Hubbard and Katy Stockdale.

Introduction

A couple of years ago, I embarked on a series of journeys to extreme places. Over the course of twelve months, I managed to visit the coldest, hottest, wettest and driest inhabited places on Earth, a voyage of discovery that took me from Siberia's permafrost to the stifling heat of East Africa's Rift Valley, from the rainswept hills of north-east India to the arid coast of South America. I discovered not only how people managed to live in these places at all, but also why they settled there in the first place and, most intriguing of all, why on Earth they stayed.

Seeing how people coped with the planet's most excessive weather whetted my appetite for extremes. Back in the familiar surroundings of my home in Oxford, I got to thinking about even more remote and inhospitable environments. For my next project, I wanted to go where there are no permanent towns, to places where the habitats are so hostile to humans that survival requires a lifestyle completely in tune with Nature's rhythms. What were the day-to-day challenges of life in places where the natural world still reigns supreme, where the physical geography is so raw and unforgiving that only the toughest survive?

I was looking for extreme environments inhabited by traditional peoples, and I started my quest in the library of the School of Geography and the Environment at Oxford University, where I teach. I had an idea of the sorts of places and people I wanted to investigate, but only after weeks of ploughing through textbooks and research monographs, atlases and maps did I finally decide upon four habitats that I, as an inhabitant of the comfortable mid-latitudes, would find particularly unpleasant. They were ice, jungle, sand and swamp.

For ice, I would go to Greenland, the largest island in the world. Wreathed in a permanent ice sheet, it is home to the Inuit who hunt narwhal, a fabled, tusked whale. These annual hunting expeditions are still conducted from a tiny kayak with a wooden harpoon, an age-old confrontation between man and beast on the edge of fragile sea ice.

My jungle location was not difficult to choose, since I've always longed to venture into the dark tropical forests of the Congo Basin. Here, the real experts in jungle survival are the Biaka pygmies, probably the first inhabitants of Central Africa's forests, whose lifestyle has changed little over several thousand years.

Choosing which of the world's many sandy deserts I should explore was more difficult, because when I wear my academic hat my speciality is hot deserts and I have worked in several. But after some searching I came across mention of a group of Saharan nomads about whom I knew nothing. Members of the Tubu tribe cross the vast expanse of dunes that make up the Ténéré Desert each year to buy dates from the oases to the north.

For swamp, I decided to head for one of the least-explored places on Earth, the Indonesian side of New Guinea, an area known as Papua, to find the Kombai people. They are a remote group, tucked away in a waterlogged land, whose Stone Age way of life has been known to outsiders only since 1980.

Mobility appeared to be a common element to survival in all four environments, each group of people I'd chosen being more or less nomadic. For me, therefore, the timing of my trips was going to be important because I could see that simply finding these people would be a challenge in itself.

The Congo's Biaka and the Kombai of Papua's swamps are both

groups of hunter–gatherers, combing the jungles and marshes for animals and plants to nourish them. But in both cases, periods of roving are punctuated with interludes in more permanent settlements, consisting in the Kombai's case of lofty tree-houses designed to avoid the waterlogged terrain.

Hunting is the only means of survival in northern Greenland, there being no vegetation to speak of in the icy wilderness. The Inuit are the most permanently settled of the four groups I'd be looking into, but their forays into the untamed Arctic often last for weeks on end. Here, the most bountiful time for hunters comes in a short summer window of opportunity, when the sea ice melts and the narwhals arrive. In the Ténéré, where neither hunting nor gathering yields enough sustenance to survive the burning desert sands, the Tubu rely on trading to support their lifestyle. Like the Inuit's quest for their biggest prize, the Tubu's annual trek across the dunes is carefully timed, to coincide with the date harvest in the northern oases.

I was heading for the farthest outposts of habitation, four isolated communities each wandering their own wilderness and adapted to survive their treacherous terrains: the frozen fjords of Greenland, the steaming jungles of Congo, the shifting sands of the Ténéré, and the mosquito-ridden swamps of New Guinea. Having worked out my schedule and renewed my life insurance policy, I was ready to embark on the first of my new journeys to the planet's extremes.

ICE

Greenland

ONE

Kim Petersen was a Dane who worked in Kangerlussuaq at the post office. It was a part-time job. He was ready at any moment to stop sorting mail and don the gear for his other occupation, that of ice-sheet rescue worker. Kim had agreed to take me up on to the ice sheet to show me what was what. He made all the arrangements for the trip. We would have to take supplies for two days, he told me. 'There is no wildlife on the ice,' he said, 'so no food up there.'

Four-fifths of Greenland is permanently buried beneath its blanket of ice. Look at any atlas and you'll see that this giant island, the world's largest, is dominated by white nothingness fringed with tassels of green. People talk about going 'up' on to the ice sheet because it's shaped like a vast flattened dome with a summit more than 3,200 metres above sea level. It's like one enormous mountain, only it's made of frozen water.

No one lives on the ice sheet. A Danish company, Saga Maps, which sports a Viking longship logo, produces detailed sheets of the inhabited parts of Greenland around the edges of the ice. Their cartography adorned the corridor walls of my hotel in Kangerlussuaq, but the greens and browns were edged on almost every sheet with bald white patches depicting permanent ice, marked only with the words IKKE OPMÅLT (UNEXPLORED). They were reminiscent of European explorers' maps of Africa in centuries past, where a lack of knowledge about the dark interior was disguised by an artist's impression of the dangerous creatures that might lurk there. Saga Maps' cartographers indulge in no such frivolities, and not only because romance has been removed from the twenty-first-century map-maker's arsenal. They have learned enough about this icy wilderness to know that animals and plants simply cannot exist in its harsh terrain.

Kim is unusual. Few people venture voluntarily on to the ice sheet. For most Greenlanders, it's just one big no-go area thanks to its bleak and lifeless topography. 'None of the locals, the Inuit, ever go,' he told me as we followed a rough track that led out of Kangerlussuaq towards the ice. 'They know there's nothing there.' We were bouncing along in a strange vehicle that looked like a prefab cabin mounted on wheels. The track followed the sandy bed of a fjord more than 200 metres wide on which Kangerlussuaq is situated. Appropriately enough, its name means 'the big fjord'. Kim told me that the modest stream that wound its way over the sands would become a major river as summer progressed, melting the snow. Snowmelt sometimes built up behind barriers of ice, he said, until the mounting pressure of water burst its frozen dam and a raging torrent would surge down towards Kangerlussuaq. 'On such occasions, half the village must be evacuated', he told me.

The snowmelt season that begins as spring fades into the long Arctic summer is important for many in Greenland, not least for the Inuit who make their living as hunters in this wild country. Prolonged summer days open the way for extended hunting trips and, far to the north, my ultimate destination, great tracts of ocean that spend the winter locked in an icy embrace are briefly liberated as the sea ice thaws, fragments and gradually returns to a liquid state. This is a window of opportunity in which, for a few months, Greenland's hunters can pit their wits against the biggest prize that nature has to offer in this, or any other part of the world: whales. Still caught using a harpoon cast from a tiny kayak, these giants of the deep, while protected elsewhere, continue to be fair game for Inuit hunters using their age-old techniques.

But while the sea ice was my eventual goal, to join a hunt for the fabled narwhal, I thought it would be apt to begin with a sortie on to the ice sheet that so dominates this most northerly of islands. From Kangerlussuaq, the ice was relatively accessible overland thanks to the track we were following. Kim would introduce me to the do's and don'ts of life on the ice and instruct me on how to stay alive in such a barren environment. As we made our way further inland towards the ice, we passed the scattered remains of a crashed aircraft. 'These are the unexpected visitors to the ice sheet,' Kim told me. The twisted metal fragments had lain in this position since 1968, but were so well preserved in Greenland's dry air and low temperatures that they looked much fresher. A US Air Force fighter, en route from North America to Germany, had planned on a refuelling stop at Kanger-lussuaq but poor weather had prevented it from landing. If you're low on fuel over Greenland you have few options. The pilot had used his ejector seat and watched helplessly as his aircraft smashed into Greenland's ancient rocks.

Aeroplanes and helicopters can still get caught short by the unre-liable weather, often a reason for Kim to drop the letters in his sort-ing office and assume his rescue role. Others who venture forth into the ice-bound wilderness do so with a purpose: scientists bent on unlocking the secrets of the ice sheet, and adventurers who hanker after the thrill of crossing the ice by foot or dogsled. I'd come across a Norwegian guy in Kangerlussuaq while he waited at the airport to fly home. He'd been airlifted out from his quest with two friends to ski the 500 kilometres from Kangerlussuaq in the west to Isortoq on the east coast. He and his companions had made thirteen hours a day for six days before growing blisters had forced Richard Larsson to radio for help. Beyond the range of Kim's helicopter, the rescue workers had arrived in a plane fitted with skis. They were forced to cut off the heel from one of Richard's £400 boots.

He looked Nordic and tough and had all the proper gear. A gymnastics teacher, he'd trained on Norway's small ice cap for this expedition, but his first visit to Greenland had ended in ignoble failure. He looked sad and dejected as he limped gingerly on his damaged foot.

'It is as much a mental task as a physical one,' he told me. After four days of skiing, his team had been hit by a whiteout, swirling snow obliterating the horizon and reducing visibility to as low as a metre. 'For a full day, I could see only the front of my skis.' This was when he first realized the deteriorating state of his foot. He had carried on for another forty-eight hours before giving up. His cheeks had been reduced to peeling crusts highlighted by the outline of his sun goggles. He told me his cracked and desiccated lips had been bleeding as he ate his breakfast in hospital that morning.

My encounter with the Norwegian gymnastics teacher had filled me with a respect for the ice, mixed with a minor feeling of trepidation that offset Kim's boyish enthusiasm. Kim never tired of the place and had jumped at the chance of another excursion on to the ice. The ground all around us was rough and marshy, dotted with grey tussocks of grass. Every so often the marsh gave way to frozen lakes that were starting to melt from their shores inward, like winter scabs beginning to heal in the sunlight.

Kim pointed beyond a small lake towards a steep slope where two large creatures stood studying us from the hillside. 'Musk oxen', he said quietly. They were dark, lumbering beasts approximating to cows but more like yaks in appearance. From this distance, their long shaggy coats gave the impression of a couple of medieval jousting horses taking time off to graze the lifeless grass. Their name in Greenlandic, *umimmak*, roughly translates as 'one with a long beard'.

Above us in a perfect blue sky the sun was shining. It had been shining in Kangerlussuaq for a couple of days. Virtually non-stop. Most of Greenland lies inside the Arctic circle, that imaginary ring with the North Pole at its centre enclosing an immense area where the tilt of the Earth on its axis means that in summer the sun never sets and in winter it does not rise for many days on end. This is the land of the midnight sun, and the sunshine in Kangerlussuaq, my point of arrival, had confirmed the stereotype rather nicely. It had been troubling me since I'd first set foot in Greenland. The curtains in my hotel room were ineffective and I'd been experiencing difficulty in sleeping. It wasn't the best preparation for my two-day introduction to ice-sheet survival.

But the ice sheet was already in sight, a great grey blob sitting ponderously on the horizon as if it was taking a breather before swallowing up another hillside like something out of a third-rate horror movie. As we drew closer to its edge, dirty with sediment gouged from the earth below, it took on the appearance of a vast ceramic sculpture. Towering ridges and cracked cliffs twisted and turned in an arrested motion. From the plane flying into Kangerlussuaq, the ice sheet had looked like the rough hide of some ancient ice-age beast and here too it was cracked and textured like the skin of a rhino, a maze of crevices, fractures and crevasses.

Kim sighed. I turned to see him smiling as if at a familiar friend. 'Another month and it will be perfect,' he said. 'Later in the summer, when the snow melts, there are many more cracks and crevasses. Then you can see its true beauty.'

The track was climbing steeply towards the ice edge, where we would leave our Tonka-toy vehicle and climb aboard a snowmobile to continue our journey. Kim momentarily became serious. 'Nick, when we're on the ice you don't walk anywhere unless I say so. There are many crevasses here that you cannot see because of the snow cover.'

It's curious to think that a gigantic blanket of ice like this one, which is second only in size to the Antarctic ice sheet, is created by the accumulation of snowflakes. Admittedly, you need hundreds of thousands of years of snowfall to make an ice sheet several kilometres thick, but it still seemed strange to me that this vast expanse of frozen water that stretches 2,500 kilometres from north to south and 1,300 kilometres across could be produced simply by the gradual build-up of delicate, feathery snow crystals.

But that's how it happens. When snowflakes land they are slowly compacted by the weight of overlying snow and converted into ice crystals interconnected by air spaces. As more and more snowflakes float down to land these ice crystals are compacted further until most of the air spaces are squeezed out and pure ice is formed. In polar regions like Greenland, where the extreme cold means that winter snowfall rarely melts, this process can take a few thousand years. Each year the snow builds up to form layers in the same way that annual tree rings show periods of growth. This is why scientists are such frequent visitors to the ice sheet, because these layers are natural archives, used not only to decipher the age of the ice but also the atmospheric and climatic conditions at the time the snowflakes fell. The scientists study cores drilled down through the ice, and the deeper the core is drilled, the further back in time it probes.

Research on the ice sheet is relatively comfortable. The scientists might sleep in tents but hot meals are served in a heated prefab building. Kim was going to instruct me on how to survive should I ever get caught short, without shelter of any kind. We had finally arrived at the very edge of the ice, a spot known as Camp 660, though 'camp' appeared to exaggerate its importance. There were just a couple of snowmobiles parked haphazardly alongside a rusty shipping container. The name of the place dated from the first survey of the area. The hill we had just climbed was thought to be 660 metres above sea level. 'A better survey says the hill is closer to 580 metres', Kim told me. But the name still stands.

We left our four-wheeled vehicle and proceeded on to the ice riding a snowmobile, a cross between a small boat and a motorcycle to look at, with two skis at the front and a caterpillar arrangement beneath the seats. The terrain here was flatter than before but the snow and ice took on a thousand shapes and textures. In some areas the residual covering of snow had been sculptured into aerodynamic shapes reminiscent of sand dunes, all pointing in the direction of the predominant winds, their crests sparkling into the distance in the late afternoon sunlight. We sped past twinkling sugar-coated ridges and small blue pools fed by constant trickles of meltwater. Here the vista was smooth as only snow can be, there rough and wind-hewn with elongated crystals directing my gaze to some far-off vanishing point.

Half an hour in, we stopped briefly at a metal box the size of a small garden shed wreathed in snow two metres high on one side. I had to dig at the drift where it had been whipped round to almost obscure a door. Inside were two bunk beds, a two-way radio mounted on a small table next to a carton of rations, a box of matches and a stack of candles. I paused briefly to drink in the calm of this oasis in a land of ice. A light wind was blowing outside, little more than a breeze but enough to bring the air temperature down well below zero. It had stung my face and numbed my fingers. And so I realized the importance of shelter, but it struck me that anyone in trouble out here would have to be very lucky or extremely skilled with their compass to come across this haven practically buried by snow.

Kim stopped more frequently after that. He would cut the snow-mobile engine and unfold a thin length of metal more than a metre long, rather like an extended dipstick, and walk in a direction testing the depth of snow with it. 'We need the right conditions,' he kept pronouncing. On the first occasion, I ambled along behind him, and Kim reminded me of the dangers of wandering off his course. 'Only follow me,' he instructed. 'This is very important.'

By the fourth stop, I still hadn't made out what exactly Kim was looking for, but he announced that the place was appropriate for our shelter. 'There are no hidden crevasses here and the depth of snow and ice is good,' he said. 'We cannot dig down too deep so we will have to build up also with snow. We call the shelter an "ice grave".'

Kim returned to the snowmobile to unload two red shovels and a large saw. He took in my questioning look. 'For cutting through the ice,' he said, holding up the saw. 'You dig your own grave and then you lie in it.' He smiled. 'If you don't survive, this will save time later – it is pre-prepared.'

Where we had stopped, a couple of hours inside the rim of the ice sheet, Kim reckoned that we were standing on ice about a kilometre thick. It was nearly 9 p.m. by the time we started to construct our ice grave. Kim began by outlining an elongated coffin-shaped patch with the tip of his saw. 'Why so long?' I wanted to know. 'We will sleep up this end,' he replied, 'and enter through this end.' He walked to the entrance end and drew a much shorter rectangle at right angles to it. 'Steps down here,' he pointed, 'and we make the entrance just big enough to squeeze through. The corner will make sure no wind disturbs our beauty sleep.'

He knelt down and began to saw through the ice at the corner of the coffin-shaped patch, cutting a half-metre square. 'Shovel,' he said, extending his hand, and he levered up the square block that was about 20 centimetres thick. Manoeuvring the hefty slab to one side, Kim sank the shovel into the square hole. 'This powdery snow we must dig out,' he told me, 'about to waist-height. Below that is solid ice on which we can sleep.'

He handed me the saw. 'You cut while I dig.'

I found getting the saw into the ice to be tricky but, once in, cutting it was fairly straightforward, like sawing through reinforced polystyrene. There the resemblance ended, however. The ice block itself was surprisingly heavy and difficult to lift. I levered it up and pushed it over to one side but Kim told me to be careful with the slabs. 'We will need them later', he said, though I couldn't imagine why.

When I'd cut two more blocks, opening up a sizeable gap in the ice, I joined Kim standing in the hole to dig out the powdery snow. The operation was surprisingly hard work, but at least it kept me warm. Since we'd arrived on the ice sheet, and the sun had begun to get low in the sky, the temperature had dropped markedly. I asked Kim when was the last time he'd had to dig one of these for real.

'Four or five years ago,' he said, pausing to rest on his shovel. 'It was just for me, though, so smaller than this one. I got caught in some bad weather. It was changing so frequently, very strong winds, sometimes snowing, then a whiteout with zero visibility. In these conditions it is best to wait for it to blow over because it's changing so much. Often you cannot see where you are going and it is very easy to lose your way, even with a compass. But I was lucky,' he grinned, 'I only had to wait for twelve hours. It could have been two or three days.'

We continued to dig, shovelling the powdery snow out from our growing hole. Kim had set about sawing the next sections and carefully laying the slabs of ice to one side. I asked him why we were keeping them. 'These we will use for the roof', he explained.

After a couple of hours of almost non-stop digging and sawing we had excavated a waist-deep trench some three or four metres long and a metre wide. My wrists were hurting and I had worked up quite a fug inside my thermal jacket. 'Almost there,' I said hopefully. 'Maybe half way,' said Kim.

I'd thought he was joking but he stood in the trench and began to dig into the walls at the sleeping end, hollowing out a person-length cavity for sleeping in. 'The area between us we keep clear – it is room for turning round in.'

Neither of us could pause to rest for very long because a fresh wind was blowing and it soon reminded me that being exposed to the wind when you have a minor sweat going inside your clothes is not a good idea. Our only significant rests came when we drank long draughts from a waterbottle. Despite all the petrified water lying around us, the atmosphere was very dehydrating. 'It is necessary to drink a lot up here because it is so dry,' Kim told me. 'Perhaps five litres a day. You must boil water at night and during the day keep it next to your body so that it does not freeze. Never eat the snow,' he added, 'it is too cold. It might ease a thirst, but it can cause you to have very bad stomach cramps.'

It was midnight, and I was feeling exhausted, by the time we came to the roof. Even the sun had sunk low in the cloudless sky, as if it too could do with a break. We each wrestled one of the ice slabs we had sawn into position, facing each other across our trench, and carefully lowered the top ends to rest on each other forming part of a V-shaped roof. Several ice slabs broke as we continued to build the roof and fresh ones had to be cut, so it took the best part of another hour to complete the operation. It was well after 1 a.m. by the time we dug the steps and covered those too with a roof.

Kim led the way, head first, crawling down the steps and squeezing through the entrance hole. Inside, our ice grave was bright and remarkably comfortable. Although I suspected that lying down anywhere would have been a welcome relief for me, our shelter offered total protection from the wind and was therefore surprisingly warm. Its interior was bathed in an eerie blue light filtered through the ice blocks that made up its roof.

Kim was settled in his sleeping hollow, his head at the entrance end. He smiled and pointed to one of the red shovels that had been left just inside the squeeze hole. 'If you need a shit, you do it on that shovel and throw it out.'

Safely inside our ice grave, I discovered another, less orthodox, use for the saw. Kim had brought some bread and cheese for our rather late evening meal but the bread had frozen solid. The saw was the only implement capable of cutting it.

Just before we finally allowed ourselves to fall into a much-needed sleep, I crawled out of our ice grave to take a leak. It was approaching 3 a.m. and the sun had finally sunk below the horizon, but its light was still strong – it might have been early evening at home. Kim had said that it would rise again in about an hour.

The vista had become a minimalist painting. The two-dimensional icescape was featureless to a sharp horizon cutting the picture in two. A slight variation in the sky's tone faded from darker to lighter blue as my eyes ascended. Sitting in the middle of an otherwise unfathomable atmosphere was a small, radiant three-quarter moon.

TWO

I boarded a Greenlandair flight going northward up the coast, bound for Ilulissat. Kangerlussuaq held no further attractions for me. Although it had celebrated its official designation as a village just a few months before I arrived, it was still little more than an airport. The prefabricated metal boxes that passed as its housing had been there for more than sixty years, but the place had yet to shrug off its temporary feel.

My propeller-driven aircraft crossed an endless landscape of lakes, fjords, ice, snow and rock. The terrain was wild and untamed, a primeval wilderness seemingly untouched by man. The vista fitted the facts: Greenland's rocks are among the oldest on Earth, some no less than 3.7 billion years of age. And each time I gazed out on this timeless scene, I saw the ice sheet sitting like Nature's mentor watching over her domain. She had dispatched portly glaciers to ooze down towards the coast like rivers of white lava gouging canyons as they went, spitting out icebergs into the cobalt waters of the Davis Strait that separates Greenland from Canada's Baffin Island.

This was physical geography in the raw, better than any textbook diagrams I had ever come across. But in numerous other respects, I was forming an impression of Greenland as one big geographical anomaly. Although a territory of Denmark, it has many of the hall-marks of a country in its own right, with a capital city, flag and national language and a government for home rule established in 1979. But its impersonation of a country came up short, at least by the standards I had in my mind. There weren't enough people living there for a start. Although Greenland is the world's largest island – Australia is bigger but is considered a continent – its population is only about 55,000. This is partly because so much of its territory is permanently concealed beneath the ice. People can live only in a sprinkling of settlements around its margins. Put Norway, Sweden and Finland together, double the size and cover with ice, and you get close, but you'd still have to remove most of the people and replace them with polar bears.

However, even in those peripheral bits that are habitable, the trademarks of human occupation were few and far between. The tell-tale indicators available in most other parts of the world are simply absent in Greenland. One aspect that immediately struck me was the lack of roads. The location of a town is betrayed in most places from the air by a network of transport links, but Greenland's settlements are not connected by roads. Journeys between places are by dogsled or snowmobile when there's enough snow on the ground, otherwise people travel by air or by ship. And, of course, the settlements them-selves are small. Nuuk, the capital, is by far the largest 'city'. It has a population of around 13,000. By the time my plane had landed, I realized that I needed to recalibrate my mental images rather swiftly. There was a small hoarding outside the airport at Ilulissat welcoming travellers while proclaiming it to have been 'city of the year' in 1993. Ilulissat has a population of under 4,000 people. We have villages bigger than that in England.

But after Kangerlussuaq, Ilulissat did almost feel like a city with its tarmac roads (some punctuated with street lights), busy harbour and rows of neat wooden houses. Painted in yellows, greens, reds and blues, their pastel shades lent a welcome splash of colour to the bare, snow-patched hillsides. But Ilulissat was still no ordinary city. Clear plastic bags bulging with water intended, I was told, to keep the flies away, hung in the porch of each wooden dwelling. Gardens were there none. It would be pointless to try in such a harsh climate so backyards were put to a more practical use instead, as holding grounds for teams of dogs. They barked, snapped and growled as I walked past, a cacophony of madness and bared teeth as they strained on their three-metre chains. They shared their marshy ranges with rough wooden assemblies that at first I thought were outdoor clothes horses, but turned out to be drying racks for fish and meat. Many were hung with row upon row of small dun-coloured objects that I learned later were filleted halibut, obtained from the city's fish factory, being dried for dog food.

Another oddity hit me at 1 a.m. on my first night. Unable to sleep, thanks once again to inadequate curtains, I set out to roam the streets, thinking I might sneak a glimpse of this mini-city at rest. Not a bit of it. Right outside my hotel, small children were busy making mudpies in the dirt by the roadside as their slightly older brothers and sisters raced up and down on rollerblades. Down the hill a couple more children were playing catch in the bright sunshine with a blue rubber ball. Youths were hanging out by the entrance to the main supermarket, which was at least closed, and an impromptu game of football was in full swing on a patch of waste ground with makeshift goalposts. As long as the sun was shining, it seemed, Ilulissat did not sleep, which all things considered must have been exhausting. I was certainly finding it so. Perhaps the residents of Greenland simply put off sleep until winter. In these parts, the sun sets at the end of November and doesn't show its face again until January.

Most unusual of all was the view. Ilulissat is situated on a bay hemmed in by an island that, according to legend, had been pulled here by two hunters from the south. Considering it an obstacle to their vocation, the two men got so annoyed that one day they climbed into their kayaks, lassoed the island and pulled it northwards to its current position. It wasn't the island that made Ilulissat's panorama unusual but the bay it enclosed. It was a mass of ice, much of it broken into meaningless fragments littered across the seawater, but this icy debris was interposed with more hefty icebergs in a range of shapes and sizes. There were ragged pieces of burnt charcoal, the smooth and aerodynamic curves of ice dunes and blobs of meringue straight off a giant cook's spatula. This in itself was a breathtaking sight but, during the week I stayed in Ilulissat, the view was constantly changing. Ilulissat stands at the snout of one of the world's most productive glaciers, a colossal conveyor belt exuding 20 million tonnes of ice a day – enough to supply New York City with water for a year. The inexorable, lumpen surge averaging a metre an hour provided a kaleidoscope of Arctic variability.

Unsurprisingly, Ilulissat means 'icebergs' in Greenlandic. The name of the large island across the bay, Qeqertarsuaq, means just that, 'large island'. I was growing accustomed to the Inuit penchant for naming places according to their topographical features, and I liked their no-nonsense style.

My reason for visiting Ilulissat was to find a woman who had been recommended as someone who might be willing to teach me the basics of kayaking, a skill I would have to master rapidly if I was to stand a chance of joining a narwhal hunt. But Rikke was busy for the next few days and therefore I had time on my hands. I was so taken with Ilulissat's bay of icebergs that I wanted a closer look, so I took to hanging around the harbour in the hope of persuading one of the many fishing boats to take me out into the bay.

I struck lucky on my second day. Late in the afternoon, I got talking to a guy who was setting out with his father on a seal hunt. Aqqalu looked like a young polar bear, broad in the shoulder but fresh of face, with beady brown eyes that held firm when he looked at me. 'Seals are now coming in from Newfoundland,' he told me, 'so we should have some luck.' His features hinted at a trace of European blood in his Inuit ancestry, an impression Aqqalu confirmed when he described himself as fourth-generation Greenlandic.

I wondered how long we might be out on his boat, a 28-footer, as Aqqalu eased it cautiously past the harbour entrance and into the mass of ice. 'One hour if we're lucky,' he said, 'but it could be much longer. It might be thirty hours before we catch a seal.'

Ominous grinding noises were emanating from below the water level as we nudged past the floating chunks of ice. Although most stood less than a metre above the level of the lapping waves, every schoolboy knows that boats and icebergs don't mix, but since the ice was densely packed for some distance beyond the harbour entrance there was no avoiding it. I assumed that the hull of Aqqalu's boat must be specially reinforced to withstand unavoidable collisions of this sort.

'Has the hull been toughened to deal with all this ice?' I asked, confident of the answer I was about to receive.

'No,' came the reply. 'It is all about glancing off the icebergs. You never hit them head-on.' So I decided not to look until we reached open water.

I knew when this was, because Aqqalu opened up the throttle and we gained speed. Standing in the small cabin alongside him, I breathed a secret sigh of relief. We were heading towards the outer reaches of the bay, where we would turn in towards the bigger icebergs floating in front of the snout of the Ilulissat glacier. Aqqalu told me that the seals often liked to hunt for fish among the icebergs or to take a breather while lying on the ice.

Aqqalu shot his first seal when he was ten years old, but had left the pursuit of wildlife to go to school and college. By the time he had finishing training as a supermarket manager two years earlier, he had made up his mind to become a hunter like his father. Seals were his main quarry, although he couldn't hunt them in February or March when the weather was bad and the days more or less continuous night. Twenty-four-hour sunshine and breaking ice represented the best seal-hunting conditions, but the summer thaw also presented other opportunities among the icebergs: molluscs could be collected along the shoreline and salmon were there to be fished on one of the sounds. Seals have long been a staple of the Inuit huntsman, their meat providing food for both the hunter and his dogs, their skins used for clothing and boots, their sinews as thread and for fishing lines, and in times past their blubber was burnt as fuel. 'We have no cows or sheep here,' Aqqalu told me, 'so we hunt seals instead.'

He would sell today's catch to a kindergarten in Ilulissat or the old people's home. 'Everyone eats seal meat', he said.

Although Aqqalu was following in the time-honoured footsteps of his forebears, he cut a thoroughly modern figure of a hunter with the Global Positioning System and radar fish-finder in his cabin and a mobile phone that played the Hornpipe when it rang. And it wasn't hard for me to understand his choice of career as I savoured the fresh taste of the Arctic air and tracked a gull gliding just above the surface of the glistening water. Greenland had lost a supermarket manager and found another hunter.

It was approaching 11 p.m. by the time we found ourselves among the grown-up icebergs spawned by Ilulissat's colossal glacier. Some reached the height of four-storey buildings, shot through with multiple veins, one for each year of snow falling on the ice sheet far inland. We were floating in the company of giants, and their eerie presence took my breath away.

Most of the icebergs that reach the North Atlantic Ocean are produced, or 'calved', from the major glaciers of West Greenland. Where a glacier meets the ocean, these gigantic lumps of ice are weakened and broken off at the snout by the action of the rising and falling tides. The new icebergs float because glaciers are composed of fresh water which is less dense than seawater.

West Greenland is the iceberg capital of the northern hemisphere. Each as individual as a snowflake, tens of thousands of these majestic behemoths are calved from this coast every year. Although most melt long before they reach the Atlantic, perhaps one in a hundred is large enough to continue its journey into the shipping lanes. There's a good chance that this was the starting point of that most infamous of iceberg disasters, the termination of the supposedly unsinkable *Titanic*.

Stately and timeless they may have looked, but static they clearly weren't. I was startled the first time I heard a deep rumbling that broke the primordial silence, and Aqqalu pointed beyond the leviathan that loomed over us to a far iceberg that was shedding a curved overhang. Minutes later, our boat bobbed on the resultant wave that reminded us to keep our distance.

I hadn't been expecting it, but seal hunting turned out to be a very tiring business. We returned to Ilulissat just after lunch the following day, seventeen hours after setting out in Aqqalu's boat. Most of our time was spent searching among the towering icebergs, the tranquillity of the ocean occasionally broken by the far-off thunder of falling ice.

Merely spotting a seal was difficult. Aqqalu and his father took it in turns to stand motionless on the foredeck, scanning the icy scene with binoculars while the other manned the wheel. Aqqalu would point beyond a bit of floating ice in the distance and whisper, 'There', carefully pick up his rifle and, by the time I thought I might have seen what he was pointing at, it was gone. The seal would pop up its head to survey the scene, take one look at us and duck back under the water.

I was fascinated by the process, although not looking forward to the result. The requirements for seal hunting were infinite patience while being constantly alert. A hunter must have 20-20 vision, lightning reactions and the skills of an Olympic marksman. If you see a bobbing head at 150 metres, you just have time to raise your gun and fire a single shot. Or not.

They tried guessing the direction in which the seal was swimming, and for fifteen minutes the tension was high as the man at the helm would swing the wheel and swerve to stalk the prey. But they had made six sightings and fired five shots, hitting nothing, by 5 a.m. when I left them to it and climbed into my sleeping bag on the rear deck.

Some hours later, I emerged to find that little had changed. I rejoined Aqqalu on the foredeck to scan the water. I was tired and cold and the thrill of the chase had long passed. When he did eventually shoot one as it lay on a low slab of ice minding its own business, I was still able to muster a feeling of sorrow. But it was leavened with respect for the hunter's persistence.

Only when Aqqalu hooked the seal and found a flat sheet of ice on which to skin it did my sense of sadness briefly dominate. I swallowed a sweet-tasting slice of the animal's liver, a traditional delicacy still warm from beneath the blubber, and by then I have to admit that my emotions had been invaded by a selfish feeling of relief that the hunt was over.

Rikke was sunning herself on the small veranda at the back of her house. She had strawberry blonde hair that was nicely complemented by a flash of white teeth when she smiled. It was her suggestion that I start my kayaking career not in the sea but in a small mountain lake not far from her home. For this I was relieved, because I had been half expecting a gung-ho expert who would take great pleasure in throwing me in at the deep end, both literally and metaphorically.

I had never been in a kayak, or a canoe, and I was blissfully ignorant of the difference between the two. Indeed, I didn't need the fingers of one hand to count the number of times I'd even been sailing. Although I'd read that despite its size and apparently flimsy construction, the kayak is among the most sturdy and seaworthy vessels available, I was still rather concerned at the prospect of making my debut in a little-known region of the Arctic Ocean.

And that, of course, would be just the start of it. I'd spent the morning lying in my bed mentally pacing up and down and marvelling at just how stupid a scheme my whole Greenland escapade was. The idea of joining a narwhal hunt was the stuff of *Boy's Own* adventure stories. But I had to face the fact that I was no longer a boy and that one of the supposed benefits of maturity is a clearer understanding of one's personal limitations. Somehow along the way, I seemed to have lost sight of these simple facts.

I was proposing to join a group of hunters, who, like Aqqalu, had probably shot their first seal before puberty and had no doubt learnt to pilot a kayak prior to walking, and paddle into a recently frozen stretch of Arctic Ocean to do battle with a whale up to five metres in length and weighing in at more than a tonne. The whole project seemed impossibly foolhardy. If I hadn't come up with it myself I'd have thought someone was trying to do away with me.

But I had come this far and, by some strange twist of my own fate, I didn't appear to be turning back. As I made my way to Rikke's house on the outskirts of Ilulissat, I clung on to two possible let-out clauses. Perhaps I would turn out to be such a poor kayaker that I would have to downgrade my scheme to some sort of observer's role. This plan had the added advantage of absolving me from direct participation in the hunt. If I'd learned anything from my sortie with Aqqalu, it was that I was sorely out of touch with the hunter–gatherer in me. I hadn't got the staying power, I rather doubted my accuracy as a marksman and I was not confident of my ability to deliver a fatal blow. I just didn't have the stomach for it. It wasn't that I didn't see the difference between hunting for sport and hunting for subsistence, and let's face it, an animal that expires suddenly, courtesy of a bullet through the head, knows little about the matter and must have lived a rather more natural life up to that point than most of the poor dead creatures served up on the average European dinner plate. But when it came down to it, I'd spent too much of my life wandering the supermarket shelves to hold out much hope of becoming a real hunter. And all this was quite apart from the fact that what we were talking about here was a whale, that most hallowed of conservationists' icons.

And, then again, even if I was able to master a kayak, it was unlikely that any self-respecting Inuit would actually let me get close enough to a narwhal to cause it a problem.

Rikke led me to get the kayaks down a set of upturned wooden pallets that served as a ladder of sorts descending the sharp incline in front of her house. They were balanced on top of a drying rack hung with several rows of evil-smelling halibut fillets. When her team of dogs saw her reach up towards the racks, they exploded into an apoplexy of howling and barking.

Supremely unconcerned, Rikke began untying the kayaks, but I was still labouring under the West European delusion that a pack of ferocious dogs doing a good impression of rabid wolves was a situation best avoided. Some of the larger beasts looked as if they might wrench themselves free of their restraining chains at any minute.

'You are quite safe,' Rikke said with her confident smile, 'they are just hungry.' I didn't tell her that this was precisely my reason for hesitating; all I could do was help her to untie the kayaks as quickly as possible.

We carried them up past her house and across a patch of waste ground into the hills behind the city. It was only about 500 metres, but in just that short distance we found ourselves on the edge of the wilderness. A small meltwater lake no more than 25 metres long and less than a dozen wide nestled between two spurs, its glassy surface all but clear of floating ice.

The sight of this tranquil pond, which Rikke assured me was only waist-deep, did wonders for my confidence, further boosted by the drysuit she produced for me to pull on. While a wetsuit is designed to admit a film of water that is warmed by your body heat, it is not much good when the water temperature means that, if you go in, your body would be producing heat for only a few more minutes before you would expire from hypothermia. The much more spacious drysuit is designed for you to pull it on over the warm clothes you are wearing.

Suited up and ready, Rikke gave me a guided tour of my vessel. Made of canvas stretched taut over a wooden frame, it was long and thin and had three holes in it. The largest, central one was for me to sit in. Rikke produced a large canvas sack that she stuffed into the hole and secured around its rim. Should water enter the kayak, it would be held in this bag only. I might get wet, she said, but the kayak would still float. The other two holes were covered with roundels of canvas held in place with tough elastic.

'This is a European kayak,' she told me. 'Traditional Inuit kayaks do not have these other two holes, used for storing things.' She passed me a double-ended oar.

'First I want to introduce you to the biggest fear in kayaking, which is not the water, not the kayak, but yourself. You have to be confident.' She smiled, giving me another flash of her white teeth. 'Remember, the kayak is your friend. The most important thing is to maintain your balance, and this you do with your oar and your hips.' Hers were wiggling in simulation.

'So what we're going to do now is put you into the kayak.' Her hips stopped wiggling and she moved over to her kayak. 'Watch how this is done', she said as she slipped into it, her legs fluidly disappearing into the central hole. The moment was similar to that first time one of your junior school friends shows you how to ride a bicycle. It all looks so easy. But at this point our kayaks were still on dry land and of course this getting-in procedure was going to have to be completed when it was in the water. The ice-cold, mountain-lake water somewhere well inside the Arctic Circle.

'Perhaps you could just do that again,' I suggested, 'maybe a little more slowly.'

Rikke pulled herself out. 'The oar you use to maintain balance,' she explained, pointing out the end of her oar tucked under a leather strap. 'When it is out over the side of the kayak like this' – the oar was pointing out with the flat part of its outer paddle parallel to the ground, a bit like a one-sided stabilizer on a kid's bicycle – 'the kayak cannot tip over this way.'

With her legs on that side of the kayak, she sat on it behind the hole and swung her legs over to slip her feet into the bag. 'You see? It's easy.'

Of course it was easy. These things always are when you know how. Rather less fluidly than Rikke, I managed it in my own kayak. There I sat, pretty happy with my achievement, until I realized how absurd it was to feel elated at simply getting into a kayak while on solid ground.

Then it struck me that getting in was one thing, but getting out was perhaps more important. If I was to roll over while on the water, I wanted to know that I could exit the craft just as rapidly. This wasn't a standard Inuit procedure, of course. If an Inuit rolls over he just keeps on rolling until he pops up on the other side in the manoeuvre known in kayaking circles as an 'Eskimo roll'. I didn't seriously fancy my chances of mastering what is known to be a complex operation in just a single lesson. Hence, for me, learning a speedy way out of my craft was crucial. In fact, without wanting to be overdramatic, my life depended upon it.

I grabbed the rim and lifted myself out. Not too difficult. I got in and out a few more times, just to make sure my first effort wasn't a fluke. Admittedly, this was just a simulation. The real thing, should it happen, and I thought it highly likely, would have to be conducted under rather more harrowing conditions: upside-down in freezing water with the clock ticking rapidly towards the point at which I would drown. But putting that harsh reality aside for a moment, I thought I was ready for the lake.

Not quite. While I was still sitting inside my kayak, Rikke instructed me to push my knees one to each side of it. 'Push them as far as they can go, and then relax. Splayed like this, your knees help you to balance.' I did as I was advised. 'Now wiggle your hips so if you fall to one side you can get back to the right position with some kind of explosive movement of your hips.' I could understand what she was getting at, and despite the fact that we were still on land, I thought I was getting the hang of the wiggling hips.

I was ready to attempt the procedure in the water, and needless to say it was slightly more difficult when the kayak was floating. But with

Rikke standing in the water holding it steady, somehow I managed it. I tried a hip-wiggle and if she hadn't been there I'd have tipped myself straight out again. 'Not so violently', she said, and after a few more less vigorous wiggles I thought I had it. Deep down I was concerned that without a Rikke to help me actually get into the kayak, I might still experience some problems but, for now, I was growing in confidence under her calm assurance.

'Shall we go for a paddle?' she suggested. So we did.

Of course we couldn't go far in the small pool but, once I was inside the damn thing, actually moving was surprisingly straightforward. We silently glided up the pool and I exceeded my expectations by turning round without too much difficulty, taking mental notes while watching Rikke's expert manoeuvres beside me. Kayaking was all hip-wiggling, balance and self-confidence. My hip-wiggles were improving rapidly, and I was becoming more stable by the minute. After a few lengths of the meltwater pool, I felt the early stirrings of belief in my own ability.

If I'd left it at that, I'd no doubt have gone on to become an expert. But Rikke had one more manoeuvre she wanted to put me through. 'Now you should roll over and go in', she said matter of factly. My heart sank. 'Is that really necessary?' I wanted to know. I'd thought I was doing rather well.

'You should do this to see how it feels', she said. In my mind, I thought I had a pretty good idea of how it would feel: cold and wet and potentially very dangerous. But annoyingly I knew she was probably right. As she explained, it was much better to experience the shock of going in for the first time while I was under her watchful eye. So reluctantly, I agreed.

Rikke was once more standing in the water, holding my kayak, and there I was sitting inside it taking deep breaths and pretending to be confident. 'Ready?' she asked. I wasn't, but then I really didn't think I'd ever be.

As if in slow motion the kayak rolled gently over, and abruptly my world was inverted. But it was worse than that because in this upside-down world someone had replaced the crisp mountain air with iced water. Fortunately, I was so focused on exiting the vessel that I hardly registered the rush of freezing liquid all around me. My heart was pumping and my head was saying, 'OK, let's get out of here.' My arms heard the message and coerced my hands into grabbing the kayak's rim to haul my legs out of the hole. Before I knew it, I was back in the world I understood, gasping with the shock of it all and laughing with relief at having survived.

I'd been right. Tipping over felt cold and wet and potentially very dangerous. Perhaps I really was getting the hang of this kayaking business.

THREE

Greenland is a misnomer. It's not green at all. They say that the grass becomes verdant as the summer progresses, but in the early months of the midnight sun the snow and ice melt slowly to reveal tired hummocks of grey vegetation emerging from the long darkness of winter. The only green thing I saw during my month-long stay was a beer can made by Carlsberg.

The island's name started out in life as a con trick and has stuck. Greenland was given its handle by Erik the Red, a tenth-century Norwegian sailor who explored part of its southern coastline and founded the Norse colonies there in 985. To be fair to him, Iceland had already been spoken for, and neither Whiteland nor Greyland has much of a ring to it. But according to the Saga of Erik the Red, he chose the name deliberately to attract settlers.

Probably unbeknown to Erik, the island already had some inhabitants of its own. The first Inuit had arrived some 3,500 years before, crossing from North America. Inuit means 'people', and is what the native inhabitants of the Arctic call themselves in Greenland, Canada and Siberia. When I was at school these people were referred to as Eskimos, but Eskimo is now considered a derogatory term. It has its roots in Athapaskan, one of the indigenous North American languages, and means 'eaters of raw meat'. The Athapaskan view of their northern neighbours was firmly down the line of the nose, although curiously the term Eskimo is still used in Alaska to distinguish this group from other native populations. Greenlanders refer to themselves as *kalaallit*, and they know their island as Kalaallit Nunaat, or 'land of the people'.

It was far up in the northwest of the island, where I was heading, that the first Inuit crossed over from today's Canada. They were probably following in the tracks of the musk ox, lured into a new land by the prospect of fresh hunting grounds. Greenland has long represented the outermost frontier of human settlement. Those first immigrants lived in conditions bordering on the very edge of what people can survive, but they did better than that. They made it their home.

And what a home it was. Up on the ice sheet and out among Ilulissat's icebergs, I'd grown accustomed to being overwhelmed by the scenery of Greenland, but the setting that met me at Qaanaaq airport reached new heights of wonderment. The small town was perched on the edge of an ice fjord, a tract of ocean frozen into an ethereal plain and hemmed in by mountains spliced seamlessly by glaciers glistening in the afternoon sunshine. Studded with giant icebergs fixed in suspended animation, it was a landscape that could exist only in dreams. An enchanted world of make-believe, it made the Grand Canyon look like a drainage ditch and reduced Ayers Rock to the status of a carbuncle. I'd never seen anything like it and I was unlikely ever to see its like again. It was almost enough to make me believe in Santa Claus.

No town could ever be good enough for this prospect fit for an Arctic paradise, but it still seemed as if Qaanaaq hadn't really made much of an effort. The world's most northerly palindrome fell some way short of its fairytale setting. It was the usual assortment of prefabricated wooden housing criss-crossed by cruddy dirt tracks and punctuated with chained teams of gnashing dogs.

The further towards the poles you travel on this planet, the more someone like me has to leave behind the touchstones of Nature I'm familiar with in the mid-latitudes. Ever since leaving Europe I'd been mentally ticking off the geographical frontiers as I'd crossed them. Greenland has no trees to speak of, so I'd passed the treeline even before arriving. Likewise the so-called permafrost line, because all of Greenland's territory consists of perenially frozen ground. I was now several hours' flying time inside the Arctic Circle, though still 1,400 kilometres short of the North Pole. However, unknowingly I'd also crossed another boundary of sorts. I'll call it the sewage line. While Kangerlussuaq and Ilulissat had boasted piped systems, here in Qaanaaq things were a bit different. Failing to secure lodgings in the town's small hotel, I eventually managed to rent a room in the otherwise deserted Danish Meteorological Department's northernmost guesthouse. Denmark has done wonders for Greenland's infrastructure, but a sewage system in Qaanaaq had obviously been beyond them. Like all the other dwellings in town, the guesthouse's toilet facilities consisted of a familiar-looking bowl to sit on, but that's as far as the similarities went.

I could never quite get used to the fact that there was no chain to pull. Its absence always left me with the residual feeling of a job not quite completed. And I admit to a minor sense of horror when I was informed that I had to leave the front door open every other morning at around nine o'clock for the 'shit man' to come and remove my offerings. I never actually met the man, so I can't report on the demeanour of the gentleman with the least-enviable job in Qaanaaq. All I can say is that, a bit like the tooth fairy in reverse, he completed his task on schedule each appointed day. It just wasn't quite the sort of fairy that the scenery had led me to expect.

But for me Qaanaaq offered other possibilities for enchantment, because this was the place from which I hoped to join a narwhal hunt. On my first stroll around town my pulse had been sent racing when I passed the municipal offices sporting on its door a plaque depicting a blue shield with a star at the top. Below the star, its tail fin curled, was a silhouette of the mighty beast outlined in white, its tusk pointing skyward. I was definitely on the right track.

The day after my arrival, a Sunday, I set about my task of finding some hunters who might be prepared to let me tag along. My initial enquiries were unrewarding. A man I approached outside the post office-cum-bank told me I was too early for narwhals. 'Maybe next week', he suggested. I received a similar response from another character who was hanging around outside Qaanaaq's shop. The population here appeared to be predominantly Inuit, whereas further south I'd seen a much larger proportion of European faces. Not many people here spoke English and, although those I approached who could do so had been civil enough, they answered my questions with little interest. Like Aqqalu in Ilulissat, they all had a rather stoical manner. It crossed my mind that their attitude might be a Greenlandic version of the mañana complex, so when one man told me I should find some hunters at a nearby house celebrating their children's confirmation, I headed straight over there.

The streets of Qaanaaq were not only littered and muddy that first day, but they were also pervaded by a powerful and very unpleasant smell. It seemed to follow me round as I walked, a pungent blend of rotting flesh underlain by the delicate aroma of dog. Earlier I'd surreptitiously checked the soles of my boots, but found nothing. As I approached the house that had been pointed out to me, a standard red wooden abode surrounded by a gaggle of people eating and drinking, the stench grew progressively stronger. It hung in the air like an invisible toxic cloud and by the time I came within earshot of the throng of people, the reek was almost overpowering.

I got talking to a middle-aged Danish woman on the edge of the gathering. Behind her, tables were spread with plates of small pancakes and lines of paper cups beside urns of tea and coffee. People were tucking in, the children who had just been confirmed dressed smartly in brightly coloured and intricately patterned sweaters and long white moccasin-type boots, although they extended high up the thigh. Tufts of white fur protruded from their tops.

The kids had just been confirmed into the Lutheran Church, by far the most dominant religion in Greenland thanks to centuries of Danish influence, the woman told me. She was a schoolteacher, she said, not in Qaanaaq but in a smaller village somewhere further to the north. 'Siorapaluk is the northernmost settlement in Greenland', she said without any hint of pride.

I noticed a badge pinned to her jacket depicting the same shield with star and narwhal motif that I'd seen outside the municipal offices. I told her about my mission in Qaanaaq and she confirmed the reactions I'd already received elsewhere in town. The narwhal season had not yet begun because the sea ice had not quite melted sufficiently. But her pupils' fathers, most of whom were hunters, were expecting to set off on their first narwhal hunting trips the following week.

'While you wait, you could visit Siorapaluk,' she suggested. 'There's not much there, but it's a remote community. You might find it interesting.' Then she surprised me by offering to let me stay in her house. 'I'm off to Denmark for the summer holidays, so it's just sitting there empty', she said.

It soon became clear that Eva considered herself to be a bit of a misfit, although she seemed normal enough to me, if unusually kind and trusting. 'I don't really fit in here,' she said, 'but people don't bother me. They recognize that I'm a bit different.' She told me she got away with it because she was the schoolteacher. The Inuit made allowances accordingly.

I was trying to make out precisely in what way she considered herself to be out of the ordinary, when she astonished me by saying, 'I don't like all the dogs.' I just stood there with my mouth open. 'And this smell is terrible,' she grimaced, waving a hand towards a further table that I hadn't noticed until now. It was low and partially obscured by a man kneeling in front of it, apparently eating. I could just make out a red mass on the tabletop, source, it seemed, of the mysterious odour.

'This is as near as I can go', Eva concluded.

'What is it?' I asked.

'A local delicacy,' she said. 'It's a seal stuffed with seabirds, "auks" I think you call them in English.'

Interesting, I thought to myself. But unusual though the ingredients were, I still couldn't decide why their smell was so awful.

'They remove the seal's innards,' Eva went on, 'and replace them with the birds, feathers and all. Then they bury the whole thing for a few months until it's ready.'

'They don't cook it?'

'Oh no, that's why it smells so terrible. The Inuit love it.'

There was movement behind Eva as I stood there taking in this information. An Inuit woman was talking to her and Eva translated. 'She says you are very welcome to try it if you like.'

My mind went into a spin as the horrible realization that I'd been outmanoeuvred dawned on me. 'You don't have to', Eva was saying, but the kind face of the woman behind her was gesturing me towards the bloody table.

'I don't want to deprive anyone of their lunch', I said, trying to sound nonchalant but inside feeling increasingly desperate.

'Don't worry, they'd be happy for you to try', Eva replied.

I had hoped she might have been an ally, but she probably thought she was just trying to be helpful.

'I won't come with you', she added as I moved off, holding my breath, in the direction of the appalling spread.

The table was covered with the bloody remains of rotting flesh and a few flies that were busy gorging themselves on the entrails. Beside it, a cardboard box was filled with a mass of small bones and blood-spattered feathers, the remains of the auks that had filled the seal's cavity. Congealed blood and guts were everywhere, but to my intense relief it seemed that the platter was all but consumed.

'Oh what a shame,' I managed to stutter to a young woman standing behind the low table, 'I was looking forward to sampling some of this.' In my mind it was the most obvious lie I'd told in a long time, but my concentration was focused on other things. I was frantically trying to hold back my intense desire to vomit under the influence of the incredibly powerful stench.

The woman smiled. 'I'm afraid so,' she said with a slight American accent, 'but try some of this.' She patted a large chunk of unidentifiable flesh that sat on the table beside the disembowelled seal carcass.

'Thank you,' I said stupidly, and, 'What is it?' as she cut a thick slice from the lump with a large hunting knife.

'Narwhal liver', she said.

To my eternal credit, I managed to swallow the portion of rotting liver without throwing up, but I've never felt so relieved in all my life as when I thanked her and made my exit from the confirmation party. The incident had left a significant dent in my resolve to join a narwhal hunt.

Later that afternoon, I made my way down to Qaanaaq's shoreline where Eva had told me I should be able to find a dogsled heading for her village of Siorapaluk. It didn't look like a shoreline due to the absence beyond it of sea. The only thing that gave it away was the haphazard line of small boats wrapped in tarpaulins. What lay before me was the sea, of course, it was just that it was frozen solid. The town itself was largely clear of snow and ice, and the meltwater streams had already started trickling down the hillsides to carve their way through Qaanaaq's dirt streets. But here the gravel and grime of the town gave way to a vast ice-covered expanse. I was standing on the edge of the impossibly beautiful view, and although far off the icebergs still looked stunning locked in their wintry procession, up close the scene was blighted by snoozing dog teams, petrified half-eaten seal carcasses and the occasional empty sled.

The one sled that wasn't empty was being loaded by two figures busying themselves with lengths of rope. One was a mountain of a man dressed in dirty blue overalls and Wellington boots. On his head he wore a baseball cap, and as I drew nearer I saw a pair of cat's eyes embroidered above the peak over the words 'No Fear'. I called hello and the big fellow slowly unbent himself to stand upright, turned his head and studied me from beneath the rim of his fearless cap. He had at least half a dozen chins, and it looked as if some of them had slid down under the force of gravity to join his substantial belly.

I asked him if he spoke English. 'Yes,' came the reply, so I asked if he was heading for Siorapaluk. 'Yes,' he said again, so I followed up with the key question. Might there be room for me on his sled? 'Yes,' he said a third time.

For a moment it occurred to me that 'yes' might be his only word of English so I introduced myself and was relieved when he said his name was Hans. 'This is Odaq', he said pointing towards his accomplice, a round-faced man with a broad grin.

I paused to look over his sled. It was a considerable size, a good four metres long, much bigger than any sled I'd seen in England.

'Yeah,' Hans said, 'they're big here.' He was just a man of few words.

The construction was simple, two runners held together by cross slats with two upright pieces of wood at the back end. The whole thing was bound together with lengths of rope. There was not a nail in sight.

'Makes it more flexible,' Hans told me, 'when you go over rough ice.'

An hour or so later, once I'd been back to the Danish Meteorological Department's guesthouse and collected my bag, we eventually pulled out of Qaanaaq and I got an immediate sense of what Hans meant by rough ice. Close to the shore, great domes rose up like metre-high blisters where the sea had frozen over boulders and there was no alternative but to plough straight across a couple of them. Odaq was walking ahead, cracking his whip to keep his team of dogs all pulling more or less in the same direction, while Hans brought up the rear pushing the sled across the uneven terrain.

'Be careful,' Hans called to me as we approached an ice blister at some speed and the whole sled creaked as it nearly tipped over. I hung on for dear life to the ropes lashed across the caribou skin laid over the rear end of the sled.

Hans put on a surprising burst of speed to run alongside the sled and plonk himself down in front of me. 'You OK?'

We were out past the blisters and here the ice was predominantly flat, punctuated only by an occasional small iceberg that was easily avoided. The dogs were gaining speed and Odaq slowed his trot, ran alongside the sled and neatly leapt aboard on one knee in front of us.

'How long to Siorapaluk?' I asked Hans.

'Maybe six, seven hours', he said.

The route we followed took us out into the middle of the ice fjord towards a mountainous mass marked on my map as Herbert Island. Siorapaluk was located around the headland and two fjords further north from Qaanaaq, a distance little more than 50 kilometres as the crow flies, but melting sea ice meant that our course was not exactly a direct one.

The chill wind generated by our speed made me grateful for the padded jacket and trousers I'd brought along for the trip. I was less prepared for the smells that came with it. The dogs in front of us regularly produced unpleasant whiffs as they broke wind or slowed to defecate. The stink was only marginally offset by my admiration for how they managed to have a crap while running. A dog would slow to a scamper and squat down, constantly looking over its shoulder to ensure that it was not going to be rudely interrupted by a sled up its backside as its companions raced on. Each dog's line was roughly three metres long, so it had about six metres' worth to complete the operation: three to bring it level with the sled and another three as the sled passed it.

It was not long before I could distinguish the experienced dogs from a couple of novices because the novices often failed to realize that if they didn't complete before their six metres was up they would be dragged unceremoniously along by their harness. The first time this happened, the dog in question yelped piteously and I assumed Odaq would stop to enable it to regain its footing. Not so. The sled just kept speeding along and the dog was dragged some distance before finding its feet once more and rejoining the team.

Despite the fact that I'd been fearful of these menacing creatures since first coming across them, I couldn't help but sympathize when I saw them in this distressing situation. But dogs in Greenland are not pets and there is no quarter given.

We had travelled for a couple of hours in the bright sunlight towards Herbert Island before Hans pointed into the distance beyond it where a bank of cloud sat cotton-wool-like on the horizon.

'Maybe fog', he said.

As we continued, the cloud bank moved slowly in towards us, engulfing all before it, until we found ourselves surrounded by a damp and clammy fog. It clung to everything like a cold sweat. Odaq had put his foot out to drag on the ice, slowing our progress until the dogs stopped to look round, their tongues long and panting.

'We have to wait till it clears', Hans said. With visibility this bad, it would be easy to stray on to thin ice, he explained.

We had stopped in the lee of a large iceberg, but Odaq made the dogs pull us another ten metres away before finally allowing them to rest. 'Dangerous', he said, pointing at the towering block of ice and waving his arm to mimic it toppling over or shedding some of its mass.

The dogs settled down, some grabbing the opportunity to scrape snow with their jaws to quench their thirst. Others rolled over in the snow like puppies before curling up and shutting their eyes. I asked Hans how long he thought we'd have to wait.

'You can never tell up here. The weather forecast said today will be sunny but they're often wrong. They don't really know.'

Odaq busied himself untying and retying the dogs' lines. We'd had to stop several times already when a dog got tangled. They were adept at skipping over the ropes as they ran, jockeying for position, but it was inevitable with ten of them that occasionally one would be unable to unscramble itself from the mass of lines that ran from the front of the sled. Odaq would bring us to a halt and grab one of the ropes to haul a squealing dog backwards or up in the air to disentangle its leg. At first I'd thought this act might represent a kindness towards the dog, even though Odaq's help was rough-handed. But when I saw the dog being dragged along after failing to relieve itself in time, I realized that stopping to unravel tangled ropes simply constituted good dog team management. A dog with a broken leg was no good to anyone.

'Maybe we could go fishing', Hans suggested.

From the sled he produced a small shovel and a long stick with a pointed metal end and trudged off at right angles to the iceberg. 'We can dig a hole and drop a line through it.'

It took us half an hour to hack a small hole through the ice which was more than a metre thick. When we were through, Hans left me to widen the hole while he rummaged around in the large canvas sack that hung from the rear end of our sled to find a couple of fishing lines with large hooks on their ends.

He waddled back to the hole, handed me a line and we dropped them through the ice. He hadn't baited the hooks. 'No need', he said. After unravelling what must have been a good 50 metres, we set to, rhythmically pulling the line up with a sharp swing of the arm to attract the fish before letting it down again.

'What are we fishing for?' I asked him.

'Polar cod', he said.

'Are they good to eat?'

'They taste like fish', he told me.

After quarter of an hour without luck, we let out some more line. The sea below us was 200–300 metres deep, Hans thought, and the trick was to find the level of a shoal. Within the next five minutes we had caught three. Odaq set up a small gas stove and we boiled them. They did indeed taste like fish.

FOUR

It was two in the morning by the time we reached Siorapaluk, but after a few weeks in Greenland I wasn't surprised to see a couple of small girls playing catch down by the waterside. The fog had begun to clear soon after our fish supper and we had continued on our way towards Herbert Island. As we passed its soaring peaks our progress was slowed when Hans announced that we'd come upon 'bad ice', a phrase that for a time became our mantra as we stopped frequently for Hans and Odaq to walk ahead and test it with their metal-pointed poles. The bad ice forced us to take long curving detours, sometimes backtracking before we found a dependable stretch.

Siorapaluk looked out over a fjord where the ice had largely melted to leave white fragments littered across the glassy sea like smashed pieces of polystyrene. The settlement clung to a steep fan of sediment deposited by the meltwater streams that flowed down from its mountainous backdrop. This was as far north as anyone lived in Greenland and the place was pervaded with a sense of clinging to the edge of Nature's void.

Most of its inhabitants were hunters, Eva had told me, and evidence of their work was all around. Each of the small collection of wooden houses was twinned with a drying platform, most laden with amorphous lumps of blubber and meat, sometimes accompanied by a walrus tusk or set of antlers. The ground here was still largely covered with snow and ice, but abandoned bones and partially decomposed sections of skeleton poked through from the frozen substrate. In areas where the snow had gone, the sodden earth had become a concoction of thawing putrid flesh, blubber and dog's muck. It was an indestructible, sticky gunk that quickly became moulded to the soles of my boots. I didn't warm to the place. It was as if the whole settlement was oozing with mud and crawling with crud. Even the dog teams, which sniffed at me as I passed, seemed more menacing here. It was like a village of death.

This initial impression was confirmed when I moved to check out a small boat tied up at a section of bank where the sea ice had completely melted. Four hunters were unloading the fruits of an expedition. Great chunks of flesh and blubber were being hurled ashore from the boat. I counted the severed heads of seven walruses, their eyes closed in eternal rest, stiff whiskers sprouting over their ivory tusks. Hans pointed out that the hunters had also caught a small beluga whale. When I looked where he was pointing, I could just recognize its tail fin sitting among the morass of bloody flesh.

But further up the hill was the most disturbing casualty of all. Suspended from one of the rough wooden drying platforms, hanging by its neck, was a dead dog. Its mouth open and back legs barely touching the ground, its front paws hung limp as if it had been caught in the act of jumping up to catch a morsel thrown by its owner.

After the initial shock of seeing the dog, my mind began to race with questions. 'Maybe it was too old to work, or got sick', Hans offered by way of explanation. I'd become accustomed to the idea that these animals were not pets, but I hadn't taken the next logical step of wondering what became of a working dog when its working life was over. It didn't look as if it had been hanging from the drying platform for very long, but why, I asked Hans, had they left it hanging there at all? It was almost like a warning to other dogs. 'They probably gonna skin it tomorrow,' he said, 'otherwise they just throw it away in the sea. They'll use the hide for something.'

Hans told me they hanged their old dogs in Siorapaluk because local wildlife law forbade them from using guns. The village was close to a large nesting ground for seabirds and they weren't to be disturbed. The following week I was offered other explanations for not using a gun on a dog that had outlived its usefulness. Another hunter told me he wouldn't shoot a dog because bullets were expensive. But the most bizarre explanation of all came from one of the narwhal hunters. He'd already told me that he couldn't live without his dogs and I'd been touched by this mutual sense of reliance between man and beast. But I soon realized the danger of imposing my own sentimentality where it wasn't appropriate. When I asked him how he dispatched those that had outlived their usefulness he too said he hanged them. When I asked why, he said, 'We don't shoot our friends.'

After all the fatalities, I passed an unsettled night in Eva's house, a place that fitted her status as a bit of an oddity in Siorapaluk. From the outside, it looked like all the other prefab sheds, but its interior revealed a Scandinavian ideal home with polished wood floors, colourful rugs and pictures of living wildlife on the walls. I awoke early wanting to leave town as quickly as possible but, having travelled this far, I thought I should at least look up one of Eva's friends, particularly since he was currently residing in a cabin a half-hour's walk outside the village. From Eva's description, Ikuo sounded like another misfit. For a start he was Japanese, not a nationality I'd expected to find represented in Greenland's northernmost settlement. Apparently he had lived here for thirty years and had become a respected hunter.

I found him sitting outside his cabin at the foot of a steep boulder-strewn slope just along the coast, drinking tea in the morning sunshine. He wore an ancient grey anorak, baggy trousers and stout hiking boots. His smile was broad and mischievous from beneath a battered grey cap with woollen ear-warming flaps turned up at the sides. The view from his cabin looked out over a translucent sea scattered with broken fragments of virgin-white ice. The water was calm and the atmosphere clean, its early morning edge now gone in the sun's growing warmth. Silence reigned but for the shrill chatter of small black and white birds as they wheeled and turned en masse in the air above us.

'Little auks,' Ikuo said, squinting as he looked up into the sun's glare, 'I think they can also be called "dovekies". They have their homes here. Very good to eat.' Little auks have long been an important food source for northwest Greenland's Inuit, and Eva had told me that Ikuo was a bit of an expert at catching them. His long-handled net, rather like a butterfly net but with a larger mesh, rested against the cabin behind him. I'd seen similar specimens leaning against the buildings all over Siorapaluk the night before.

With his thirty years of experience, I assumed Ikuo must be a very skilled hunter by now, but when I suggested this, he answered modestly. 'Not really,' he said, 'I am still learning. After ten, maybe fifteen years, I could live as a hunter, but every day I am still learning.'

Like all the local hunters, he hunted seal, walrus, narwhal and the occasional polar bear but this morning his quarry was auk. He told me they were best caught in the morning as they returned from their feeding grounds out past Herbert Island where they dined on plankton. 'Then they are flying and fat after eating. This is the best time for catching,' he said. On a good day he might catch 400 of the chubby little birds, but his personal best was a staggering 900 in just 4 hours. 'But other times only ten,' he said. 'It depends. There are many different factors. Good wind is important so they all fly in the same direction. Also they must not see you, so you must hide.'

We had begun to climb the rocky slope behind his cabin, Ikuo leading the way carrying his net, a canvas bag slung over his shoulder for his catch. Tens of thousands of auks were all round us, perched on every rock, gathered in groups on patches of snow, and swirling high above us like swarms of mosquitoes squawking and chattering as they flew.

Ikuo told me that biologists reckoned there were between 20 and 100 million of these birds along this northwestern coastline. 'This is a guess only,' he emphasized, 'but certainly there are many.' He stopped as a flock of auks nearby, disturbed by our passing, rose up from a snowpatch and swept down the mountain like an avian avalanche. He threw his head back and laughed loudly. 'Greenpeace people need not be worried,' he said. 'There are many animals. Also, few hunters.'

As we scrambled further up the steep scree, I asked Ikuo what had brought him to Greenland in the first place. 'Oh, this is very complicated,' he told me. He walked on. This was clearly to be his only comment on the matter, but he did tell me that he came originally from near Tokyo, 'a terrible town', as he described it. He had been back to Japan just twice in the last thirty years. 'I don't like it,' he said. 'I have to pass through Tokyo to get to my father's house. Those people in central Tokyo, ooh they are like a monster. It is quite dangerous for me. My life is much better here with Nature.'

Ikuo had stopped, announcing that this might be a good place from which to try. He pulled his canvas bag over his shoulder and placed it between two rocks as we made ourselves as comfortable as possible, facing out to sea among the ragged boulders. The net was resting on a rock below as he held the long handle, bent slightly under its own weight, down in front of him. A few auks flew across our line of vision and Ikuo flipped the net up, but the birds were beyond its range. 'Too high', he muttered, and then he immediately launched the net up into the sky once more, this time snatching an auk in mid-flight.

Hand over hand, he pulled the net towards him to get at the struggling bird, carefully extracting it from the net, its wings now caught in his grip. The little auk, scarcely bigger than a starling, sat snugly in his hand, a look of puzzlement in its beady eyes. Then Ikuo ruffled the bird's downy feathers, pushing his thumb into its chest just below one of its wings. In just a second or two, the auk hung limply in his hand and he dropped it on to a small patch of snow among the rocks beside him. He let out the net and looked back up into the sky.

I was amazed at how easily he had dispatched the auk and was about to ask him how he'd done it when he whipped the net into the air once more and brought it back down with another one. 'How do you kill it so quickly?' I asked as Ikuo pulled the net towards him.

'You find its heart and press,' he explained as he repeated the procedure, killing the bird swiftly, as if turning off a switch. He dropped it down beside the first one.

I picked it up to ruffle its plumage, silky soft black and white feathers, and returned it to the growing pile. Ikuo glanced down and told me to keep them out of the sun. 'Not too hot,' he told me, 'to keep them fresh.'

Over the next twenty minutes the pile of little auks between us grew steadily and, having watched Ikuo, I asked if I might have a go. He grinned and handed me the net.

It was not as easy as it looked. My first few efforts were woefully inaccurate. 'Always too early,' Ikuo told me. 'The bird must be above you before you launch the net. Otherwise they see your movement and avoid it.' I tried again, but my timing was still poor. Ikuo laughed. 'After they have passed,' he said again, 'always after.' But try as I might, I continued to fail miserably.

After about an hour, we gave up and picked our way back down across the scree towards Ikuo's cabin. Our catch must have numbered about thirty birds, not a great total by Ikuo's standards, but we had started late and some of the time had been wasted with my inept efforts. But we had enough for a late breakfast. 'The easiest and most tasty way to cook them is just boil up, in slightly salty water. You boil for more than thirty minutes,' Ikuo told me. 'But today I think we can fry these. I have some dried onions. They are also very tasty with onions.'

After my experience with the stuffed seal in Qaanaaq, I was concerned that Ikuo might not pluck the birds before frying them. I needn't have worried because in keeping with his efficient way of killing the auks, he showed me an amazingly proficient way of dealing with its feathers.

Ikuo grabbed a half-plank of wood from beside his cabin and wedged it in between two of the planks that made up the sort of platform on which he had been drinking tea when I'd arrived earlier. In the upstanding half plank, two nails protruded a centimetre or so apart. 'For the head,' Ikuo said as he picked an auk from his sack and fitted the bird's neck between the nails.

'So,' he said, 'with your knife...' he opened the blade of a penknife that he'd pulled from his pocket, 'you remove one wing.' Holding the bird in one hand, he skilfully nicked the wing at its shoulder and twisted it off.

'And then... like so.' With the bird secured by its head, he pulled the remaining wing sharply downwards and the bird's entire body cavity popped out, leaving its plumage hanging from its head. Ikuo sliced the wing off the small piece of meat and dropped it. He was left holding a perfect little breast with not a feather on it. It had been faster than unwrapping it from cellophane.

Part of me had seen enough of the consequences of hunting by the time I returned to Qaanaaq and resumed my quest for a narwhal hunt to join. I hadn't been disturbed by the auk-netting, and the fruits of my outing with Ikuo had tasted excellent fried with onions, but the horrors of Siorapaluk still weighed heavily on my mind. Hunting was a way of life here, and I understood that my problem with its results was simply a matter of conditioning. I wasn't familiar with the process of butchery; it was the blood and guts that perturbed me, not so much the killing itself and certainly not the meat that came afterwards, although the partially decomposed seal stuffed with auks had certainly tested my resolve.

Yet in my mind I kept returning to the ultimate goal of my projected final hunt. I badly wanted to see a narwhal, the whale with the spiralling tusk which until the early seventeenth century was thought in Europe to be the horn of the legendary unicorn. Priceless objects made from the horn are still dotted around the palaces and museums of Europe. Several of the treasures of the Habsburg empire are made from *ainkhürn*, an ancient dialect word for *einhorn* – the unicorn – including the sceptre itself, symbol of its imperial power and authority. Queen Elizabeth I had the Horn of Windsor valued at £10,000, a sum that in the sixteenth century would have bought you a castle and a large estate to go with it. Denmark even has a Unicorn Throne, its legs and armrests made entirely from narwhal horns. But just to satisfy this curiosity to see one of these whales, was I really prepared for the reality, still a harsh reality in my mind, of being witness to an almost mythical creature's demise?

Greenlanders have a small quota of whales that they are allowed to kill annually and the method used is centuries old: a hunt with a harpoon, from a kayak. It would be a spectacle beyond compare, an age-old confrontation between man and beast. The whole existence of the Inuit here in this northwesternmost corner of Greenland had long depended on the narwhal, a creature hunted from some time in June for a season that lasted just a few months. From the time the sea ice began to break up on the edge of Qaanaaq's fjord to the moment it returned to its frozen state was a small window of opportunity quickly closed. Hans had told me that when the sea ice formed again around 10 to 15 October, it did so very fast. He said he once saw some hunters go out to sea from Qaanaaq in a boat and by the evening they couldn't get back because the ice was already too thick around the shoreline. They were forced to leave their boat and walk home.

The meat of a whale lasted a hunter's family much longer than that from any other animal, and the narwhal's vitamin-rich skin, the *muktuk* said to taste like hazelnuts, was a cherished delicacy. This had always been the case. In times past, in a land with no trees, where even a small piece of driftwood was a rare and precious commodity, its tusk had taken the place of wood. The Inuit used the spiralled tusks as tent poles, fashioned them into arrows and harpoons, and carved them to make runners for their sleds. Even in the early twentieth century, narwhal tusks were still used as handles for auk nets. Today, when wood can be imported, the tusk remains an esteemed prize with a high commercial value. When hunters set out in their kayaks – never alone, for most cannot swim and may need help if they capsize, should their Eskimo roll not work – it is the one whose harpoon is first to stick who carries off this, the most precious trophy. The cash received from its sale is critical to help pay the rent, buy heating oil, ammunition and clothing at the village shop.

I'd become doubtful of my desire to see a narwhal caught when I'd first returned to Qaanaaq. However, as the days dragged on, and my enquiries about joining a hunt seemed to be getting me nowhere, my craving to get out on to the frozen ocean once more, indeed to put my new-found kayaking skills to the ultimate test, had been rekindled. I couldn't win. When I assumed that joining a hunt was just a formality, my courage began to desert me, but as the possibility looked increasingly remote, I only wanted it more.

All these deliberations remained academic until one morning when I was woken by a hammering at the door of the Danish Meteorological Department's guesthouse. For a confused moment, as I tumbled out of bed, I assumed I'd got my days confused and my visitor was the shit man come to empty my toilet. When I opened the door, I was met by the face of Hans looking intently at my bare legs from beneath the peak of his 'No Fear' baseball cap.

'I found you some hunters,' he told me. 'They're leaving to catch narwhal today. You better get ready.'

FIVE

The big fellow marched me across town to get kitted out. The hunters would spend up to a week out on the sea ice, he told me, and it could become very cold, so I needed some proper gear. We crossed a wooden bridge over a small gully that in the time I'd been in Siorapaluk had already grown from a trickle to a sizeable meltwater stream, and arrived at the house of Hans's friend. He would lend me the clothes necessary for my trip. He had a store of such things in his garage.

Hans's friend was also named Hans but he was a much smaller version. His garage, like garages the world over, was packed to the roof with stuff. It was like a treasure trove of Arctic paraphernalia. Piles of fleeces and hides rubbed shoulders with cardboard boxes full of old magazines and lengths of wood in various shapes. An assortment of rifles stood in one corner while up above a collection of wooden harpoons was balanced between the rafters. A musk ox skull stared blindly out at me from one of the shelves as little Hans disappeared into the back of his garage. He returned a moment later carrying a pair of trousers. These were no ordinary trousers. They were three-quarter length and voluminous, a bit like a clown's outfit with a pair of braces attached at the waist. Woolly and white, they were made of polar bearskin.

'These should fit,' said little Hans, handing them to me, 'and you'll need some *kamiks* too.' He bent down and removed a kayak oar from the top of a wooden box, opened the box and produced a pair of sealskin boots. They were also white and came up to the knee. He placed them at my feet as I struggled into the polar bearskin trousers.

'Now just something for your top,' he said, disappearing again into the dark recesses of his garage to make rummaging sounds behind me. I had the bearskin trousers on and took a perch on a jerrycan to grapple with the *kamiks*.

'Warm, eh?' said big Hans, gesturing at my trousers. They were, extremely warm.

The *kamiks* were stiff yet supple at the same time. 'You know how they make them soft?' big Hans asked rhetorically. 'Women bite the leather with their teeth to make them that way.' The boots came with insoles of felt and an inner bearskin sock. They were incredibly soft inside and immediately very warm.

Little Hans emerged once more with a heavy anorak-type top in pale blue. Beneath the blue cotton it was made from sheepskin. I pulled it over my head and little Hans handed me a pair of leather mittens lined with fur. 'That's it,' he said. 'I think you're ready now.'

I worked up quite a sweat inside my new outfit while walking down to the shoreline, where big Hans introduced me to a party of five hunters busy getting their dogsleds ready, but by the time we set off, and the wind began to whip past me as we sped across the sea ice, I was grateful for all the animal skins and fur. I was riding on a sled with a hunter named Mads Ole, a wiry individual who told me he came originally from the far south of Greenland where his grandfather used to herd sheep. His family had moved to Qaanaaq when he was a boy.

We were heading out along a similar route to the one I had travelled with Hans and Odaq, in the direction of Herbert Island. But this time we skirted to the south of the island, its steep slopes plunging down to the petrified sea, out towards the mouth of the ice fjord. The first time we stopped for Mads Ole to unravel one of his tangled dogs, he hesitated before returning to the sled and told me the conditions weren't the best for our hunt. 'The wind is towards us,' he said. 'It is better if it blows out to sea. That way it clears the broken sea ice.' The breeze was so light I hadn't even noticed it.

We had started in convoy, a procession of sleds each with a kayak lashed to its length, but after an hour or so Mads Ole and I were lagging far behind the others. 'I don't like this slow motion', he complained. The dog team wasn't his, he told me. He had had to borrow his father's team because some of his dogs were sick. 'My father he likes to go slowly, slowly. My real dogs take maybe three hours to get there, but these dogs: six hours.'

Mads Ole said he always trained his dogs up in the mountains, the best place if you wanted them to be fast. But his father never did. Worse from our point of view, his father's dogs had been fed the day before. That always made them slow.

The other hunters stopped and waited for us to catch up so we were more or less altogether again when we finally arrived at the edge of the ice. A light wind was still blowing up the fjord, so although the sea ice stopped abruptly at a clean edge, which Mads Ole and his colleagues tested with their spikes to ascertain its strength, we were not met by open sea but large fragments of drifting ice clogging up the water. They continued on towards the horizon as far as I could see.

I could appreciate that if the wind changed direction, to blow down the fjord, these ice chunks would be dispersed. As it was, there were only a few gaps left, like ponds between the icy debris. The largest of these was perhaps 50 metres across and 30 wide, but others were just a few metres across.

'Do you think the wind will change direction?' I asked Mads Ole.

'Maybe', he said.

The hunters secured their dogs some distance back from the ice edge, each using a sharp knife to excavate two small holes angled diagonally towards each other some 10 centimetres apart to leave a tiny ice bridge on which a rope could be tied. Small thought it was, each of these tiny ice bridges was strong enough to hold a half dozen dogs. We set about making camp, the sleds acting as platforms on which we slept with tents pitched over them. Mads Ole pushed his alongside that of Frank, one of the other hunters, and the two sleds had more than enough room for the three of us to sleep on.

I stood looking out to sea, surveying the scene across the mass of ice. To my right were the slopes of Herbert Island riddled by gullies clogged with tendrils of ice. Far off to my left was the southern shore of the ice fjord, a procession of rounded mountains partitioned by sun-spangled glaciers. And behind me sat the frozen plain we had just crossed, a snow-white tract punctuated by its giant icebergs and bordered by the mountains that backed the now invisible town of Qaanaaq. I felt as if I was standing on the very edge of the world.

And so began up to a week of waiting. The hunters placed their kayaks on the ice edge, positioning them by the largest debris-rimmed pond. I had trouble believing any narwhals would appear in such a small opening, although Mads Ole assured me it was possible. But we had few options. I could see that to hike across the ice fragments towards distant open water would be too dangerous, particularly while carrying a kayak. All we could do was wait and be ready, while hoping the wind would change and ease the ice fragments out to sea.

The narrow top of each sleek kayak was loaded with a harpoon and coil of line attached to a float. I watched as Mads Ole blew up his hunting bladder, a whole clean-shaven sealskin gradually growing to become a bizarre parody of a child's inflatable toy. When it was fully puffed up, he slipped a wooden peg into the blow hole and showed me that the float was secured by a line to the harpoon's detachable point, a metal blade held in a setting carved from a walrus tusk. On impact, the harpoon point disengages from the wooden shaft, he told me, and the inflated sealskin float drags behind and tires the whale. When the animal resurfaces, other hunters move in with their harpoons to speed the kill. Since the harpoon had to be thrown from a sitting position, a special detachable piece of wood was secured half-way along its shaft with an ivory pin. The hunter holds this wooden slab and throws it with a flicking motion to help propel the weapon through the air.

Their hunting equipment prepared, checked and rechecked, the hunters took it in turns to stand and look through their binoculars, surveying the scene for signs of activity. Several hundred metres away along the ice edge, towards the fjord's southern shore, a mini-iceberg just a metre high provided an observation platform. Someone stood on it round the clock because narwhals might appear at any hour of the day or night. I took off my wristwatch and buried it in my bag on the first day. Its time had often been little more than a confusion during the previous few weeks, but now that all I could do was wait, it seemed supremely inconsequential.

For me the first twenty-four hours were tinged with a tense expectancy, heightened by the need for quiet because the whales would be put off by any loud noise or sharp movement. 'Always still, always ready,' Mads Ole told me in hushed tones. 'No loudness. Now we must follow hunters' rules.' The need for silence meant we became attuned to the stillness of the ice, a calm broken only by the call of an ivory gull or the barely audible sound of sea ice fragments grinding as they were gently moved by an otherwise imperceptible current.

Day blended into night and night into day. I slept fitfully, snatch-ing at periods of rest lest the narwhals should appear while I was dozing. I'd let go of time but without my watch I came to recognize Nature's smaller diurnal rhythms: the height of the sun in the Arctic sky, the stream of little auks returning from their nightly feeding grounds. We fired up the stoves when we were thirsty, making tea or coffee with melted snow scraped from the ice, and ate when we were hungry, the hunters taking it in turns to boil seal meat which we ate in a rich broth.

As time lost its value, so space also took on a new meaning. Distances were difficult to estimate out on the sea ice, and I'd already seen Arctic mirages over the ice sheet, phantom pools of water that I'd more commonly associated with hot deserts. But I was wholly unprepared for a more extraordinary type of mirage that I learned later is known as fata morgana. I was scanning the ice fragments through binoculars when I came across a series of three towering icebergs that I had not seen before. They loomed like a trio of toadstools on the horizon. Their shape surprised me, since none of the icebergs I'd seen previously had been anything like this. Their slender height appeared to be in defiance of the laws of gravity. Any iceberg so tall and willowy should topple over and lie on its side, but I decided that perhaps the three towers were all part of the same structure, a joint base making their gravity-defying posture possible.

But when I looked again after a cup of coffee, the toadstools weren't there. I swept the entire horizon to find them but they had simply disappeared. It was only after I returned to England that I read about fata morgana, a strange form of Arctic mirage that makes distant features appear as spikes, turrets or towers, objects with great vertical exaggeration rising up from the horizon. After my experience, it didn't surprise me to read that closer to land, these ghostly apparitions can seem like large and significant landmarks. Early Arctic explorers had been deceived by these topographical spectres, mapping headlands and mountains that were never seen again.

One evening, Mads Ole and Frank decided to venture out on to the ice fragments that were still lodged in front of us. Clutching their spiked poles, they asked if I wanted to come along. We hopped from one ice floe to the next, Frank leading the way, testing the edges as he went. We leapt over the cracks as if playing a giant game of hopscotch. Several hundred metres from camp, standing in the middle of a sizeable slab of ice, Mads Ole bent over from his waist as if to peer at a spot on one of his *kamiks*. He had a look of intense concentration on his face, his elbows resting on his polar bear knees.

'Listening', whispered Frank in answer to my questioning look as he too bent over to eavesdrop on an invisible world. After a while, Mads Ole straightened and gave me a single nod. 'Narwhal', he said simply and pointed out beyond Herbert Island. Now I bent down and strained my ears, but I wasn't tuned to the secret airwaves.

When they came, I wasn't ready. I'd been expectant for several hours after our sortie on to the ice floes but had finally laid down for a rest. I'd just drifted off into a deep slumber when I was awoken by the sound of the zip on our tent and Frank's head appearing through the flap. Again, just the one magic word, 'narwhal', and he was gone.

I pulled on my *kamiks* and hurried out. Mads Ole was already in his kayak on the edge of a large pond some distance from our tent and Frank was quietly slipping into his nearer to. Far to my right the other hunters were making their way to their kayaks as silently as possible. Under other circumstances the sight would have been comical, a trio of small men waddling along in their polar bearskin trousers. The pattern of ice ponds had changed since our arrival and the kayaks had been moved accordingly. I managed to get into my kayak alongside Frank who was sitting in the smallish pond nearest to me. He held his finger to his lips as I did so, his face fixed with no expression.

We sat. Waiting. Stock still. Beyond Frank, I could see the other four hunters positioned across the icescape, as motionless as figurines carved on a polar frieze. A light wind was blowing, rippling the water in our icebound pond, as four gulls glided silently above us. Time passed and nobody moved. For some reason, now that the moment was near I wanted to know what time it was. The chill air had that extra bite to it that came when the sun was low in the sky and behind the tents the dog teams were all splayed out on the ice asleep. I decided it must be around midnight. I was sitting in the calm of the Arctic, but I could hear the blood pumping in my ears.

An unspoken decision had been made at some unspecified time

that I would not throw a harpoon. Mine would be an auxiliary role. Resting behind me on my kayak was an inflated sealskin float that I could introduce into the proceedings when called upon. But my nerves were still taut, both with the expectancy of seeing a narwhal for the first time and the anxiety of a hunter's novice assistant.

Frank manoeuvred himself away from the ice edge and I looked urgently around, but saw nothing but the ripples on our pond. Frank paddled noiselessly across the water and glided in to rest on the opposite side. Now time seemed to stand still as we continued our vigil. As the adrenalin subsided, my fingers began to throb with the cold and slowly I flexed them round my double-ended oar. On a far ice floe one of the gulls that had been circling swooped down to land and strutted along as if inspecting our formation. It was the only thing that moved across the otherwise static backdrop.

I don't know how long we sat there waiting for the narwhals but they never came. One of the furthest hunters levered himself out of his kayak, pulled it out from the water and trudged off back to his tent. One by one, the others followed. I was already back in bed by the time Mads Ole ducked in through our tent flap. He didn't say a word as he lay down to rest. Frank remained out there scouring the horizon with his binoculars.

You know you're in a strange place, far from home, when you wake up next to the round sun-burnished face of an Inuit who's dressed in polar bearskin trousers. I left Frank to sleep and emerged from the tent to find that a steady snowfall had wreathed the camp in its tender embrace. Herbert Island had disappeared and the slumbering dogs had snowflakes for eyelashes. The breeze was still blowing in from the sea and the flakes were arriving in gentle, near-horizontal flurries.

Someone had been out and caught a seal, perhaps partly in frustration after the narwhals' false alarm, and its stout corpse lay thinly disguised beneath a layer of snow. A red bloodstain was barely discernible around its head.

Some of the hunters were playing cards in the lee of a tent and I joined them for a few hands. I asked whether they thought the narwhals would come today. 'Maybe', was Mads Ole's only reply. It seemed to be the Inuit hunter's favourite word.

They were all better than me at cards, their impassive manner ideally suited to the game of bluff and deception. My rudimentary capacity for infinite patience while being constantly alert, the qualities I'd first seen on the seal hunt with Aqqalu among the icebergs, had worn me down since our arrival on the ice edge. But these guys were blessed with a staying power that I'd rarely seen before. It wasn't that they were unfriendly but, as I looked into their faces, I realized that not once had I ever been able to tell what any of the hunters I'd met was thinking. Like predators, their eyes told me nothing, yet with one look it seemed that they could see right through me.

The snow stopped later that day, and Mads Ole asked if I'd like to accompany him on a seal hunt. His dogs needed food, he said. We partially dismantled our tent, just enough to extricate one of the sleds, hitched up the dog team and set off across the fresh snow away from the sea edge.

Mads Ole had seen a seal on our journey out from Qaanaaq, a distant speck lolling beside a hole in the ice. On that occasion he had stopped and grabbed his rifle, taken aim, fired and missed. The seal had slipped back into its blowhole unharmed. This time he called the dogs to a halt and unhooked a wooden contraption from the back of his sled. The device was like a small sled, with strips of polar bearskin nailed along its tiny runners. Mads Ole unfurled a piece of white cotton that he fixed to the front of the small sled, pulling it taut so that it looked like a miniature sail. He took his rifle and laid it along two upright wooden struts, securing it with string. The gun's barrel pointed out through a slit in the small sail. He gestured for me to follow as he crouched down and sneaked forward, holding his rifle with the sled and sail contraption attached to its end, in the direction of the dark spot on the horizon some 200 metres away.

Somehow his dogs must have known we were after their dinner because they had all curled up to lie silently on the snow. Mads Ole crept forward, whispering to me that it was important never to approach a seal from upwind because it would be able to smell us. 'They see good too,' he murmured, 'so we use the shooting screen to get closer.'

He was now lying down, spread-eagled on the snow, pushing the mobile screen in front of him. Stretched out behind, I paused to peer through Mads Ole's binoculars. A fat seal was lounging on the ice far in front of us, sunning itself beside a blowhole. If it had turned its head to look in our direction it might have been able to make out a little white object against the snow, but it would no doubt have looked like a small, unthreatening iceberg.

We edged nearer and nearer until we were within shooting range. Mads Ole squinted through his gun sight and put his finger on the trigger. Through the binoculars I saw the seal's body judder briefly a moment after the sharp crack of the shot being fired, and then lie still. Mads Ole scrambled to his feet, walked back to his dogsled and we sped across the ice towards the seal.

It lay dead, a shot clean through its head, a dribble of crimson blood staining the snow beside it. Mads Ole took a hooked pole and dragged it the short distance to his sled and I had to help him lug the heavy body on board.

My first dead seal, the one shot by Aqqalu out among the icebergs, had aroused in me feelings of sorrow and guilt, mixed with a hint of anger. But this one stirred no such emotions. After seeing several dead seals lying prostrate in our camp, being cut up for our pot or fed to the dogs, I'd lost the ability to mourn its death. I was surprised, and a little perturbed, at how quickly I'd crossed an emotional threshold somewhere in my conscience and become desensitized to the loss of life.

Our wait for the narwhals continued. I played cards, read books, and peered for long minutes through the binoculars. Ivory gulls would float past our camp to land and strut their stuff on the ice, and one day Frank pointed to a pair of different birds beating their wings across the skies in the direction of Herbert Island. 'Eider ducks', he said. I felt the warmth of the sun on my back as I tracked them away into the distance across a bank of cloud hanging phantom-like over the island's slopes.

As the hours merged into days, I sensed that my ability to tolerate the tedium of waiting was developing. I'd stopped being anxious and the tension had drained from my limbs. I found myself lapsing into neutral, a mental limbo in which one part of my mind was alert but most of it was far away, musing on other things. I realized I'd felt it before; it was the mindset of long bus or train journeys when you gaze out at the passing scenery while thinking of life back home.

Every so often, my heart would miss a beat when a seal broke the surface of one of the icebound ponds in front of our camp, and frolic for a while, before disappearing again beneath the Arctic waters. Little did they know their luck was in because no one would shoot them from our camp for fear of scaring away the narwhals.

As we sat killing time, I asked Mads Ole how his hunting year panned out. He caught narwhals in summer, he told me, walruses in the months of February, March and April. 'What do you do in the winter?' I asked him. 'Is it possible to hunt in the dark?'

'Winter here is hard, it can be minus forty degrees Celsius, and the darkness also makes it difficult. But I hunt seals with my dogs. They are difficult to see but the dogs can smell them. Seals I hunt all year round.'

I had asked the same question of Ikuo, the Japanese hunter in Siorapaluk, and he'd told me that he hunted only small animals like Arctic hare in winter. 'You cannot shoot in the dark,' he'd said, 'but they have tracks. We can set a trap on their tracks.' Perhaps, as he'd intimated, he really was still learning.

But summer was the time of maximum opportunity. The seals were easier to spot and the narwhals arrived. Food secured and preserved during the months of the midnight sun would supplement the meagre pickings of winter.

Mads Ole said he had shot his first seal while out hunting with his father when he was twelve years old, and harpooned his first narwhal when he was eighteen. 'Once I harpooned three narwhal in one day.' His record for seals was twenty-four in a single day. 'But other days, nothing,' he said. 'Sometimes, one week just one seal. You never know how many.'

On what he said was the sixth day, Frank told me that we were running short of coffee and tea, and our sugar supplies were low. The snow had begun again, a light dusting of fairy powder settling on our camp. We would have to head back to Qaanaaq the following day, he said.

The delicate flakes were still falling when the narwhals came. I knew immediately that the churning of the water in the pond directly in front of me was not made by any seal. I couldn't see their tusks, but their size was unmistakable. No one had to utter the magic word this time.

Frank and Mads Ole were slipping into their kayaks in a silent flash but I could only stand, rooted to the spot, watching as the glistening backs of a dozen animals broke and rebroke the surface. In those few, fleeting seconds I realized that my kayak training had been for nothing. Now that I was confronted with these majestic beasts easing their flanks in and out of the water, I recognized that I couldn't be a part of any hunt. My heart wasn't in it and my head told me I'd be foolish to try.

For a brief moment, it seemed that the hunters' movements had frightened the creatures away. The sea became calm once more as they sat in their kayaks staring as if they too had now become immobilized. They had reverted to being motionless figures engraved on the polar icescape.

When the water churned again it was just a single narwhal, letting off a sharp hiss as it expelled the air from its blowhole. On the far side of the pond, Mads Ole was already moving towards it, gliding with silent strokes from his double-ended oar. He stowed his oar beneath a leather strap on his kayak and with one fluid movement raised his harpoon above his shoulder. I caught my breath as he launched it, not with a powerful thrust, but in a gentle arc that seemed to take a long time before its point struck the mass of gleaming skin. A coil of rope leapt up like a snake from his kayak to follow it.

The harpoon glanced off and made a slight splash as it hit the water.

Nearer to where I was standing, Frank too had moved smoothly away from the bank. The narwhal was coming towards him twisting and rolling in the icy water. He had already stowed his oar and was feeling the weight of his harpoon in his hand as the snowflakes swirled around him. With a flick of his wrist he tossed his weapon through the air. It too glanced off the surface of the whale and splashed into the swell, its leaping rope curling behind it to land with a muted spatter on the surface.

And it was gone. As suddenly as they had appeared, the narwhals had vanished, leaving just ripples behind them. Both hunters seemed to know it, because they were slow to retrieve their harpoons floating on the water. They stayed in their kayaks for another twenty minutes, ready to rejoin the fray, but somehow I could sense that they knew their chance had gone.

They were left to watch as the narwhal's wraithlike ripples spread out gently across the pond like the reverberations made by a loud noise in a glass of water. Only this brief conflict had been conducted in a timeless silence, punctuated by the ghostly eddies of the falling snow.

When Mads Ole finally returned to shore, I asked him if he thought the narwhals would return. I already knew how he'd reply.

'Maybe.' But this time, I didn't think so.

* * *

The morning we left was silent but for the mournful cry of a solitary gull as it glided across the wintry wonderland. The sun was low in a cloudless sky, its rays making the ice crystals sparkle like diamonds. The wind had died away but the ice was still clogged up against the ice edge in another fresh arrangement, the water in its ponds as still as glass, reflecting the snowcaps above the slopes of Herbert Island.

I'd spent a week on the sea ice, beneath the Arctic skies, in the company of mountains half as old as the planet itself. The hunters were returning disappointed, but my hunt for the narwhal had ended in a strange sense of satisfaction. I'd witnessed an age-old confrontation between man and beast and, although by now I'd been accustomed to the sight of death, I was pleased that this time the hunters' stealth had failed to catch the gentle giants of the icy sea.

I'd been uplifted by my venture to an island that time forgot, a thousand miles from anything familiar, a world away from home. And I was sad to be leaving one of Nature's last strongholds, now shrugging off its wintry mantle.

It was a magical place where the sun shines at night; where glaciers, not trees, fill the valleys; and where wildlife roams as free as the wind, until it crosses a hunter's line of vision.

JUNGLE

Congo

ONE

It was the termites that finally put me off. I could cope with the idea of bats and caterpillars but for some reason the termites got to me. Actually the reason was clear. I'd only pondered the idea of eating caterpillars and bats, but I got to taste a couple of termites. They sat in two neat conical heaps piled on top of a large green leaf laid out on the ground in the Total market. One of the piles was still alive, a mass of tiny white bodies that I realized were still wriggling and crawling only when I bent down to take a closer look. The others had been smoked, my accomplice, Annaelle, informed me.

She asked the old woman crouched behind the heaps if I could try one. The woman nodded and Annaelle pointed to the blackened pile. 'Try one of those,' she said, 'the others haven't been cooked yet.'

Carefully, I plucked a couple of the glistening dead insects off the black heap and popped them into my mouth. They were crunchy and didn't taste of much. Contrary to what Annaelle had said, I didn't think they had been smoked, more like fried in butter that had gone off in the heat. They weren't really that unpleasant, sort of like eating rancid grit, but the thought of consuming them on a regular basis over the coming month was definitely off-putting. It struck me that if termites were on the standard forest bill of fare, I'd probably have to eat a lot of them because I couldn't believe that they had much nutritional value.

Annaelle seemed satisfied. 'There you are, you see. Now do you understand what I'm saying?'

She had been on at me to make my sortie into Congo's forests a brief one since I'd revealed that I was intent on spending a month in the jungle. We'd got along very well until that point, mostly because I came from England and Annaelle had spent an extended period living with relatives in south London. She loved Lewisham, she told me, but her favourite part of England was Catford. When she asked me what I was intending to do with my stay in her country, the Republic of Congo, she obviously expected me to say that I'd be spending my time enjoying the sights of Brazzaville, the capital. When I told her I was here to visit the forest, she looked puzzled.

'What for?' she asked.

I said I wanted to see how people lived in the immense tropical lowland forest that occupied the Congo Basin. I was keen on making contact with some Biaka pygmies, whom I knew lived in the northern parts of the country. Annaelle didn't look convinced. 'How long are you going for?' she asked suspiciously. I told her.

'One month!' she shrieked, overdramatically I thought. 'What are you going to do for a whole month?'

I tried to explain further. The Biaka were probably the first inhabitants of Central Africa's forests, and they still lived from hunting and gathering. These were the true experts in jungle survival. Their lifestyle hadn't changed much in a few thousand years. It had to be interesting.

But I was already too late. Annaelle wasn't listening. 'One week, that's enough,' she declared with a wave of her hand. 'There's nothing there, just animals and nasty things to eat.' At which juncture she'd insisted on taking me to the Total market to prove her point.

It was strung out along a muddy street leading away from a

defunct petrol station that had given up the ghost some months before, when Congo's supply of petrol had dried up. They were repairing the refinery down on the coast, Annaelle told me, but no one quite knew when those repairs would be finished. Meanwhile, a brisk trade in illegal imports from Kinshasa, a quick boat trip across the river Congo, had sprung up on street corners to supply the taxis that still plied the streets of Brazzaville. The petrol was sold by the litre in old glass bottles.

The market was a typical bustling African scene consisting of row upon row of wooden stalls selling everything from shoes and toiletries to mounds of sugar and salt towering out of deep plastic sacks. Small children darted in and out between the shoppers, many of whom were women with fantastic hairdos twisted into braids. Some of the braids had been wound up so tightly that they'd become soft bobbles on a cranial pattern of perfect football-like pentagons, others carefully secured close to the scalp to give the impression of a crocheted skull-cap. A few had simply left their braids to burst from their heads like astonished spikes.

The day was muggy and overcast, the tropical sun unable to penetrate the thick layer of cloud. Single hawkers wandered between the stalls holding up their wares to potential clients. One man sold towels, another specialized in mosquito nets, a third had catapults strung all the way up one arm. Another held out his hands to display two bunches of bats hanging upside-down. I couldn't tell whether they were dead or alive.

Annaelle pointed out the bats to me with a gleeful grin as she wafted her way through the throng. 'That's what I mean,' she said. 'That's what you'll have to eat in the forest.' She was a striking woman in her figure-hugging dress adorned with bright prints of the Virgin Mary surrounded by religious slogans. Her outfit was rounded off by a pair of black winklepicker shoes which made her careful to avoid the worst of the large muddy puddles that punctuated the street we were following. In retrospect, it was the shoes that should have given her away immediately as a city girl. The bright print dresses I saw throughout the market, and everywhere I went in Congo, but winklepickers were not standard country footwear. However, by this time I'd certainly marked out Annaelle as a metropolitan woman thanks to her serious antipathy towards the forest.

'I don't go there – I am afraid', she announced after I'd sampled the termites and checked out a wriggling pile of bright green live caterpillars proffered by another woman nearby.

I asked Annaelle what it was that scared her. It was only a forest after all, I suggested. 'No, no, you don't understand. It is full of wild animals,' she insisted. She paused as a battered motor car inched its way past us through the crowd and then she turned to look at me. 'It is also a place of bad magic,' she added more seriously. 'You must be careful.'

This comment came as a surprise because what with all the pictures of the Virgin Mary on her dress I hadn't put down Annaelle as someone who'd give more than a second thought to so profane a set of beliefs. But there was no doubting her sincerity because when it became clear to her that our visit to the Total market had not succeeded in deflecting me from my mission, she insisted on taking me to see a *fetiche*.

I had an inkling as to what a *fetiche* might be, but I asked anyway.

'You'd call him a witch doctor. He can protect you from the dangers in the forest.'

So far, this hadn't been the start I really wanted, given the concerns about my trip that I'd brought along with me from home. The Congo has a reputation. To the European mind, it comes with a lot of baggage, much of it menacing. It is one of those geographical regions that conjures up powerful imagery, an icon of mystery and darkness. It was an impenetrable jungle, a vast tropical forest that harked back to a time before people, to an era when vegetation could still riot unhindered on the earth. It was the testing place and deathbed of countless intrepid explorers, victims of its seemingly endless menu of deadly diseases. And it was that river, a coiled serpent that snaked its way through the heart of Conrad's darkness.

I'd been down to take a look at the river the previous day, hailing a taxi to drive me to a set of rapids just outside town. It was the beginning of a stretch of the river where Henry Morton Stanley finally realized that his mission to descend the Congo in the late 1870s had become impossible. Swirling brown water was gushing over a maze of hidden boulders that for Stanley and his companions, ravaged by smallpox, starvation, dysentery and ulcers, turned out to be impassable. These cataracts, the wildest stretch of water Stanley had ever seen, continue for 300 kilometres, almost to the Atlantic Ocean. Clumps of water hyacinth were speeding past me, tossed and turned in the angry currents, like phlegm spat out by the forest as it cleared its throat. And I couldn't help but feel a sense of foreboding, standing there on the edge of this colossal jungle, contemplating my journey that would take me up several of the tributaries lacing the forest, feeding these waters of the mighty Congo.

This trip had already set off a struggle in my mind, between the impassive scientist in me and the emotions entertained by my more literary side. I'd considered the evil of the forest and its spiritual hazards to be simply fictitious Western creations, but Annaelle's view on the matter indicated that it wasn't solely a product of European imagination. And there was also some cold hard evidence of evil that still lurked beneath the murky image. The sinister Ebola virus, most recent creation of this fetid breeding ground, may largely remain a mystery to medical science, but the horror of its effects has been plain for all to see. This terrible exterminator, named after the Ebola river, a tributary of the Congo, appears to liquefy the body organs of its victims. People literally melt away, from the inside out. In other branches of science too, the vast Central African rainforest is still the least studied of the world's tropical forest regions. In more ways than one, I was definitely venturing into the unknown.

As our taxi sped away from the Total market, the driver having first nipped across the road to buy a bottle of petrol, I turned to ponder another of the challenges I would have to face on my jungle journey. My termite snack had led me to think about insects, which, like other forms of life, run riot in the tropics to become an unavoidable annoyance in the daily routine. It had put me in mind of something I'd read some months before, written by Mary Kingsley, an English traveller who roamed widely through the jungles of Africa in the late nineteenth century. She reckoned that 75 per cent of African insects sting, 5 per cent bite, and the rest are either permanently or temporarily parasitic on the human body.

It's common knowledge that most of the millions of insect species thought to roam the planet – no one knows just how many, the estimates vary widely, from 2 million to 100 million – are residents of the world's tropical forests. I felt my skin begin to crawl as I thought of the numerous specimens licking their mandibles at the thought of some fresh white meat. Mary Kingsley's advice, if approached by an insect, was to take no notice. Just keep quiet, was her recommendation, and hope they go away. Some hope. But then I thought again of the two piles of termites I'd been faced with in the market. I suppose turning the tables and eating the damned things was one approach to the problem, but the taste of rancid grit reminded me that I didn't even fancy that.

Our taxi had passed through the wide boulevards of central Brazzaville with its remnants of French colonial buildings and entered a less salubrious zone. It looked like a down-at-heel industrial area. Here the vehicle had to veer to avoid potholes in the tarmac, but this wasn't a problem for long because we soon turned off the sealed road on to a track of bright orange dirt. The sky had darkened and now looked more menacing. Far off, flashes of lightning had begun to spark on the horizon.

We pulled up outside a gate that Annaelle led me through, past a low-slung house and into its back yard, to an open structure with a corrugated iron roof. It seemed that the *fetiche* conducted operations from his garden shed.

Two men peered out at me from their perches on small wooden stools inside the shed. Each was bare-chested except for a sash of vegetation strung from the right shoulder to beneath the left arm, and in both cases their left arms sported a long white stripe on the outside extending down to the wrist, rather like the stripe you would see on the arm of a sports shirt. A similar dab of white paint had been applied to the outside of each man's right eye. One of the men wore a pair of bright pink silk trousers held in place with a leaf belt around his waist. This man's chest sash was made from palm fronds, while his accomplice, whose sash consisted of a bushy green vine, wore a wrap-around black print skirt.

Both men looked me over with no expression in their eyes as Annaelle explained to them what we'd come for. As she spoke, I was able to take in the paraphernalia of the *fetiche* business. The ground at the feet of the man with pink trousers, who, judging from his central position, I took to be the boss of the outfit, was strewn with shiny brown gourds, plastic buckets and unidentifiable objects wrapped tightly in hessian and bound with string. An old plastic water bottle, now filled with murky brown liquid, stood beside his foot. A wicker basket held bones, dried pieces of animal skin and what looked like porcupine quills tied in a bundle.

On a low table behind him was an array of other baskets overflowing with roots and tubers. Lengths of old rope, bits of rag and branches of green leaves drooped down from the table-top. In one corner of the shed, where I now saw another man in the shadows bent double and slowly rocking back and forth on his own tiny stool, more brown gourds hung from nails in one of the stout wooden posts that held up the roof. The post was chalked with numbers. At the base of the post, an assortment of animal horns poked out from an ancient wooden box.

I was surreptitiously trying to make out what was going on with the rocking man when Annaelle announced that the *fetiches* were ready for me. I nodded, now somewhat unsettled about what I was letting myself in for. Still throwing furtive glances over towards the figure in the corner, I crouched down on the small upturned box that Annaelle motioned me to sit on.

The man in pink trousers, who was now sitting directly opposite me, looked me up and down and said something.

'You must take off your glasses', Annaelle told me. I did so.

Without taking his eyes off me, Pink Trousers murmured something to his skirted accomplice, who took a short length of palm frond from the table in the background and tied the two ends together to make a ring. He took a step towards me and placed the fronds on my head, making a rough sort of crown. Meanwhile, Pink Trousers had begun to mutter to himself as he bent over and picked up one of the shiny brown gourds lying at his feet. He pulled a rag bung out of its top, dropped it on the ground, and slipped his index finger into the gourd's hole. His finger came out covered in a red-brown paste. He sprang up from his stool and leant over me. Still muttering, he placed his finger on the bridge of my nose and smeared a line up the centre of my forehead to my hairline.

'This will make you invisible to animals', Annaelle told me, as if this were the most normal thing in the world.

I didn't have much time to react to her announcement because having retreated, Pink Trousers was already back in front of me, this time holding a wooden bowl containing what looked like a black paste. He blackened his thumb and smeared the sooty mixture on the outside of my eyes.

'This allows you to see all potential aggressors clearly', Annaelle explained.

I glanced over towards the figure in the shadows. He had stopped rocking back and forth and now sat stock still on his little stool.

The sorcerer's assistant now came forward. In one hand he was holding another, rather larger, wooden bowl filled with green foliage;

in his other hand he held a plastic water bottle. He poured some water over the leaves and offered me the bowl. I took it.

'You must sniff the leaves,' Annaelle explained to me, 'breathe it in.'

'What's this one for?' I asked as I held the bowl under my nose and sniffed. 'This is a special protection against snakes', she replied.

The leaves didn't smell of anything other than wet leaves, but I was happy to be getting such a thorough set of defences.

I wasn't finished yet. It was Pink Trousers' turn again and he crouched down in front of me to draw a circle on the ground with a piece of white chalk. His assistant passed him a flat stone that he pulled from the mass of material behind him and Pink Trousers proceeded to draw another smaller circle on this.

'This is the circle of innocence,' Annaelle told me. 'You must sit in it.'

I moved to sit on the stone.

Pink Trousers was rummaging in one of the baskets at his feet and pulled out a long piece of brown string. Towards one end, the string had been carefully wrapped around a small twist of dark blue cotton material. He stood up and came towards me, holding the string in both hands.

'You must wear this whenever you are in the forest,' Pink Trousers explained through Annaelle. 'It will protect you against bad spirits.'

He gestured for me to stand up and he pulled my shirt out from my waistband. I held my shirt up as he secured the string round my middle. 'Only wear this in the forest,' the explanation went on. 'You can take it off when in camp.'

Annaelle approached from the side of the shed and told me the ceremony was finished. 'You can step out of the circle', she said. Pink Trousers and his accomplice were busying themselves with their gourds and sprays of foliage. Annaelle looked me up and down. She seemed satisfied.

'I still think you're foolish to go into the forest,' she said, 'but at least now you're properly protected.'

Flying to Ouesso took me north, across the Equator and into one of the most sparsely populated regions of Africa. Most of the Congo Republic's three million inhabitants are tucked away in the southern corner of the country, between Brazzaville and the coast, leaving the northern regions to the trees. They were laid out below me in an impenetrable carpet of green, their crowns rounded and pimply like an endless sea of broccoli heads. It was only as the aircraft came in to land that I got my first glimpse into this dense mass of vegetation, briefly making out slender trunks wreathed in vines and lianas. The creepers dangled from the canopy like primeval streamers, lending the forest edge an air of forgotten festivity.

The tropical lowland forest of Central Africa is among the largest in the world, second only in size to that of the Amazon Basin in South America. These tropical forests are renowned as the richest assemblages of life-forms on the planet and, for the first leg of my journey, I was heading for a particularly remarkable corner of Congo's jungle, the Nouabalé-Ndoki National Park. When a man from the ministry of waters and forests first ventured into the area in the late 1980s, accompanied by an American ecologist, the two biologists were so struck by the abundance of wildlife in this remote pocket of jungle that they set about persuading the government to conserve it permanently.

Their expedition, undertaken at a time when ivory-poaching had reached crisis proportions across the continent, had been in search of forest elephants. There turned out to be elephants in abundance, along with hippos, gorillas, chimpanzees, leopards, antelopes, pigs, buffaloes and nine different types of monkey, as well as countless species of birds, plants and, of course, insects. The region was literally teeming with wildlife, perhaps a greater concentration than in any other part of Africa. The Nouabalé-Ndoki forest is also very rare in Central Africa because it has never been logged. Following its desig-

nation as a conservation zone in 1993, its wildlife treasures hit international headlines as one of the few undisturbed natural sanctuaries
left on the planet. *National Geographic* magazine called it 'the last
place on Earth'; *Time* dubbed it the 'last Eden'. It sounded like just
the sort of place I was looking for.

As you might expect, reaching the last place on Earth took some
time. Making my way there alone was not an option, so I'd arranged
to meet up in Ouesso with Patrick Boudjan, a local ecologist conduct-
ing research into elephant migrations. He had agreed to guide me to
the park. After flying across 650 kilometres of solid forest to reach
Ouesso from Brazzaville in a clapped-out Soviet airliner, I now had a
six-hour boat journey up the Sangha river to look forward to. This
would take us to a village called Bomassa, Patrick told me as we
emerged from Ouesso's dilapidated, roofless airport terminal and
headed off towards the river. From Bomassa, we'd be able to hitch a
lift in a pick-up until the track petered out. We'd then have to take a
canoe down a smaller river for an hour, followed by a thirty-minute
walk to a base camp on the fringes of the park. From there, it was a
six-hour trek through the jungle to the small research camp he was
taking me to.

We strolled down Ouesso's main street, a long ribbon of brick-red
soil that descended to the banks of the Sangha river. For the first time
since my arrival in Congo, the sun had broken through the barrage of
clouds but although the brightness was welcome it did nothing to
relieve the mugginess of the air. Now it was clammy, oppressive and
hot. Previous days had been clammy, oppressive and warm.

Patrick stopped at a stall selling cassava that had been cooked and
wrapped in leaves to buy supplies for the trip upriver. He told me you
couldn't find cassava in Bomassa. 'People can't grow it there because
the elephants trample the fields.'

The Sangha was perhaps 100 metres across at Ouesso, its water
chocolate brown and flowing at considerable speed. We clambered
down its steep bank to where several long pirogues were tied up, each

vessel fashioned from a single hollowed-out tree trunk with an outboard motor attached to one end. We climbed aboard one and settled down in the wooden armchairs lined up in a procession along its length. It looked as if at least this leg of my journey would be a comfortable one.

It was another two days before we reached the research camp we were aiming for. Within minutes of leaving Ouesso, the banks of the Sangha, a major tributary of the Congo, disappeared as the forest closed in. A tangled mass of plants – trunks, boughs, leaves and reeds – rose up to tower above us as inscrutable walls. The foliage came in a hundred different greens, leavened only by the brown of the water and the occasional purple bloom of water hyacinth amassed in mats by the side of the river or floating past us downstream in itinerant clumps. Trees leaned over from both sides to drape their branches and creepers in the passing flow. It was as if the jungle was sagging at its edges, great waves of vegetation crashing down to engulf the progress of our pirogue, which now seemed small and fragile among the giant trees.

The chugging of our motor became a comforting sound in the otherwise brooding silence of the river, although as night fell it sparked an upheaval of noise from chattering crickets and burping frogs, and a blizzard of insects materialized from the darkness to bombard my face. But through it all, as lightning flashed on the shadowy horizon, we just motored on, ploughing our lonely furrow deeper into the immense forest, as if we were travelling back to the beginning of time itself.

TWO

We reached the village of Bomassa and fell into our beds, hungry for sleep, rising too early the following morning for the next leg of our journey: a bumpy truck ride and another pirogue along a smaller, winding river before we took to our feet. Finally, I was actually entering the forest.

It was darker and cooler beneath the trees as we forged our way into this strange world ruled by plants. It was a world pervaded by stillness, without wind, not even a breeze, as saplings silently struggled to find a way to the sky between the solid tree trunks. The forest floor was littered with large dead leaves and flat, leathery seed cases the shape of footprints. They were grey-brown and looked as if someone had discarded thousands of old insoles.

We followed a path, constructed by elephants Patrick told me, which sounds as if the hike was easy-going. But a tropical forest path is not quite the same as a path through a forest where I come from. Looking ahead as I walked, there was clearly a way through the foliage, but the ground was a confusion of obstacles lying in wait to trip the unwary. Roots riddled the trail, snaking across the path to snatch at my toes, and fallen branches lurked to graze my shins.

Whole tree trunks lying across the track had to be clambered over in brief shafts of welcome sunlight. And as soon as I had tuned in to the obstructions at my feet, an aerial contingent took over to hinder me. Head-high creepers and vines reached out like tentacles to scratch my face or garrotte me.

Towards the end of our trek the hidden sky arrived from beyond the towering canopy, heralding its presence with thunder that sounded like great doors slamming in the clouds and huge boulders rolling in heaven. They rumbled and tumbled with unnatural volume, bigger than any boulders you could ever see. Immense flashes of lightning followed the deafening crashes, enough to make me jump in disbelief. I heard the rain before it reached me, the trees of the forest being so densely packed that drops falling on the canopy took minutes before they reached the ground. But once they'd started to filter through, they came tumbling down into the jungle in a cascade of water that drenched me in seconds.

The final stretch before the research camp meant wading through a waist-deep river. I was exhausted, sodden, scratched and bruised, but we'd arrived. I truly felt as if I'd penetrated the heart of darkness.

The following morning, the neat little camp was an oasis of sunshine in its clearing surrounded by the soaring trees. It was an assortment of tents and makeshift wooden shelters with rush roofs that served as a base for researchers studying the forest and its wildlife. Paths led away from the main camp to smaller satellite clearings where Patrick and I had pitched our tents, and another led down to a little wooden jetty that had been constructed over a stream for bathing.

The area we were in is known as the Goualougo Triangle, a wedge of forest on the southern border of the Nouabalé-Ndoki National Park hemmed in between the swampy floodplains of two rivers, the Ndoki and the Goualougo, one of which we had waded through late the previous afternoon. The few natural scientists who have explored this area believe that these geographical barriers have for centuries discouraged people from venturing into this spot, leaving the Goualougo

Triangle undisturbed by man. The area's biodiversity is extraordinarily rich, and many of its animals have never seen a human being. The triangle's apes, for example, respond with little fear to the presence of humans, and often descend from the canopy to gaze in curiosity at those who enter their territory. This is exceptional in Africa, where most apes know that people have proved untrustworthy in the past and are best avoided.

So Goualougo's apes presented a unique opportunity for Crickette Sanz, a young woman from Washington University researching chimpanzees. She had offered to let me tag along on her daily walks looking for her subjects of study and noting their behaviour. Assembling at seven o'clock that morning ready for the off, Crickette introduced me to her trackers, three Biaka pygmy men from Bomassa village: Koba, Djokin and Mbio, all wearing identical tan T-shirts and an assortment of plastic footwear. They looked bashful and embarrassed as I shook their hands in turn and Crickette described them as her eyes and ears. She couldn't do her research without them, she explained. Although she'd been working in Goualougo for two years, she seldom ventured far out of the camp alone for fear of losing her way on the maze of elephant paths. These men were also much better than she was at recognizing the calls of the chimpanzees, and spotting them in far-off treetops, despite her two years of experience in the area.

Before we headed into the forest, Crickette briefed me in her down-to-earth manner on what to do and what not to do if we came across any gorillas or elephants. On first meeting her, I'd been struck by her fresh-faced air of innocence, her pale complexion no doubt due at least in part to the amount of time she had spent in the twilight world of the forest. But I thought her Alice in Wonderland appearance was in one sense entirely appropriate, given the fact that she was working in an area previously untouched by people. Goualougo was a wonderland, although it wasn't without its dangers. Both her feet needed to be firmly on the ground. A male gorilla might treat us to an aggressive display if we disturbed him, she told me, particularly if we inadvertently positioned ourselves between him and a female. 'He might howl, slap the ground or beat his chest, which some people can find pretty disturbing', she said. Given the size of a male gorilla, I thought that I might be one of those who'd find it pretty disturbing, so I was glad she'd taken the time to explain how I should react.

'Don't run away,' she said, counter-intuitively. 'Although he may look dangerous, he won't charge if you just keep still. You might inch yourself closer to one of the guides, but don't make any sudden movements. Usually what happens is the male will make his way round us to his female and we can continue on our way.'

Elephants, on the other hand, appeared to be a slightly different matter. I had quizzed Patrick on the subject during our trek to the camp the previous day. Since the path we were following was an elephant highway, it struck me as a pertinent question to ask. He turned to smile at me when I did so. 'Run,' he said cheerfully. 'Very fast', he added.

As we clambered in turn over a fallen tree trunk covered in bright white toadstools, Patrick went on, 'The pygmies often climb a tree to get out of the way', but he said he couldn't climb fast enough. 'Sometimes it is OK just to hide behind a tree,' he explained, 'but I prefer just to keep running.' It had sounded like solid, if slightly alarming, advice.

Crickette's view on the issue was that I should take my lead from one of the trackers. 'They know what to do', she said. So I mentally reverted to Patrick's recommendation.

'One more thing before we go,' Crickette added. 'Stay within sight of the person in front or behind you all the time. I've asked Koba, Djokin and Mbio to look out for you but if you do get lost, stay exactly where you are until someone comes to find you.'

In my own mind I'd already decided to do just this should I get lost. The track we'd walked on the day before had been constantly dividing and sprouting side paths, all of which had looked the same to me. I'd realized at an early point the importance of keeping Patrick in my sights at all times, which, given the difficulties I was having with the obstacle course of roots, branches and creepers, was no easy task. But a supremely necessary one. On one occasion I had lost sight of Patrick for just a moment thanks to a particularly virulent creeper that had grabbed hold of my rucksack and wrenched me back as I'd tried to pass, nearly pulling me off balance. In the few seconds it took to untangle myself, Patrick had disappeared. It was as if he'd been swallowed up by the trees. I hurried to reach the next bend in the path, stumbling on a large root as I did so. When I reached the bend, Patrick was still not visible and the track divided. Right or left? I asked myself. I had no idea. Instinctively, I pinched the folds of my shirt to find the string given to me by the *fetiche* in Brazzaville with its small twist of blue cotton as protection against bad spirits in the forest.

I plumped for right, but after a few tentative steps I called out, just to be sure, and seconds later Patrick emerged from the undergrowth. He was on the other track. The ease with which I could happily have taken a wrong turn and continued marching into oblivion had been all too apparent. My stomach had lurched when I'd seen him, I suspect just to give me an idea of what panic might feel like.

The moment had come back to me as I'd wriggled down into my sheet sleeping bag that night. For an instant I'd felt really lost at that fork in the path. As I closed my eyes, I tried to decide if there was a difference between 'lost' and 'really lost'. I hadn't come up with an answer before drifting off to sleep.

We set off with Djokin leading the way, followed by Crickette and myself, Patrick, Koba and Mbio bringing up the rear. The jungle was the by-now familiar riot of plants scrambling for position on the forest floor, a blanket of dead leaves and branches slowly mouldering back to whence they came. Djokin carried a pair of secateurs, occasionally snipping rogue creepers and small branches that dangled across the track to hinder our progress. On our walk into the camp, Patrick had been wielding a machete for the same purpose, targeting thicker specimens, but now that we were in the park disturbances were deliberately kept to a minimum. It struck me that Crickette's quest to study the chimps would have been ten times more difficult without this network of paths maintained by the elephants.

Every so often, Djokin would pause to look down at the ground, pointing out signs of animals that had passed this way. He indicated a mass of little round pellets, like brown *petit pois,* the droppings of small forest antelopes known as duikers. Further on, he gestured to an area where the decaying leaf mould had been slightly disturbed, signs that a red river hog had been rooting for something to eat.

The time slipped by as we continued our patrol. We walked in silence, conversing when we had to in hushed tones, in keeping with the stillness of the forest. I noticed that none of our trackers ever trod directly on any of the fallen branches and boughs that littered the path. I mentioned this to Crickette, who I saw was also careful to lift her feet over even the largest tree trunks that lay across the track. Just the sound of a snapping twig could alert animals to our presence, she whispered. I tried to follow suit, but found it virtually impossible to avoid every obstacle in my path. Part of my trouble was that I was still being hassled by dangling obstructions. Djokin's efforts with his clippers were fine for Crickette, who was of a similar stature to her trackers, but my extra height, though marginal, was enough to mean I continued to suffer from the mid-air hazards.

We paused below a soaring fig tree to look for its fruit on the ground. Crickette showed me one of the tiny figs, scarcely bigger than a marble. 'It's nearly ripe,' she said softly, splitting open its tough brown casing with her thumbnails to reveal the white flesh and tiny seeds. 'Chimps like to eat figs, so we might see some here.' Djokin and the others were scanning the ground around the base of the tree for signs of chimpanzee droppings, but there were none to be seen so we moved on.

Slowly my eyes were being opened to the workings of the forest, the tell-tale signs of animals passing and traces of their endeavours.

Beside a termite mound built up against the giant trunk of a tree, Crickette ducked down to pick up a short stick from the ground. She beckoned me over to the mound. 'Goualougo's the first place in Central Africa we've found evidence of chimps using tools to eat termites.' She poked the stick into a small hole in the hard mud. 'See? They poke holes in the mound with these dowel-like twigs and fish for the termites with a different type of tool.' She turned to scan the ground and picked up another, longer twig. 'Like this', she said.

Crickette pulled out an exercise book from her rucksack to scribble down a note, a sign I was pleased to see that the others took to mean it was time for a rest. I slumped to the ground, still weary from the days of travelling to get here, only for Crickette to look up and tell me that it was probably better not to sit directly on the forest floor. She had produced a small sheet of plastic from her rucksack to sit on. I looked at the others. Djokin and Koba were perched on a fallen tree trunk, while Mbio was squatting on a spread of leaves that he'd pulled from a sapling. Patrick was still standing, inspecting the termite mound.

'You see the guys never sit on the ground,' Crickette said. 'There are parasitic worms in this leaf litter that can burrow into your skin through your clothes.'

It's a long time since I've stood up so fast.

We continued on our way, a route of about 20 kilometres that was roughly circular and would take us back to camp before nightfall, Crickette explained. Within minutes of leaving the termite mound, Djokin stopped at a thick log lying at right angles across the track and pointed to a sizeable pile of droppings beside it on the path.

'Gorilla', said Crickette, pulling out her notebook again to record the finding. I peered over her shoulder to look. Given the situation, it was almost as if the gorilla had been sitting on the log to conduct his business, I thought to myself. The parallel with the human *modus operandi* was too much for me, and I had visions of a huge black ape reading a copy of the *Forest Times* as he squatted there in the middle of the path. I wasn't going to say anything, for fear that my thoughts were too irreverent, but then I did anyway.

'It's almost as if the gorilla was sitting on the log to do it.'

'That's exactly what he was doing', Crickette smiled.

I just stood there with my mouth open for a few seconds before walking on.

But although I'd now seen plenty of evidence that we were surrounded by creatures, we were yet to actually spot one, despite being several hours into our trek. I have to say that I found this surprising. We were, after all, trudging through a habitat renowned for its abundant wildlife. Forests in the humid tropics are the most biodiverse environments on the planet, thanks to their year-round warmth and copious amounts of rainfall: ideal conditions for life to thrive in. The riot of plantlife was plain to see, but where were the hordes of animals? I'd seen none, not even a single bird. Indeed, other than a small number of ants, even Mary Kingsley's legendary insects had been few and far between, although I wasn't too upset by their non-attendance. It was the absence of actual animals that frustrated me. It wasn't that I'd expected them to stroll up and introduce themselves, but I had thought they might be rather easier to see.

But then it was difficult to see anything much, what with all the vegetation and the murky light; and, despite our attempts to make as little noise as possible, our big group must have been easy for wildlife to hear and steer clear of. And of course a lot of life must have been going on above our heads, high in the trees. But it was still disappointing, and still surprising to my mind that we hadn't caught at least a glimpse of one of the big mammals, like a gorilla or an elephant. By this time, part of me had become quite eager for a confrontation with an elephant, even if it did mean running for my life. At least it would prove that the droppings and other supposedly tell-tale signs of abundant wildlife weren't all part of some elaborate hoax.

In fact, large mammals aren't really supposed to be very abundant in wet tropical forests. Their profusion in this region of the Congo is due in no small part to the existence of natural clearings, bald patches in the forest, known in Nouabalé-Ndoki as *bais*, where grasses, sedges and herbs thrive in the sunshine. These pockets of pasture, virtually devoid of trees, comprise only a tiny percentage of the total forest area, but they act like magnets to a whole range of animals that would otherwise have to spend all their time among the trees browsing on woody plants.

I'd read about the *bais* before coming out to Congo, and when Crickette mentioned that we were fairly close to one, I asked her if we were heading that way. She replied that we weren't, because chimps rarely ventured into them, but she was happy to take a detour and show me. Good, I thought to myself, since all sorts of big animals, including gorillas, elephants, buffaloes and pigs, are supposed to regularly turn up to dine in these areas, so my chances of finally seeing some creatures should be good.

The eating habits of these animals help to maintain these open-air snack bars in just the way they like them. Grazing, digging for roots and churning the mud with their feet all tend to keep these zones as pastures, free of trees and shrubs. Elephants are particularly effective at ploughing up the *bais* while they feed and wallow in the mud, but they also make a more conscious effort towards home improvements. They often expand clearings by pushing down any small trees bold enough to encroach on to their pastures. Larger ones are dealt with by stripping their bark off, leaving them to die and eventually drop of their own accord.

As we forged off the track down a slight incline towards the *bai*, I realized that I was also keen to see one of these clearings for a different reason. I'd begun to feel a mild dose of claustrophobia. I'd felt it the previous day as well, while on the march to Crickette's camp. After an hour or two, I'd kept thinking that I must be nearing the end, or at least some hint of a clearing to relieve the relentlessness of these trees. In my mid-latitude mind I was day-dreaming of coming to the edge of the forest, perhaps seeing a road, with cars on, and a motorway service station where I could buy some food and a cold drink. This was doubly perturbing, since I hate these service stations at home and tend to avoid them whenever possible. In my defence, it was only a few days since I'd left England, and my brain must have still been catching up. I told myself that I'd probably plunged into the Congo Basin too hastily, but I was here now so I'd better get used to it. The visions of motorway service stations had been banished from my mind, but I couldn't completely get over the fact that I was missing the open air and sunshine.

One thing about the *bais* that I hadn't fully taken on board while reading about them was that they tend to be waterlogged because they are usually associated with marshes, streams or springs. I could tell we were nearing the clearing because the trees in front of me had thinned and beyond them I could see a great slab of blue sky. The ground here was marshy and a little further on I could see the trees and shrubs were standing in water.

Koba, Djokin and Mbio each picked a large leaf for himself and sat down, obviously not that interested in actually venturing into the *bai*, but Patrick had clambered on to the trunk of a tree that leant out over the water towards the opening. I followed him along the near-horizontal trunk, craning my neck to get a glimpse of what might be beyond. But the foliage of a couple more trees nearer in meant the view was too restricted and I couldn't see much beyond a mass of tall, brilliant green reeds where the water looked as if it had become decidedly deep.

For a moment I felt dejected. I couldn't see me plunging into the *bai* because I was secretly still perturbed at the thought of those parasitic worms that burrowed into your skin. I reckoned I'd been lucky once, but I wasn't going to give some other nasty insect the opportunity to take up residence in my body. But when Crickette started wading into the water in her Wellington boots I snapped out of it and decided to join her.

We pushed our way through the tangle of branches at the edge of the marsh and I felt the warmth of the sunshine on my face as the water came over my boots and we continued wading through sucking mud to where the reeds began. An electric blue dragonfly darted towards us through the reeds, hovering a few centimetres above the water. By this time the water was up to my chest and it was still getting deeper. The willowy reeds were well above our heads and I could see nothing of the rest of the *bai* which seemed to stretch several hundred metres beyond us.

We stood still and listened. I thought maybe I could hear the call of a bird in the distance, but I couldn't be sure. I shook my head.

'Nothing.'

'Sometimes you can hear elephants and buffalo swimming,' Crickette told me, 'but not today.'

After standing for a few minutes, we turned and made our way back to the shore to remove our footwear and wring out our socks. The rest of our clothes just had to remain wet. I still hadn't seen any animals, but it had felt good to stand in the sun for a while.

I got lucky on our trek the following day, although the first sizeable creature we saw had a dubious allure. Koba was leading and stopped abruptly as he was about to clamber through a dense curtain of lianas that blocked our way. He took a step back, eyes fixed on a point on the ground about a metre in front of him. He whispered something to the others and Djokin and Mbio moved silently past us to take a look. I strained to spot what it was that had brought us to such an immediate halt. All I could see was the usual confusion of dead leaves and creepers, until a slight movement caught my eye.

'It's a yellow mamba', Crickette whispered.

I could just make it out now, a short snake, no thicker than a piece of rope, slithering through the shadows across the dead foliage. It had a small frog in its mouth.

'Is it poisonous?' I asked.

'Deadly', came the reply.

We stood and watched as the snake disappeared into the under-growth and Koba gave it a wide berth as we continued on our way. Ten minutes later, Koba stopped again, turning to look at Crickette with his finger to his ear. He looked upward, scanning the treetops, and pointed. We all raised our heads to gaze in the direction he was indicating, but I could see nothing.

'Monkeys', Patrick murmured from behind me. I strained to see but couldn't make out anything among the branches and leaves silhouetted against the sky. Then a movement caught my eye, and way above my head a monkey clambered along a branch, grabbed a hand-ful of something from a bough, and popped it into its mouth.

Crickette was now pointing in another direction, further off, where another towering branch had been disturbed.

'More of them over there', she whispered.

Djokin, who had advanced to stand beside us, shook his head and said something. 'He says that's not a monkey', Crickette translated to me in hushed tones. They exchanged a few more words and Crickette pulled a pair of binoculars from her rucksack, put them to her eyes and scanned the far treetops. I couldn't see anything but the trees.

'He's right,' Crickette murmured, 'they're gorillas.' She paused. 'Three of them.'

I still couldn't see anything, and Crickette handed me the binoc-ulars, pointing towards the high distance and explaining where I should look. I followed her directions and eventually focused on a giant black ape reclining on a thick branch pulling sprigs of leaves down to eat them. Beyond it, I could just make out another two goril-las almost obscured by the foliage in a tree slightly further off.

I was astonished. Not because this was the first time I'd seen them in the wild but because I'd had no idea that gorillas climbed trees. I was used to seeing photographs of them lounging in dense vegetation on the ground or roving about on all fours through the long grass. To my mind it didn't look right to see them so high up in the trees, 30 or 40 metres off the ground. They looked out of place.

It was like walking into the engine room of a ship and seeing a couple of ballet dancers stoking the furnace.

I stood there transfixed, peering through the binoculars. The one I could see most clearly was male, a so-called silverback. I could just make out the beginning of its broad silvery-white stripe as it lay on the branch on its back. The other two were females, Crickette was telling me, but I was only half listening, my mind still coming to terms with what my eyes were telling me. These creatures were too big to be so high up in the trees. Were they stuck up there? I wondered. Did they need help? Should I call the fire brigade?

THREE

The mid-air gorillas were only the first of several surprises I had during the best part of a week I spent with Crickette wandering the elephant trails of Goualougo. I hadn't expected to be abandoned by my sense of direction, which is normally quite good, but I'd found the lack of landmarks in the forest totally disorientating. Most of the area we'd been patrolling was flat, with no distinctive features other than a few termite mounds and the occasional stream or stretch of swamp, but where these were in relation to our camp I had no idea. The elephant trails meandered back and forth and their network was so extensive that I found it impossible to keep a sense of where we were. On most days I had lost my bearings within minutes of leaving the camp. Our trackers obviously knew the paths and termite mounds, and for them there were probably numerous other points of reference, but for me the forest all looked the same.

Not being able to see the sun had something to do with my lack of orientation, and the absence of sunshine, except in brief treefall areas and on my one sortie to the edge of the *bai*, I still found depressing. This twilight world did have its benefits, however. The temperature in the forest was always very pleasant and the humidity never too high. I also suspect that the perpetual gloom had something to do with the welcome lack of flying insects.

The dearth of colour in the forest was also surprising. Virtually everything, alive or decaying, was either green or brown. As the days progressed, my ability to spot smaller life-forms on our daily sorties improved, but most of them were drab and unremarkable. Even the caterpillars were disappointing. They weren't fat and rainbow coloured with psychedelic fur, as you might expect from the humid tropics, but small, undistinguished and anaemic-looking. I did see some bright red berries the size of cherries, a favourite gorilla snack apparently, and on one occasion a solitary orange butterfly, but that was about it. Otherwise I was stuck in a monochrome netherworld.

And I still couldn't get over how difficult it was to see any animals. The gorillas would have remained invisible to me if it hadn't been for the trackers' acute senses, and it was thanks to them that I eventually got to see my first chimpanzee.

Early one morning, I ambled up the path from my tent to find Crickette in a state of some excitement. Djokin and Koba had located some chimps and they were pretty close to our camp apparently. The trackers had heard their calls the previous night and had been out at first light to look for them. Hurriedly, I grabbed my hat and rucksack and we set out to find them.

We'd been walking for less than twenty minutes when Djokin silently signalled a halt and started to peer upwards into the trees. He edged forward, off the trail, the rest of us following as quietly as we could, until he stopped again, putting his hand out to lean against a huge tree trunk. He turned to us and nodded, pointing up into the foliage. About 15 metres above our heads a chimpanzee sat looking at us, scratching her rump.

For a few minutes, the chimp, who Crickette identified as one she knew as Jane, was restless, clambering back and forth between branches and looking down on us nervously. But then she decided on a bough that hung down towards us and set about bending over smaller branches to make herself a sort of nest. Jane settled down to watch us.

Crickette had her notebook out and was scribbling away with a smile on her face, happy, I think, that she'd finally been able to show me one of her subjects of study. I could make out Jane's white lips, a button nose and perfect round ears. Occasionally she pulled some fruit off a spray at her elbow to nibble, totally at ease and apparently enjoying the show. I'd thought it was supposed to be the other way around.

A couple of days after seeing Jane, I left Goualougo and made my way to an airstrip hacked from the jungle near the edge of the Nouabalé-Ndoki National Park. Here I was able to hitch a lift on a small aeroplane flying further north, across the park, to the small town of Makaou. In Makaou I'd arranged to meet Johnnie, a conservationist who was going to escort me down the Motaba river to the village of Bangui-Motaba. Bangui-Motaba was almost my ultimate destination, because it was here that I was hoping to meet a group of Biaka pygmies who would take me into the forest to live with them.

We'd spent my final evening in Goualougo round the campfire talking about survival. I'd asked Crickette how long she thought she'd last on her own in the jungle if she got lost. She paused to consider the question.

'I suppose I could eat what the chimps eat,' she told me, 'but I wouldn't last long. Water would be the biggest problem.' Her trackers knew where to find water, stored in a certain type of liana that could be easily chopped with a machete, but she said she still got the vine confused with another species that had deadly poisonous sap. She'd also seen Biaka follow the sounds of distant cicadas which lived in a type of forest dominated by *Gilbertiodendron*, or *malapa*, trees. *Gilbertiodendron* were often found close to rivers and water courses.

Patrick told me his chances of survival would depend on the seasons. If he got lost during the rainy season, there were many fruits that he knew he could eat. They might keep him going for a few days.

Our conversation just confirmed what I'd already concluded, that scientists like Crickette and Patrick would be lost without their pygmy assistants. During my time in Goualougo I'd seen Koba, Djokin and Mbio's skills in navigating and reading the forest, but each evening we'd returned to the camp, where Koba's wife Louise was always ready with a dinner of smoked fish brought from the village of Bomassa. Other than the research camp, nobody lived permanently in the park, so I was yet to see the Biaka's knowledge of the forest put to its traditional purpose: to support their hunter–gatherer lifestyle. This is what I was hoping to do from Bangui-Motaba.

The journey downriver by pirogue took us the best part of a day, a day that started with torrential rainfall. It was the tail-end of a storm that had begun the night before with deep rolling thunder and flashes of lightning that heralded an almighty downpour. The lightning had continued to flare in the sky for hours, at first as a distant artillery barrage with occasional multiple flashes, like a neon strip light that was trying to splutter into action but never did. Slowly the storm approached, until its microseconds of light exploded right before me, each, like the crack of a whip, so brief that I was left with just a blinding image on my retina of the forest brooding before the tempest. The air had become steadily more oppressive until the rain began.

The morning had started out dry but had taken an unnaturally long time to unfold. At 8 a.m., a good two hours after the sun had risen, it was still almost as dark as night. And then the deluge began again, thrashing the river in loud, aggressive torrents. The rainstorm was demonstrating the Congo Basin's reputation as the lightning strike hotspot of the planet. Data from satellites that orbit the Earth have shown that on average fifty strikes a year zap every square kilometre of land in this dark heart of Africa. Most of Britain clocks up fewer than two, while the entire continent of Antarctica receives virtually no strikes at all.

Lightning is caused by a massive surge of electrical energy built up in towering thunderstorm clouds. Within these clouds, particles of ice and droplets of water, churned up and down by turbulent winds, become electrically charged, possibly through collisions. Particles with opposite charges tend to separate within the cloud until its upper portion acquires a positive charge and its lower part is negative. Lightning is an electrical discharge between these positive and negative regions of a thunderstorm cloud. The Congo's tropical position attracts an endless series of thunderstorms, welling up over the Equator and releasing their cloudbursts with the torrents of rainfall.

My time in Goualougo had helped to ease the initial sense of foreboding I'd felt at penetrating the Congo's heart of darkness. But heading downriver in this deluge, besieged by these mythological thunderbolts, was like a timely reminder from the region's gods of their menacing reputation for mystery and darkness. As Johnnie and I chugged our way along the Motaba river, through the uproar of the elements crashing down around us, it seemed once more that my journey was taking me on a passage to the very centre of things in this primeval jungle.

My rendezvous with the Biaka at Bangui-Motaba was not quite as straightforward as I'd originally hoped. One source of confusion lay in the fact that Bangui-Motaba was not simply a Biaka village, but two villages, or one divided in two: one part inhabited by the Biaka, the other by the Bantu.

Although the various pygmy groups were probably the first inhabitants of Central African forests, they also have a very long history of interaction with agricultural peoples, some of whom began moving into the forests up to 2,000 years ago. One facet of these longstanding relations is the fact that the language the Biaka speak has evolved over time from an ancient language borrowed from the Bantu, one of the agricultural groups, to become a distinct tongue in its own right that is quite different from that which the Bantu speak today.

Probably from the earliest times, a mutual reliance developed between the Biaka hunter–gatherers and the farmers and fishermen of the other ethnic groups such as the Bantu. Anthropologists usually describe these relations between Biaka and Bantu as symbiotic, in which the Biaka exchange meat and other forest products for crops, salt and iron implements, today brought in by traders who ply up and down the river. But this traditional relationship has changed somewhat in recent times from a relatively equal trading partnership to one that is rather less evenly balanced. The situation that met me in Bangui-Motaba looked more like a single village society with two classes. The Biaka were the underclass, employed by the Bantu to carry out the tasks they didn't feel like doing themselves, like digging their fields and preparing their food. But it wasn't simply that the Bantu employed their Biaka neighbours. It was more exploitative than that. I soon learned that, in effect, the Biaka/Bantu relationship which prevailed in Bangui-Motaba, as in other parts of central Africa, was that Biaka families were 'owned' over generations by Bantu families.

The difference in status between the two groups was apparent immediately upon our landing at a small inlet on the riverbank that provided the focus for the Bantu village spread out over a wide, open area beside the Motaba river. A few children watched us paddle in and were soon joined by a procession of adults, the women dressed in bright print dresses, the men in long trousers and T-shirts, who approached to welcome us. But also lined up on the riverbank, at a respectful distance, was an assortment of other, smaller figures who didn't come forward to shake our hands. They were barefoot men dressed in ragged shorts and T-shirts and bare-breasted women in grass skirts. They looked as if they were representatives of a different timeworld. Their role in the village became clear when one of the guys who had just shaken my hand, a lean young man with a smiling face, turned to bark some orders to the onlookers, and the Biaka men hurried forward to unload our pirogue.

It soon transpired that if I wanted to get to know the Biaka, I'd first have to spend time with their masters, the Bantu. So for my first few days in Bangui-Motaba, Johnnie and I were put up in the house of Jean Pierre, the smiley man who had greeted me on my arrival and ordered the Biaka to unload our pirogue.

Jean Pierre was a good host, eager to show me his daily routine and introduce me to all his friends, and I soon forgot the initial disquiet I'd felt at having to delay my sortie back into the forest with the Biaka. Village life revolved around the river, which acted both as a highway to the outside world and a rich source of sustenance. I joined Jean Pierre on his morning fishing trips in his pirogue, paddling up or downstream to check his nets that were stretched out across small creeks, crowded with overhanging vegetation, between sticks stuck in the mud.

In the afternoons, we ventured back out in his pirogue to collect palm wine. The swamp forest bordering the river was dotted with palm trees that had been primed for the purpose. A makeshift ladder of vines had been tied to the trunk, enabling a man to shin up the long, straight palm, about 10 metres in height. The top, Jean Pierre explained, had been sliced off with a machete and a tube inserted to drain off the sap into a plastic container secured to the trunk. Once the palm had been prepared in this way, all Jean Pierre had to do was turn up at the tree every afternoon and empty the container. The palm would produce up to 40 litres of sap every day for two or three months, at which point Jean Pierre simply had to prime another tree.

The wine was sweet and cloudy. It reminded me of the home-made ginger beer my mother used to make when I was a child. A refreshing thirst-quencher to glug down in the heat of the day, by nightfall it had fermented enough to give a strong alcoholic kick. 'This is an important tradition,' Jean Pierre told me, because 'modern wine', as he put it (meaning the French bottled variety), was both difficult to find and expensive.

Every evening we'd sit down among the strutting chickens

outside Jean Pierre's hut and enjoy the Congolese palm wine before a fine dinner of fish we'd caught that morning, complemented by a starchy stodge known as *foufou*. For me, the only shortcoming of this excellent fare was the *foufou*, which was difficult to eat and tasted of pure nothing. It was quickly reduced in my mouth to glue-like lumps that were hard to swallow.

It takes an awful lot of effort to produce this unwieldy stodge. A staple food, *foufou* is made from manioc, an edible tuber. After being dug out of the fields, the manioc has to be left to soak for several days in the small inlet surrounded by pirogues to get rid of the cyanide that it naturally contains. The tubers are then broken up into pieces which are left to dry in the sun. I saw the white pieces laid out on wicker trays on the rush roofs of every hut in the village. These pieces are then pounded with pestle and mortar into a flour. When the flour is sprinkled into boiling water it is stirred into a thick paste, and hey presto you have *foufou*.

When Jean Pierre explained this laborious procedure to me over dinner on my second evening, two thoughts came into my mind. Firstly that it wasn't worth it, and secondly that all the energy needed to process this staple food rather spoiled my image of Jean Pierre's life as an effortless idyll. But of course I was wrong. Preparing the *foufou* was women's work, and anyway it wasn't his wife who did it. Most of the sweat exerted in its preparation came from the Biaka. Jean Pierre's daily routine really did just consist of a couple of hours fishing in the morning, and an hour or two collecting palm wine in the afternoon. Every once in a while he ventured into the forest for a spot of hunting, with a Biaka to guide him.

I saw Biaka teenaged girls all over the village, squatting beside the mud-plastered walls of the houses in their grass skirts pounding manioc pieces in giant mortars and sieving the flour in wicker sieves. I broached the subject of the Bantu's relationship with the Biaka after dinner one evening.

Jean Pierre maintained that the two groups lived in harmony. He said that the division of labour in the village was based simply on ability. Any job requiring brain power was conducted by the Bantu, he told me, and everything else was done by the Biaka. Seemingly, the one minor exception to this rule came when the Bantu wanted to enter the forest to hunt. 'We use them as guides in the forest,' Jean Pierre said, 'because the pygmies know the forest. It is not a safe place, full of very dangerous animals, you know: leopards, elephants, snakes and the like.'

All in all, Jean Pierre insisted that his people had good relations with the pygmies, but his picture of harmony didn't quite fit with what I'd seen in my wanderings around the village. There seemed to be little social interaction between the two groups and communication appeared to be decidedly one-way. Affable wasn't one of the words I'd have chosen to describe the way in which the Bantu ordered the Biaka around.

From my point of view, both Bantu and Biaka were equally sociable and responsive whenever I stopped to say hello, but the difference in their demeanour spoke volumes. Bantu men and women were all confident and forthcoming. The Biaka, by contrast, looked humble and eager to please. They didn't exactly cower in the lee of the Bantu's huts, pounding their manioc or crushing their palm nuts to extract the oil, but they didn't look entirely at ease either.

I tried to probe the issue with Jean Pierre a little further. 'So there aren't any problems between the Bantu and the Biaka?' I asked innocently.

'There is a problem,' he said, 'the pygmies are always stealing from our fields.' I don't think he fully understood what I'd been trying to get at.

But life for the Bantu in Bangui-Motaba wasn't all a bed of roses. One afternoon we went out earlier than normal on our daily sortie to collect palm wine, and Jean Pierre visited not one but two palm trees to harvest their sap. The extra supplies were needed for an event scheduled later that afternoon. The villagers had been having a little difficulty with leopards sneaking into the village at night to eat their chickens. Four small goats had also been lost. When this problem had started, Jean Pierre and some of his colleagues had set a trap for the leopard, managing to catch and kill it. But a few days later, not long before I arrived in Bangui-Motaba, chickens and goats had begun once more to disappear. The trouble was obviously more deep-seated than anyone had realized, and to deal with it an appointment had been made with a group of villagers who had the power to call up the spirit of the forest for consultation. Apparently, the whole village would be turning out for the event and a large quantity of palm wine was always served at such occasions.

An air of expectancy was mounting by the time we returned and carried our plastic jerrycans of palm wine to the clearing at one end of the village where it was poured into a very large bucket. Beside it lay an assortment of plastic cups in the dust. Groups of small children were playing in the dirt as older villagers milled about and some teenaged boys began warming up on the village drums. Spread out on a wooden table near one of the huts was the hide of the first leopard that had been caught and killed.

Several women with babies strapped to their backs were distributing palm fronds for people to hold, and Jean Pierre and I took up position with a line of villagers awaiting the appearance of the spirit. Behind us, a large group of Biaka sat patiently looking on. Mostly women and children, they were huddled together in a congregation beside one of the huts, the largest assemblage of Biaka I'd seen so far, trying to look inconspicuous but just seeming rather out of place.

Jean Pierre told me the spirit was called Angli-moto, 'Angli' meaning spirit, while 'moto' was the word for man. He was an important personage in the village because he understood everything that went on in the surrounding netherworld of the jungle. 'If you respect him, he will protect you on the elephant paths in the forest,' Jean Pierre explained, 'but if not, he can cause you trouble.'

The youths were really going at the drums now, beating out a rapid rhythm as we all clung on to our palm fronds, and a collective sharp intake of breath heralded the arrival of Angli-moto. He was covered from head to toe in large brown leaves, a rustling mass of dead vegetation that was still just about recognizable as a more or less human form, but with extra-long arms and a lengthy penis. Villagers started singing and some clapped to the rhythm of the drums as the forest spirit juddered into view, twisting and turning as if taking in the scene that lay before him. His face was a mask of wood painted in black and white. Specks of orange flowers – which acted like antennae so that he could see everyone, Jean Pierre told me – were dotted about his head.

Angli-moto rustled his way back and forth in the rough circle that had closed to form around him, the villagers singing and pounding the ground in front of them with their palm fronds. He danced to and fro, veering towards people at random. Women and children scattered in all directions, screaming, but many of the men tended to remain more confident when the spirit darted towards them, stepping back and to the side, waving their palm fronds like a matador flicks his cape. The more self-assured among them even stepped into the circle, which had now begun to dance around the spirit, advancing towards him and brandishing their palms in his face. These men were those initiated into Angli-moto's world, Jean Pierre shouted to me above the commotion. 'They can touch him without danger', he cried. But if the uninitiated were to come into contact with the spirit they would break out in boils, he told me. Whenever the spirit rushed in my direction, I made myself scarce along with the women and children.

The performance continued in this vein for an hour or more as the drums rolled on, the circle of villagers rhythmically marching round and round waving their palm fronds. Angli-moto rustled with endless energy, shimmering from side to side and crouching down to strike the ground with violent slaps before moving forwards again to threaten a portion of the onlooking crowd.

And then he made his exit, fading back into the forest behind the huts, which was a signal for the palm wine to be doled out and the drinking to begin. Everyone was in a state of high excitement, quaffing the potent palm brew. I asked Jean Pierre how the ceremony had gone. 'Well, Monsieur Nick! Very well! We will be hearing no more from that leopard.' And he danced a little jig around me in celebration.

FOUR

I'd enjoyed my time in Bangui-Motaba, despite my unease at seeing
the way the Bantu interacted with the Biaka in the village. It felt good
to be back in the sunlight after my time in the forest with Crickette
and Patrick in Goualougo, and I found the ease of Jean Pierre's life
attractive. But I'd been struck again during Angli-moto's performance by the humble and unassuming nature of the Biaka women and
children as they watched the ceremony. The contrast between their
appearance and that of the Bantu was absolute. The Bantu women
wore bright, colourful cotton prints and headscarves – garish colours,
like flowers in the sunshine – while the Biaka were all dressed in natural tan colours. The women and girls wore grass skirts, but even the
T-shirts and shorts of the few men who watched the ceremony were
so old, and had been worn for so long, that they'd taken on the
colours of the earth. As a group, these forest people just tended to
merge into the background, almost as if they were melting away in the
brightness of the sunlight. Their presence at the Angli-moto ceremony breathed new life into my mission to spend time with them in
the shadows of their forest world. They looked like people with
mystery in their bones.

Jean Pierre told me he was sad to see me go, but the following day he took me to the edge of his village to show me the trail that led to the Biaka village, a short walk away through the trees. Less than half an hour later, I had entered the world of the Biaka.

The various pygmy groups are spread throughout Central Africa's forests, from Cameroon and Gabon in the west, through the Congo Republic and Central African Republic into the Democratic Republic of Congo (the former Zaire) and Rwanda in the east. Deciding which group I should head for had hinged largely on my finding someone who could help me by acting as an interpreter. Anthropologists seemed like a good bet to me, since their work meant that they had to know the language and most would have had to spend a year or more living with the Biaka. My reading round the subject had thrown up the names of several anthropologists studying these people. But early in my research I'd frequently started to come across one name in particular, Louis Sarno, who was not an anthropologist, but a musicologist. Louis Sarno had also lived among the Biaka. For the past seventeen years.

I didn't think it would be difficult to find him in the village. For a start, I wasn't expecting to discover any other Westerners in residence, quite apart from the fact that he was likely to be the tallest man there. But I'd also seen a photograph of Louis Sarno, and he had an uncanny resemblance to a middle-aged Groucho Marx.

He appeared through the doorway of one of the huts, not unlike the Bantu huts in design, in an old red T-shirt, billowy cotton trousers and sneakers. He'd lost a bit of hair since the photograph I'd seen of him had been taken, but he still had his bushy black eyebrows, significant nose and a pencil-thin moustache.

He welcomed me in a soft New Jersey twang and took me straight to meet the chief. Everybody had been eagerly awaiting my arrival, Louis told me, as we strolled along. I noticed a couple of the teenaged girls and one of the women I'd seen pounding manioc in

Bangui-Motaba and smiled hello. It hadn't crossed my mind, but of course the Biaka who'd been working in the village would have known who I was. The chief, who had a kindly round face encircled by short, slightly greying hair, said it was good that I was finally here. Was I ready to go into the forest, he asked? I said I was.

It didn't take long for people to get ready to leave. Not everyone in the village would be going, Louis explained, since some were obliged to stay and work the Bantu's fields. But perhaps a couple of dozen men and women, and a few youngsters, were soon preparing for the off. The women packed wicker baskets with pots and mats and knobbly manioc tubers, picked up a machete or knife and slung the baskets on to their backs to hang via a cord stretching across their heads just above the forehead. One of them then strolled over to a fire that smouldered outside one of the huts, pulled a large green leaf from her basket, folded it in half, and used it grab a charred chunk of wood from the embers. I looked at Louis enquiringly. 'She's bringing the fire', he said simply.

Most of the men busied themselves with heavy nets that they'd use for hunting, each man carrying one slung over his shoulder, and ducked into their huts to emerge carrying long spears. Those who weren't carrying nets held a spear in one hand and an axe balanced over his opposite shoulder, its handle down the back and the blade at the front. The chief was the only person holding a crossbow and a quiver of arrows. These people were travelling light.

Louis, who had a small rucksack at his feet, pointed to my large yellow bag. 'You're not taking that, are you?' I also had a small rucksack on my back with the bare essentials in, so with just a moment's hesitation I agreed to leave the yellow bag in the chief's hut.

We walked for half a day, in single file along the elephant trails. Every now and again, my mind would go back to what I'd left behind in my bag. All my other clothes for a start, although I had already dismissed this as a problem given that everyone else had brought just the clothes they stood up in. What bothered me more was the insect repellent, and I couldn't believe I'd been so stupid. I'd used a lot of it during the few days I'd spent with Jean Pierre, where a daily ration of *foufou* hadn't been the only downside of village life. Every evening as the sun went down the insects came out. There were a few mosquitoes, but they weren't too much of a bother. Infinitely worse was a tiny type of fly, not unlike a midge, that delivered painful stings out of all proportion to its size. These flies did their best to spoil an otherwise enchanting atmosphere of tropical tranquillity as the fireflies flashed like miniature sparks suspended in the darkness. All I could do was hope the biting flies wouldn't follow us into the forest.

The Biaka walked in family groups, every so often pausing by the side of the track as a woman rearranged the baby she was carrying in a strap of cloth under her arm. Single women always stick with some of the bachelors, since they have a great fear of running into gorillas while in the forest, explained Louis, who was in front of me.

'I've tried to reason with them. You know, I've read Dian Fossey's work, and she says a gorilla won't harm you if you just keep still with your eyes on the ground. But the Biaka say that might be OK for me, but gorillas don't like Biaka. "As soon as they see us they just go nuts," they say.'

'And then what happens?' I asked, somewhat unnerved at this revelation that the forest people weren't quite the masters of their environment in the way I'd built them up to be.

'Well, usually the gorilla just screams with terror and runs away. He doesn't want to meet a Biaka any more than the Biaka wants to meet him. He just gets the hell out of there.'

A feeling of relief came over me. 'But every once in a while a go-getting male will make a stand,' Louis went on as he negotiated a huge tree trunk lying across the path. 'He wants to prove himself or something, so he lets out a God-almighty roar.' My heart took another downturn. 'And then?' I asked.

Louis turned and smiled. 'That's the best bit. The Biaka men roar back, and *then* the gorilla runs away.'

It was way past midday, and I was starting to feel hungry, when we came to a stop. 'They say we're going to make camp here', Louis said.

Why we'd stopped in this particular spot I couldn't fully understand. We were about 100 metres away from a small stream, which was obviously important, but otherwise this area didn't look any different from much of the rest of the forest that we'd been walking through. It was the usual carpet of dead leaves, saplings jockeying for position, and the great trees soaring up towards the heavens.

Some of the men had fanned out and were gazing up into the canopy as the others put down their loads and rested. 'They're checking the trees,' Louis told me. 'They're *Gilbertiodendron*' – I remembered the name from Goualougo – 'only the Biaka know them as *bimba*. The trouble with *bimba* trees is that they tend to be kind of fragile. Branches break off easily and older trees just fall over, so they need to make sure there aren't any old and wonky ones around.'

Within a few minutes, everyone seemed satisfied and people got to work clearing the area. I lent a hand pulling up the smaller saplings by their roots while larger specimens were given the axe treatment. A couple of teenaged trees were also felled. The women were busy scraping away the leaf litter and debris from the ground by hand, down to the humus layer. In less than half a hour the underbrush had been cleared in a roughly circular area some 20 metres across.

Now we needed some *ngungu* leaves to make the huts. Louis and I marched off back down the trail with the women towards the stream, waded across it, and continued for some distance before coming to an area of tall plants with stems that grew to above head-height. Each stem sported a very large, waxy green leaf: the *ngungu*. The women set about cutting the tall stalks with their machetes and collecting the vaguely oval-shaped leaves. It looked easy, and I asked if I could do my bit to help. One of the women looked amused at my suggestion when Louis translated, but she handed me her machete and stood back to observe.

I was rubbish. The women were deftly felling each stem with a sharp tap of the machete, but when I tried, the blade just glanced off. I tried again, hitting the stalk harder, but this time all I managed was a dent in the stalk. The woman who had lent me her machete just laughed and said something to her colleagues who were rattling through the stand of *ngungu* at considerable speed. They turned to watch as I made my third attempt, this time hitting the stalk with some force. The long stem folded over, but hadn't been cut. Cue more laughter all round. The woman took back her machete, gave the bent stalk an effortless tap, and the giant leaf fell to the ground. I gave up. I'd failed my first test in jungle survival. All I can say is that it wasn't as easy as it looked.

Thankfully, I was slightly better at constructing my own hut. We returned to the camp clearing, the women carrying huge piles of *ngungu* leaves neatly tied with thin vines, and proceeded to build our homes for the next week. I watched as the women set about their task, forging into the outer edge of the clearing to select supple, slender saplings to cut expertly with their machetes. These poles were stuck in the ground in a roughly circular pattern a couple of metres across and bent over into arches and entwined together to form a hemi-spherical, beehive-shaped structure. Slightly thinner poles were then gathered to weave into the framework, creating a lattice. It was now ready for roofing, Louis explained.

The woman who had lent me her machete, Bumbu, sat down and untied her bundle of *ngungu* leaves. She turned each leaf over, snapped the main stem near to the base of the leaf, and slid her machete a few centimetres into the stem, slicing it down the middle to produce a sort of hook. When she'd prepared twenty or so leaves in this way, she stood up and began to tile her shelter by slipping the hooked leaves over the lattice of poles. She started from the bottom and worked all the way round the framework, sitting down to prepare another batch of leaves when she'd hung the first set. Slowly she worked her way up towards the apex of the shelter, each leaf overlapping its neighbours.

After each hut, all with their open sides facing the middle of our clearing, had been completely tiled with the *ngungu* leaves, the women grabbed handfuls of dead leaves, lianas and leafy branches from the forest floor just behind their huts and heaped them on to the leaf tiles as an extra layer of protection. With this final cover of loose vegetation, the huts just seemed to fade away into the forest background. They had almost ceased to be shelters and become just a few more tangled humps in the undergrowth.

Now it was my turn. Bumbu handed me her machete and I went forth to cut down some slender saplings. Once I'd gauged the correct angle at which to wield the blunt blade, I was rather better at this than I had been at cutting the *ngungu* leaves. I shoved my first stick deep into the humus in the free corner of our clearing and planted the second one some distance away, bending it over to wind its end round the first. I looked at Bumbu who was standing beside me. She nodded her approval and I continued, setting up my sticks in a vaguely circular pattern, and bending them over to entwine them together in the way I'd just seen her doing it. Bumbu had been joined by the other women and they were quick to point out the necessary spacing, lending a hand to secure some of my bendy poles.

It was demanding work and, despite the relative cool of the forest, I was soon wreathed in a clammy sweat. But I was also rather pleased with my progress so far. While I'd been securing the basic frame of my hut, some of the women had collected thinner saplings to be woven into the framework, to create the lattice on which I'd hang my *ngungu* leaves.

It was just as I started the latticework that I noticed my first sweat bee. It was small, no bigger than a gnat, and harmless in that it didn't sting. It just hovered in front of my face annoyingly before landing on my forehead. I brushed it off and continued weaving. The sweat bee came back, this time flying inside one of the lenses in my spectacles, trying to land in my eye. I had to stop work to hook it out, squashing the little pest on the end of my fingertip.

The sweat bee's relation, the honey bee, can cause you serious inconvenience, in a painful form, if it decides to sting you. The sweat bee itself, on the other hand, adopts quite different tactics. It just silently pesters you. And I soon discovered that it likes to pester you with all its friends. Before the one on my fingertip had been squashed, he had obviously sent a message back to his pals, because before long I was surrounded by them. Their interest in humankind is as a source of salt and other nutrients that we emit in our perspiration. But although by now I was sweating all over, the bees weren't content just to land on my arms and face. They had to crawl up my nose, and into my eyes and ears as well. Admittedly, I couldn't have smothered all these places with insect repellent, if I'd had any, but I hadn't. It was sitting uselessly in my bag back at the chief's house in the village, and that just made me all the more frustrated. Very rapidly, what had started out as a satisfying exercise in self-help had turned into a deeply unpleasant assignment.

Swatting sweat bees in every direction, I carried on manfully with my task. The latticework was all but finished and I sat down to prepare the *ngungu* leaves which Bumbu had kindly cut for me after witnessing my ineptitude with her machete. Slicing the stems with the blunt machete while trying to fend off the armada of hovering sweat bees was impossible. Snapping the stem was easy enough, but I just couldn't get the hang of the sharp tap needed with the machete to create the short hook. It wasn't a powerful tap – it all depended on striking the stem at just the right angle to split it. Try as I might, I couldn't get the angle right. After several failed attempts, I just sat there and hacked at one of the leaves in a sweat bee-induced frenzy until it was a ragged mess on the ground. Bumbu and the other women were in stitches. I had another sweat bee in my ear.

Bumbu took pity on me again, taking back her machete and pushing me aside. She squatted down and rattled through the leaves with effortless ease. I thanked her and took the opportunity to remove my hat and use it as a new weapon against my airborne tormentors. This was a mistake. As soon as I'd uncovered my head, the sweat bees all flew straight into my hair. They started crawling around in there, tickling like mad, and were ten times more difficult to extricate than they had been anywhere else.

I don't think I've ever felt so irritated in my life, but somehow I managed to tile my shelter. Meanwhile, the women had wandered off to get their fires going. When I'd finished I stood back to admire my handiwork. My leaves weren't as neatly hung as the others', and I could see a few gaps between them where the rain might get in, so I called my advisers over to take a final look. Bumbu and the others came across the clearing to examine my efforts, just as Louis, who had been conspicuously absent throughout most of my endeavours, reappeared from the bush. The women nodded and made a few adjustments here and there, but declared that it was a fine effort. Louis, too, was impressed. 'Yeah,' he said, 'it's pretty good.'

I'd built my very own leaf and stick shelter which had received the thumbs-up from the Biaka housing inspectorate. It made me feel very proud, particularly since I'd done it in a cloud of the world's most infuriating flying insects.

The sweat bees finally left me alone once I'd got a fire going outside my shelter. The men, who had vanished into the forest to hunt while I'd been building with the women, returned empty-handed. For dinner we made do with supplies brought from the village to tide us over, smoked fish carried in flat wicker contraptions that looked like snow shoes and the inevitable *foufou*. The fish had a good meaty texture, but was so blackened and shrivelled it no longer looked like fish and smelled of charred wood and smoke. The *foufou* was the usual stodgy morass. The Biaka were practically addicted to it, Louis told me, and it was perhaps the major reason for their dependence on the Bantu, who supplied it either by bartering for forest goods or in return for the Biaka's labour. Why the Biaka didn't grow it themselves was a mystery. But Louis assured me that *foufou* would disappear from the menu as the supplies we'd brought ran out. The hunters would produce fresh meat and the women would find wild vegetables and nuts in the forest.

After dinner, I settled down in my new home accompanied by the music of the jungle. As the evening had drawn in, the constant pulsing of the cicadas, a noise that was almost electronic in tone, faded out to be replaced by the night-shift. The clamour of wildlife produced a scintillating hum made up of whirrs and clicks, tweets and twitters, chirruping and squeaks. Distant honks were blended with bells and whistles and a rhythmic clatter that sounded like castanets in the night sky.

FIVE

Everyone was keen to go out hunting the following day, although I didn't greet the morning in the best of spirits. The first night in my shelter hadn't been a comfortable one. Someone had lent me a rush mat to sleep on, but it did nothing to cushion the ground. I'd thought that sleeping on leaf mould might be quite comfy but it wasn't at all.

The night was also cold. I'd taken off my sweat-sodden shirt to let it air, but soon woke up and had to put it on again, silently reprimanding myself for not bringing at least one change of clothes. It was the first of several times I was awakened by the low temperatures, rousing myself just enough to push a log further into the embers of my fire. I finally gave up at 4.30 a.m. The only positive aspects had been the lack of insects and the fact that only one of the Biaka had snored. It also hadn't rained.

By this time, most of the figures sleeping around me were also beginning to stir, some already huddled round their fires. An ethereal mist was mixed with their smoke as it twirled gently up towards the forest canopy and slowly the light of morning began to dawn.

It didn't take long to get ready for the hunt. The men grabbed their spears and slung their nets over their shoulders as the women picked up their empty baskets and we all filed out of the camp into the forest. One of the men, a brawny character named Bimbula who wore a tattered red shirt, started unfurling his net not far away, attaching one end to a handy sapling with a wooden hook and moving away quickly and silently through the forest, stringing out the waist-high net behind him. It was woven from a type of vine, Louis told me, and measured a good 20 or 30 metres in length. It looked like an extra-long tennis net. A teenaged girl and a woman with a baby strapped under her arm followed the man as he went, securing the net at intervals to roots and branches. I looked around and saw that we were alone. Everybody else had disappeared to set up the rest of the nets in a similar fashion, to create a giant circle. Or at least it was nearly a circle, Louis said, but for some reason that he didn't understand they never completely closed it. I had to take his word for this, because I couldn't even see the end of the net. I was standing next to as it tapered off into the undergrowth.

I only heard the hunt. Louis and I stayed by the net we'd just seen being set up, and as we waited for the action to begin, Louis explained how it all worked. Once the near-circle of nets had been strung out around a section of forest, the men entered the enclosure to look for game while the women took up positions around the perimeter. The idea was that the men would drive any animals they spotted towards the nets, shouting directions to one another through the trees. As an animal comes dashing out of the bush and into one of the nets, it is the women's job to jump on it, to stop it breaking through, until a man rushes up to deliver the coup de grâce with his spear. Co-ordination and teamwork were thus very important. Once an animal hit the net, it usually didn't take long to break through, so the women had to be alert to grab it quickly. Their most common prey were duikers, the small forest antelopes, and hogs, although larger duikers could leap over the net and vanish into the forest. The only animal the women wouldn't fall on immediately was a porcupine, for obvious reasons. In these cases, they just had to hope a man was close enough to spear it in time.

A whooping sound broke the silence of the forest, the sign that the hunt was beginning, followed by another and then another, as Louis and I crouched down beside our net. The rising whoops and yelps continued to emanate from beyond the trees, and I thought I could just about make out the sound of running through the undergrowth, but still I could see nothing but the forest.

The hunting cries died away for a moment, and then started again, only louder. 'Porcupine,' Louis whispered, 'they've spotted a porcupine.'

I could definitely hear people running now, an unmistakable sound of crashing through the scrub. My eyes scanned the jungle in front of me, straining to see some of the action that was obviously unfurling not far from where we were crouched, but there were no visual signs to corroborate what we were hearing. Then the tone of the cries changed, from a rising clamour to a broken series of faltering sounds.

Louis cocked his head, listening intently. 'They've lost it,' he said. 'They had a porcupine, but it got away.' He stood up and stretched his arms above his head, relieving the tension we'd both felt listening to the invisible hunt. A couple of minutes later, the woman with the baby strapped under her arm reappeared, unhooking the net, followed by Bimbula who was gathering it in.

'We're going to move on,' Louis said, 'look for another place.'

But the porcupine that got away had set the scene for the rest of the day. We continued walking, more or less in a large circle around the camp, Louis said, although I had completely lost my bearings, setting up the nets and looking for dinner. Without success.

At one stage we walked with Bumbu, who showed me a wild yam that she'd dug up somewhere along the way. Later, she paused to gather some leaves from a wiry creeper clinging to a tree. They were *koko* leaves, which would be chopped and lightly boiled to be eaten as a vegetable. Louis said they were the only leafy green the Biaka ate from the forest, something I found extraordinary given the vast number of plants all around us.

Otherwise, the only bit of excitement in an altogether disappointing day came when we happened upon a column of driver ants filing across one of the elephant trails. The guy up ahead stopped abruptly, cried '*Zaku!*' and started sprinting along the track. Louis and I stood watching as he leapt over the crawling insects and disappeared at high speed round a bend.

I remained where I was as Louis performed a similar routine, but when my turn came I crept up to the column of ants on the path to take a look before jumping over them and trotting on. They were just ants, albeit rather large ones. Or so I thought, until I realized that several had crawled up my foot and were now biting my leg with incredible force. Hopping up and down, I rolled up my trouser leg to brush them off. But you don't brush off driver ants. They sink their pincers into your flesh and just cling on. It took me a very painful minute to disconnect them from my leg one by one.

When we made it back to the camp that evening, I was tired and hungry. I was grateful to Bumbu who gave me some of her *koko* leaves as a side order to go with my *foufou* and smoked fish. But the leaves didn't really taste of anything, and they hardly made up for the distinctly meagre portion of blackened fish.

There was a slightly cheerless air about the place after the second unsuccessful day of hunting. Louis also said that the *foufou* reserves were running low. This worried me too. I didn't like the stuff, but there wasn't an awful lot else.

Actually this wasn't totally true. Concerned that the forest fare might not be totally to my liking, I'd buried in the bottom of my rucksack a small tin of sardines I'd bought in Brazzaville at the beginning of my trip. It was my emergency rations, and after the unsatisfactory dinner I decided that now was the time to break it out. Later that evening, as everyone was preparing for bed, I sneaked into the undergrowth behind my hut, tugged at the ring-pull and got stuck in to the succulent fish swimming in oil. I could still smell the oil on my fingers as I lay down to sleep that night.

Hunting and foraging were on the agenda again the following day. We walked further from the camp before setting up the nets, crossing two streams as we went. I'd got bored with the number of times I'd waded across a river and either walked on with boots sloshing full of water or been forced to sit down and pull them off and wring out my socks. I'd been reluctant to take off my footwear for weeks, fearful that some unpleasant tropical nasty would seize the opportunity to burrow into my feet and set up home there. But neither my socks nor my boots ever properly dried after a night by the fire and the prospect of contracting trenchfoot had also started to bother me.

I'd been warned about jiggers, tropical fleas that burrow into your skin, especially round the toenails, to lay their eggs. Once in, the flea swells to the size of a small white pea and itches like crazy. The only way to get rid of the flea is to dig it out with a needle and I didn't fancy that. The dangers of walking round without shoes, as all the Biaka did, had been brought home to me afresh when the chief had trodden on a thorn on the walk from the village. He'd been confined to his shelter ever since we'd arrived with a big toe swollen to the size of a small balloon, looking very sorry for himself. This wasn't just bad news for the chief. No one else knew how to use his crossbow, so we'd all lost another potential way of getting meat.

But when we came upon the first stream that morning and Louis squatted down to pull off his sneakers, I finally gave in to the prospect of waterlogged footwear for the rest of the day and incipient footrot. So I sat down on my hat, still mindful of Crickette's warning about parasitic worms in the leaf litter, to unlace my boots.

The first attempt at hunting that morning was, like the previous two days, a disappointment. As people were unhooking their nets, ready to move on, Bumbu and another, older, woman named Dokuli, announced that they were going to concentrate on foraging for the rest of the day, and Louis and I decided to accompany them. Bumbu, who was wearing a sprig of leaves round her neck this morning, and had slipped a small twig through her pierced ear, told us that they'd noticed a *payu* tree nearby on the previous day's hunting expedition and that this was where they were heading. They cajoled one of the men to come with us as protection against gorillas.

'Oh good,' said Louis, '*payu* nuts are one of my favourites. They're delicious roasted or they make them into a sauce for meat.'

The tree was one of the tallest around, its mighty trunk towering arrow-straight into the heavens for a good 30 metres before its first branch spread out to hang over the forest floor like a giant hand. All around its foot the undergrowth was littered with spherical green furry balls not unlike sweet chestnuts to look at. Louis and I set about helping Bumbu and Dokuli to collect them before they sat down to extract the nuts by holding them on the upturned blade of an axe, clamped tightly against the ground beneath one foot, and bashing the seedcases with a stout stick.

As I watched them split each furry case to reveal a shiny brown, coin-shaped nut that was tossed into the basket, I saw that one of Dokuli's big toes and two of her fingers were permanently bent backwards at unnatural angles – remnants, I supposed, of breakages that had been set badly. Later, she told me, the nut's glossy brown skin would be carefully peeled off with the fingernails to reveal a thin white disc that was roasted over the fire.

The women were in good spirits as they cracked the *payu* nuts and I thought it might be an appropriate time to ask them how they thought I'd fared so far on my crash course in jungle survival.

'Ha! You'd die in a day', Bumbu told me with a cheeky grin.

This struck me as a bit harsh, so I pointed out that I could make my own shelter, and that now at least I could identify a *payu* tree and knew how to extract its nuts.

'All right,' Dokuli conceded, 'maybe you wouldn't die until the second day.' And they both fell about laughing.

We continued foraging, stopping to pick more *koko* leaves when we saw them or to dig up roots. Bumbu let me excavate the thick brown earth around the base of a long stringy vine which she had identified by its leaf as belonging to a wild yam. The leaf looked just like all the other leaves around it as far as I was concerned, but secreted just below the surface was a large tuber that Louis assured me would taste like a potato when boiled. While I was uncovering the yam with Bumbu's machete, Dokuli had wandered off to do some digging of her own. She returned with some short white roots that looked like albino carrots and came with the unmistakable odour of garlic.

As we made our way back along the trails to camp towards the end of the day, I reflected on my time so far with the Biaka. Although my eyes had been opened wider to the possibilities of survival in the jungle, I had to agree with Dokuli's conclusion that I still wouldn't last long if left alone in this environment. I could now identify a *payu* tree, but their nuts wouldn't keep me going for long, and all the other supplies we'd found today would have remained invisible to me on my own. I was also yet to see any wildlife in this part of the forest, sweat bees and driver ants notwithstanding, although I was hardly alone in this. None of the hunters had yet managed to catch anything either. But despite my continued inability to feed myself, being here with these good-natured people had largely dispelled my apprehension of the forest. Its sinister reputation in my mind had dissolved like the ethereal mist that enshrouded our camp each morning, burning off in the first shafts of sunlight. This was still a place of mystery and murky darkness, but it was now not nearly as menacing. My deliverance from its threatening grip was symbolized for me by my decision to remove my boots and wade barefoot through the streams.

And I wasn't the only one who had felt a sense of release during my time back in the monochrome netherworld. I'd also been struck by some sharp differences in the Biaka's conduct between forest and village. Largely silent and unassuming in Bangui-Motaba, they had cast off this veneer of reserve almost as soon as they'd slipped in through the wall of vegetation, chatting and joking among themselves seemingly without a care in the world. This transformation had even been formalized in a short ritual that had taken place round a large tree near the area where we'd established our camp on the first day. After pulling up the saplings and scraping away the leaf litter, everyone had gathered around the giant trunk on the edge of the clearing, brandishing uprooted saplings and branches chopped from nearby trees.

They stood round the tree facing in towards its base, beating the ground with their leafy boughs, singing and chanting. It was a sort of liberation song that lasted just a few minutes. What were the words? I'd asked Louis.

'It's in appreciation of being back in the forest,' he told me. 'They're singing "Fuck the Bantu".'

Liberated they might have been, but the hunting still wasn't going according to plan. For the third day in a row, the hunters returned empty-handed. The atmosphere in the camp was again subdued as the last helpings of *foufou* were handed round, supplemented by the fruits of the forest gathered that day. Louis and I passed on the *foufou* and made do with wild yam and *payu* nuts for dinner. The yam delivered little excitement for the tastebuds on its own, but the toasted nuts gave it a delicious smack of roasted almonds. It just wasn't really enough for a full meal, that's all.

After dinner, Louis joined the men in what looked like a pretty serious discussion about the unsuccessful hunting. Not eating enough food is one of the theories put forward by medical scientists to explain why pygmies are small. My new Biaka friends weren't that vertically challenged, but even the tallest were still shorter than me, and I stand well short of six foot.

It's during puberty that pygmies lose out, apparently, their bodies having reduced levels of an insulin-like growth hormone throughout the maturation process. While outside their forest realm, adolescents tend to put on a spurt of growth, in pygmies this enlargement is blunted. Quite why this is so remains a matter for conjecture. It may be because of reduced food intake throughout their lives, or a tropical forest survival factor that is yet to be documented. Conversely, some put it down to a simple accident of genetic history. In the current circumstances, I was tempted by the lack of food theory.

Louis wandered back to my shelter after half an hour with a puzzled look on his face. 'It's curious, y'know,' he said thoughtfully, 'but they're saying that the animals in this area have been frightened away...' he looked at me with his brow furrowed, 'by a bad smell.' He looked unconvinced. 'One of them reckons it's a fishy smell.'

Assuming they meant the supplies we'd brought from the village, I asked if smoked fish was known to have this effect. 'No, no,' replied Louis, 'it's not the smoked stuff we brought with us. That's fine. They say it's a different kind of fish, with an oily smell.'

My heart missed a beat. I looked over towards the men who were still discussing with some animation the circumstances of the disastrous hunting. They were stretched out on their heaps of redundant netting, chewing *payu* nuts that they were roasting over the fire. Beyond them, fires gently crackled in front of the other shelters. A small boy was carefully chipping the end of a long pole with a machete, stopping every so often to address a metal spearhead to the new shaft. Dokuli was busy weaving twine from a strip of bark she'd cut and pulled from a tree on the way back from our foraging.

I drew breath and sighed, feeling terrible. 'Maybe it's this', I said, delving into my rucksack to find the empty sardine tin.

Louis looked shocked. 'Where'd you get that?' he asked incredulously. I explained myself, shrivelled with embarrassment.

'My God!' said Louis, taking the empty red tin from my hand and waving it under his nose to smell it. 'You had this all along, and you didn't share it with me.'

We ceremoniously burned the sardine tin on my fire to rid it of the smell, after Louis had shown it to everyone with an explanation of my misdemeanour. I trailed after him like a naughty schoolboy, offering my feeble apologies to all concerned. Fortunately for me, it was only Louis who seemed upset at my deception. The Biaka were just pleased that the cause of the fruitless hunting had been identified and disposed of. Tomorrow would be better, they were sure of it. But I still went to bed that night feeling like Judas.

The following day, we walked further still away from the camp before setting up the nets. Everybody was convinced of my sardine tin's culpability, but even now that it had been destroyed, they weren't taking any chances. They preferred to try in a new area, far from the slightest possibility of lingering fishy vapours. We were on the edge of the *bimba* trees, as they gave way to the more tangled undergrowth and marshy ground associated with a stretch of swamp forest.

Louis had made a few quips about my secret sardines as we'd trudged through the bush, but thankfully he was treating the incident more as a joke than an insult. I took up position with him near the huge buttress roots of a giant tree as the remainder of the party dissolved into the forest in both directions to set up the rest of the nets. The base of the tree was splayed out in fluted columns like the bottom end of a Saturn-5 rocket. My eyes followed the trunk up as it soared towards the ether, its crown lost among the other treetops. It struck me that here the trees properly had crowns, because in this forest the tree was still king.

Far off, I heard the whooping sounds that signalled the start of the hunt. They continued from beyond our field of vision as the hunters beat their way through the undergrowth in search of prey. A shriller cry caught Louis's attention and he whispered, 'Duiker!' as the clamour of voices grew louder. Louis sprang up and started running, drawn towards the yelling and screaming. I followed, crashing through the creepers like a man possessed, hoping against hope that they'd been successful, that my transgression with the sardine tin would be finally laid to rest.

When we came upon a group gathered round a stretch of netting, they were shouting and agitated. The duiker had leapt over the net and got away. It sounded as if recriminations were being made, but Louis said that they were more excited that there were animals here to be caught. All they had to do was keep trying.

We walked for just ten minutes, along the edge of the swamp forest, before unfurling the nets once more. Far above the canopy lay a perfect blue sky, a brilliant day which cast sun-dappled patches among the trees, and down here in the forest there was a wonderfully fresh tang to the air. Soon the hunting cries had begun again, the commotion steadily rising in a crescendo as the sound of running filtered through the jungle. Louis was again tuned in to the sound of voices dashing through the world of plants.

'They've seen something.' He paused, head cocked towards the distant noises. 'What is it?' I whispered. 'I don't know...' he paused. 'But whatever it is, they've got it. They've definitely caught something.' And once more we dashed off to witness the event.

A small group was huddled round the catch, a curious deer-like creature that two of the men held up for me to see. 'It's a chevrotain,' Louis told me, 'a water chevrotain. They're pretty common in these swampy areas. It's an ancient species of ruminant, and it's thought to have remained the same for about twenty million years.' It looked a bit like a prehistoric brown badger, and was certainly enough to make you start doubting Darwin. But I didn't have time to consider it further because the chevrotain was already being butchered and divided up, pieces of its meat being thrown excitedly into baskets and covered with leaves.

Complex rules govern how a catch is shared out among the Biaka, the principal share going to the owner of the net in which it is snared. As I'd seen, the men are the main net-wielders, but one or more women also often command nets. I turned to see Dokuli, with both her fists raised in the air, dancing a little celebratory jig in front of a giant treetrunk. Shadows moved, playing across her beaming face, as saggy breasts flapped up and down on her scrawny chest.

'It's her net', said Louis, smiling.

But almost as soon as the chevrotain had been dispatched, a new commotion unfolded to my right. Another gaggle of excited Biaka ran up towards us, led by Bimbula in his tattered red shirt. He was awkwardly nursing something in his arms that was clearly rather heavy. It was a porcupine, its fat black and white quills splayed out down its back. All around me, people were laughing and shouting with exhilaration. We were just two hours into the hunt and already they'd caught two sizeable animals.

Louis and I ate a snack of roasted *payu* nuts and porcupine skin barbecued on the fire while we waited for the main course. The porcupine tasted like pork, only sweeter. I asked Bimbula whether they'd be using the quills for anything and he said they'd probably feed them to their dogs back in the village. Louis reckoned the Biaka sometimes stuck them through their noses as decorations. Bumbu, Dokuli and some of the other women had returned from the hunt with blue patterns on their faces, abstract designs applied as a paste ground from a forest plant. But the Biaka's most alarming form of beautification was their penchant for chipping their teeth into points. If this group was representative, the men did it more than the women.

After our porcupine appetizer came the water chevrotain and some pieces of blue duiker that had been caught later in the day. The meat was juicy and succulent and everyone gorged themselves. That night, as the fires died down to become just smouldering embers in the darkness, our clearing glowed with speckles of luminescent mould that grew on flecks of decaying vegetation. The chief's wife began to sing a haunting five-note harmony, her rich tones echoing in the trees, reverberating through the forest cathedral.

From deep inside the black netherworld, she was answered by an extraordinary falsetto screeching, the voice of the forest spirit. Slowly, the unnerving screams approached us, the spirit's presence drawn by the mellifluous pentatonic harmony.

An insistent rhythm began on the drums as an agitated rustling came near, words cascading into our clearing in a frenzy of Mr Punch-like speech. All around me, replies came as ritualistic chants floating on the beat of the drums. Women got to their feet as the wild mass of vegetation entered our arena. They danced on the ground sprinkled with stars, their movements barely visible but for an irregular flicker of flame as they weaved their way around the spirit with the grace and delicacy of night butterflies. Otherwise I could make out just the outlines of our shelters glowing in the orange haze of the firelight, and above them the silhouettes of the giant trees

The spirit danced to a different rhythm, charging back and forth with reckless abandon in the profound darkness. It cackled and it screamed, spanking the ground with startling force, emitting a sound like planks of wood being smacked together. Then it calmed, swaying on the spot deep beneath the trees, demanding answers from the clean, pure forest. A fire flared briefly behind me, throwing my gigantic head and shoulders high against the invisible wall of vegetation and smoke. Glistening thighs, swaying hips and swinging arms flickered in the sparks and I felt myself swimming in a paradise of natural sounds: the constant pulse of the drums, the eerie chants, the bewildering shrieks. And behind it, the rich acoustic tapestry of the forest's hum: the high squeaks of the tree frogs, the fruit bat honks, the tireless throb of bush crickets laid down on a bed of jingle bells and birds singing in the darkness.

Up above, my eyes searched the treetops. The night sky was brighter than the black of the forest, my vision a constellation of twinkling pin-pricks. But down here the luminescent flecks were from a different universe, one wrapped in the soft dark glove of the forest.

SAND

Niger

ONE

Laila pulled her headscarf out to flop down over her forehead and sighed as she moved to take up position beneath the branches of an acacia tree. 'I'm a Tuareg,' she said, 'but I must stand in the shade. It's too hot in the sun, I get headaches.' Grateful for a respite from the sun's glaring rays, I joined her beneath the thorn tree, squatting down with my back against the trunk to rest my weary legs.

We were waiting for my turn in the *hammam*, or steam bath, a small pool enclosed in a square mud-brick structure fed by a hot spring. The bath at Tafédek had been described to me as something like a Saharan Lourdes. The waters were known throughout the region for their curative and restorative powers. People from all over Niger and beyond travelled to this shallow dry river bed dotted with palms and acacia trees to take its waters. Individuals with skin problems, rheumatism, persistent headaches and ailments of a more serious nature flocked to Tafédek. Others arrived for precautionary reasons, so Laila told me, viewing a dip as a sort of occasional body service to fortify themselves against the rigours of desert life. Laila had suggested it might be a good place to prepare myself for my journey into the great sandy desert of the Ténéré.

On first hearing her proposal, it hadn't immediately sounded like a rational one. The idea that immersion in hot water could be any sort of preparation for a week's walk across a sandy desert, where water would be at a serious premium, seemed inherently contradictory to me. To my way of thinking, a far better initiation would be a couple more days spent reclining beneath an acacia tree in midday temperatures that were topping 45°C (113°F) in the shade. Maybe I could intersperse my lounging with a stroll or two, I thought, although nothing too strenuous since I had to conserve my strength for what would surely be testing times ahead. Taking a bath seemed nonsensical. This would probably be the last bath I'd see for the next month.

But Laila had insisted otherwise, and by the time I'd squatted down beside her in the shade of the tree, I'd come round to the idea. Although still supremely inappropriate to my mind, I thought a bath might be rather pleasant after several dusty days of travelling to reach this spot on the edge of the Sahara, about 50 kilometres north of the town of Agadez. A group of Tuareg women were in the hot bath before me, and the giggles and playful screams emanating from behind the bathhouse door suggested that I could expect an enjoyable plunge.

I'd been awaiting my turn for the best part of the morning, hanging around as the day warmed up, watching the comings and goings of the regular flow of visitors to this hallowed spot. The male bathkeeper, a wiry individual with a squashed nose and a small black moustache, had wandered over to chat with us for a while, telling me that he had to walk to work every morning from his village three kilometres away. He had eight children, he said, but couldn't remember all of their names. 'I get up so early in the morning and return from work each day so late,' he said, 'that I never see them.'

He had disappeared again following the arrival of his next male customer, a lanky youth who strode into view with a large wooden crate on his head. He had asked Laila and me if we'd look after this object while he took the waters. Inside his crate, the open top of which was stretched over with chicken wire, was a writhing mass of lizards; twenty-five in total, the youth announced, the fruits of fifteen days' hunting. The lizards, with wide flat heads and flared spiny tails, were horny and grey but tinged with bright colours, some orange, some yellow, as if unwitting victims of a child's attempt to brighten their drab hides with poster paints.

'He will sell them in Agadez,' Laila told me. 'Some extract taken from beneath their skin is used for anti-venom against snake and scorpion bites.'

When the lizard hunter reappeared, looking appropriately refreshed, and the women trooped into the bathhouse, Laila started to explain what I should and shouldn't do to gain most benefit from taking a bath at Tafédek. As she did so, my view on the suitability of this ritual as an initiation to my march across the Ténéré Desert began to shift once more. 'Try not to move too much in the water,' she said, which puzzled me until she explained that it would be really very hot indeed. 'Ooooh! So hot,' she exclaimed, 'you'll feel that you are being boiled alive.' I was definitely starting to go off the idea again.

'If you stay still, you can tolerate it,' Laila went on, 'but moving your arms and legs will cause you much pain.' I mentally adjusted my expectations once more. On balance, maybe my plunge wasn't going to be so much fun.

But hot, of course, was something I was going to have to get used to. I'd come to the Sahara after all, the desert of deserts. It's the world's largest, occupying about a third of the African continent. Being so vast, it tends to be broken down into regional subsets. And although the Sahara is by no means entirely covered by sand, it's the sandy parts that tend to catch the imagination and get labelled. Stretches of dunes that are so immense they've been dubbed 'sand seas' make up the Libyan Desert, Egypt's Western Desert and, here in Niger, a landlocked country that straddles Arab and Black Africa, my ultimate destination: the Ténéré Desert.

To find out how life is lived in this most inhospitable of landscapes, I was aiming to join a group of desert nomads who make the journey across the dunes of the Ténéré once a year to buy dates. The dates are traded in the south for their annual household needs: clothes, soap, and millet to supplement their diet of meat and milk. Each year around late August or early September, the time of the date harvest in the oases to the north of the Ténéré, these people saddle up their camels and set out to walk several hundred kilometres across the desert. The risks are considerable. The Ténéré is renowned for its ferocious sand and dust storms. Even experienced nomads can lose their way in 'the place with no life' as Laila described the area to me, and losing your way can mean missing a water hole. If you miss a water hole, that's the end of your trip. You simply die of thirst.

And the first thing that Laila was advising me to do in preparation for this epic journey was to have a bath.

Inside, the mud-brick building was just a small dark room lined with a rough bench structure built into its mud walls encircling a sunken pit about a metre deep. The bath was about the size of a narrow mattress so that you could lie down and totally immerse yourself. The bath attendant with the eight anonymous children was busy flushing the women's water out through a plughole in the bottom of the bath as I took up position on the bench alongside two other men both also stripped to their underpants. High in the wall opposite the door was a hole to the outside where a long pipe was used to flood the bath with water. As the sunken bath was slowly refilled, the atmosphere inside the bathhouse became more humid and our torsos were soon glistening with sweat. I poked my toe into the stream of water and got a shock. It wasn't just hot, it was scalding.

Assuming the two other guys knew what they were doing, I sat back to watch as they took it in turns to immerse themselves in the water once the bath was filled. Each seemed similarly shocked as he slowly submerged his body. Although it was fairly clear from the grimace on the first man's face that he wasn't exactly enjoying himself, I asked him how he was feeling as he floated in the gently steaming bath.

'Ça va,' he managed to say through his clenched teeth. He didn't look *ça va* at all to me but he was putting a brave face on it. Bracing himself on the sides of the bath, he screwed up his eyes and slowly lowered his head beneath the water. Like him, I took a gulp of air and held my breath.

He kept himself under for a few seconds and then emerged with a sharp gasp. Ever so slowly he stood up and proceeded to rub his arms and legs with the water. The hint of a smile crept over his face, but, I suspected, not so much of satisfaction as relief at reaching the end of the procedure. He climbed out of the bath and the wiry attendant took over rubbing his limbs as the second guy stepped gingerly into the water.

The second man looked even more uncomfortable than the first. He managed to sit down, his torso half in and half out of the scalding water, but he looked far from content.

'Ça va?' I asked him, just to be sure.

'Ça va pas', he replied. This guy really wasn't enjoying himself. He stood up again, his face a picture of contortion, and clambered out of the bath. He'd had enough. Now it was my turn.

I manoeuvred myself to sit down on the edge of the sunken bath, swung my legs over the hot pool, and with a sharp intake of breath lowered them into the water. A terrible burning sensation immediately enveloped my lower legs as the rest of my body was convulsed by an involuntary shiver. Laila had been right; it was like being boiled alive from the knees down.

Chuckles of delight were coming from my two fellow victims, and the bath attendant, now vigorously rubbing the scalp of the second bather, beamed a toothy grin at me and gestured that I should stop messing around and get right in. For a brief moment I considered backing out. Laila had stayed outside during this all-male session and wouldn't be witness to my cowardice. I could tell her that I'd sat down in the water and felt the full benefit before retiring for my rub down.

I looked at my legs, now a bright shade of lobster. Goose pimples had appeared all over them as my body fought to come to terms with the ridiculous temperature. But now that my legs were still, the pain wasn't nearly so bad. As Laila had warned me, it was moving about in the hot water that caused the agony. If I could just get the rest of my body into the water, I sensed it would be OK.

I placed my hands on either side of the bath's edge, took the weight of my body on my arms, and as slowly as humanly possible eased myself down into the liquid inferno.

'*Ça va?*' asked one of my colleagues with obvious concern.

'*Ça va*', I told him, which was at least half true.

In fact, sitting up to my chest in boiling water was not nearly as terrible as I'd imagined it would be when my legs had first taken the plunge. Partly, I supposed, this was because I was getting used to it, but movement, or a lack of it, was still the key. So long as I remained stock still, it was almost pleasant. And now that I was virtually there, I decided that I'd better go the full distance and put my head under as well. I inched my bottom forward and lay back, letting the balmy waters slowly envelop my skull. An agreeable tingling sensation crept over my scalp and I heard a disembodied cheer rise up from my soulmates.

In one sense, perhaps Laila had made the right call. Now that I'd survived being boiled alive, maybe my journey across the Ténéré would seem like a walk in the park.

Tafédek lies on the fringes of northern Niger's Aïr Massif, a landscape of hard granite punched through by volcanic craters and ancient lava flows. The Aïr wouldn't really qualify as a range of mountains in most other places since its highest peak is less than 2,000 metres, but its prominence here had been brought home to me as Laila and I had left the dusty, featureless plains round Agadez and climbed on to a plateau of dark rocks and hills.

The Aïr has long been a stronghold of the Tuareg, one of many peoples that make up the population of Niger. Traditionally nomadic herders and warriors, they have ranged over vast areas of the Sahara throughout their history, from Algeria and Mali in the west to Libya and Niger in the east. No one is very sure about their origins, but some say they wandered into the desert from Crete or Asia Minor many centuries ago, and their light skin-colour and Caucasian features appear to confirm this northerly stock.

Although known to outsiders as Tuareg, the name itself is of Arab origin and means 'those cast out by God'. It dates back to the time when the Arabs tried to overpower them by force, but these proud and independent nomads know themselves as *Imazighen*, or 'free people'. The Tuareg are Islamic, but hardliners don't consider them to be true Moslems since few can understand Arabic and hence most are unable to read the Koran. Their language, Tamashek, uses an old Libyan script consisting of dots and dashes that to the uninitiated Western eye looks uncannily like a variation on Morse code. Another difference between the Tuareg and most other Islamic peoples lies in the Tuareg's matriarchal social structure in which children are considered to be descended from their mother. A child's male next of kin is not the physical father but an uncle, the brother of the mother, from whom inheritance is claimed. For these reasons, Tuareg women enjoy a position of greater respect than in most other Islamic societies. 'In some families,' Laila had told me with a knowing smile, 'the woman is treated like a princess. She needs to do no work. Even if she wants a cup of tea, a man will make it for her.'

Blessed with great self-esteem, the Tuareg have never taken kindly to being bossed around by outsiders and have always fought fiercely to retain their independence. During the colonial period, when France ran this part of West Africa, they had a few run-ins with their European rulers, notably in 1916–17 when the Tuareg laid siege to the fort at Agadez. After beating off their attackers, the French retaliated by forcibly resettling most of the Tuareg from Aïr on the plains to the south. But some Tuareg remained in the Aïr and the massif once again became their volcanic citadel in the early 1990s during an uprising against Niger's independent government.

When I finally emerged from my steam bath, feeling remarkably healthy, I found Laila, still in the shade of the acacia tree, talking to the two guys with whom I had shared my dip. They had made a two-day journey to get their dose of Tafédek's restorative waters and were about to leave for the trip back to their encampment deeper inside the Aïr's rocky terrain. Laila told me they had asked us if we could join them and I gladly agreed.

I hadn't recognized the men immediately because each was now fully dressed in a voluminous outfit rather like pyjamas, known as a *boubou*, and a lengthy cotton headdress that included a wrap-around part covering all but the eyes and tip of the nose. Given the woman's importance in Tuareg society, it should come as no surprise that she does not wear a veil – I could see all of Laila's face. Perhaps more startling is the fact that the men do. From the age of eighteen, a man hides his face beneath the folds of his combination turban and veil.

The Tuareg are said to be the only people in the world whose men go about veiled. The reasons behind this custom are as shrouded in mystery as the origins of the Tuareg themselves. Certainly, covering the face makes good practical sense during a sand storm, but this doesn't explain why the veil is still worn even inside a tent. Some say that the practice has its roots in an ancient Arab belief that warriors should go into battle with their faces covered. Others say that the veil protects a man from breathing in evil spirits. Another explanation says that a warrior on his deathbed would lose his soul through his nose and mouth if his face were uncovered.

In times past a man would not even remove his veil to eat or drink, which meant mastering an awkward technique of guiding the spoon or glass of tea into his mouth beneath it. Tuareg men also developed a complex series of minor adjustments to their veils to show moods and emotions. These customs are enforced less rigidly today but, even so, my steam bath session was the only time I saw these, or any other Tuareg men, with their heads uncovered.

It took my new Tuareg acquaintances half an hour to round up their camels, which had been left to graze with their front legs tied together so that they couldn't wander too far. All the camels were prominently marked on the face, neck or flank with deep scars notifying their ownership and each had at least one leather pouch hanging on a chain or thong around its neck to ward off evil spirits. The men, too, wore an assortment of amulets round their necks for similar purposes. There were half a dozen of them in the party, led by an elderly man named Edoua, who was dressed in a black *boubou* and deep-indigo-coloured headdress. Edoua took the lead camel by its rope and we made our way up the dry river bed, away from Tafédek and its steam bath.

As we climbed out of the river bed we left the last of the palms and acacia trees behind us. The track we followed took us up into a desolate landscape of sun-baked black boulders and rocks devoid of vegetation. We walked for a couple of hours or so before Edoua broke the desert's silence to tell me that he had been traversing the Ténéré all his life. His year was divided in two, he said. Six months were spent crossing the desert back and forth from Bilma where he bought salt to be carried to Zinder in the south of Niger, a journey of fifteen days. The other half of the year he grazed his camels in the Aïr mountains.

Bilma is one of a string of remote oases that nestle in the lee of an extended line of cliffs in the north-east of Niger near the border with Chad. The trade of salt from these oases across the Ténéré is an ancient form of commerce traditionally dominated by the Tuareg. All animals, like people, need salt as a vital part of their diet but there are few naturally saline deposits in the savannahs of West Africa, the strip of land bordering the Sahara to the south known as the Sahel, home to millions of grazing livestock. Hence, for centuries, Edoua and his forefathers have made a living carrying rough blocks of salt on their camels across the desert to sell to the herders of the Sahel.

'The Ténéré can kill even the people who really know it,' Edoua told me as we moved on across the barren rocks of the Aïr. 'You must carry enough water, food for you and food for your camels. But water is the key. The greatest danger is to lose your way without enough water. The bare essentials for a journey into the Ténéré are to take enough water and a good guide.'

The months of winter were the only time to make the crossing, he told me. This was when camels and men required least water. Few Tuareg, he said, attempt to cross the Ténéré between April and October.

My heart sank when Laila translated this last part. It was the beginning of September and I didn't want to hear that I would be attempting my journey during a Tuareg no-go period. But I would not be travelling with the Tuareg. The object of my journey when I came to make it would be dates, the other product for which the oases around Bilma are famous. And the trade in dates tends to be the preserve of another group of Saharan nomads: the Tubu.

To outsiders like me, the Tubu are perhaps the least known of all the pastoral societies inhabiting the Sahara and its fringes. Like other nomads, they are noted for their endurance and courage, but I had also heard that the Tubu have a rough and sometimes violent reputation, which concerned me for a while. Until, that is, I discovered an additional peculiarity of my quest to traverse the Ténéré: that it was only the Tubu women who made this hazardous desert crossing in search of dates. Tough, of course, they had to be, just to attempt such a journey, but women, I figured, were perhaps less likely to be quite as rough and violent as their menfolk. And when Laila had described how some Tuareg women were treated like princesses my spirits rose even further. Princesses of the desert they might be, but no princess could be that horrific.

Seeking further reassurance, I asked Edoua for his opinion on Tubu women. He pulled out a small leather pouch from the folds of his *boubou* and took a wad of tobacco from it to slip into his mouth as he considered his answer.

'Tubu women are not better than the Tuareg, but they are also strong', he said, rather diplomatically I thought.

But Laila had other ideas and she was adamant about them. 'They are tougher than Tuareg women,' she said, 'definitely.' She added, 'And they all carry knives. You must be on your guard, Nick, because they are not afraid to use them.'

To hammer home the point, Laila told me a story when Edoua called a halt and the men set about hobbling the camels for the night.

'A Tubu woman had a fiancé and she told him that for one month he could look anywhere around the group for another woman. "If you see any girl you like more than me, you can go with her," she told this man,' Laila explained. '"But if after one month we are still together," the Tubu woman went on, "you must never cross me for another woman. Because if you do this, I will kill you."'

Laila gave me a consolation smile as we spread out our blankets over the stony ground to sleep on. 'They are tough, these Tubu women,' she said finally. 'Very tough and very proud. You should never forget that.'

The rounded boulders, glistening and black as if stained by a patina of tar, shimmered into the distance as the sun slipped below the horizon to mark the end of my first day in the Aïr mountains. But with Laila's story still ringing in my ears, the desolate beauty of the scene was rather lost on me.

TWO

The camel is the mainstay of Saharan nomads, whose arid territory lies beyond the range of cattle. True, many also herd goats, but you can't ride a goat across a sand sea or load it with salt blocks and sacks of dates. It is only the camel that has allowed people to roam the desert. This creature is superbly adapted to extremes of both heat and cold (winter temperatures in the Sahara can drop below freezing), it can last many days without a drink of water, and its large padded feet are ideally suited to walking on sand.

But camels are not merely a convenient form of transport. Without their milk, and occasionally their meat, Tuareg and Tubu alike would find it difficult to survive. In the life of the Saharan nomad, camel's milk and cheese take the place of bread, which is virtually unknown in these societies. Blankets and coverings for tents are woven from the camel's soft belly hair, while its leather is worked into strong sandals, bags, ropes and sheaths for knives and swords. Even a camel's dung provides a vital resource. In a land with few trees, it's a ready source of fuel for a fire. A camel's kidneys are so super-efficient at conserving water that its faeces emerge as pre-dried pellets, which can be burnt almost immediately.

There is no doubt that camels are totally indispensable to the nomad. And they know it. They are all born with an attitude. Most camels can be stubborn, bad-tempered and vicious when they want to be, but the rest of the time every one of them is a past master at simply looking haughty and supercilious. In fact, no other animal can look so pompous. The reason for their superiority is explained by the story of Allah's last name. Allah has a hundred different names, ninety-nine of which the prophet Mohammed made known to his followers. But the hundredth name he revealed only to his trusty camel, whispering it into his ear one day as a sign of gratitude for once saving his life. Mohammed's camel was quick to capitalize on this invaluable piece of information and wasted no time in telling all his mates. To this day, no man has ever learned Allah's hundredth name, but all camels know it. Hence their incredibly condescending demeanour.

The following afternoon, Laila and I reached the Tuareg encampment where Edoua and his colleagues were based. The spot, known as Tidene, came as a surprise after the hard, dark volcanic plateau we had walked across. It was an abundant gash of lush grasses and acacia trees. Birds swooped and twittered overhead as camels grazed and herds of goats strutted back and forth through the rainy season pastures ruffled by a gentle breeze.

I'd been glad on our walk to Tidene to have had the opportunity of renewing my acquaintance with the nomad's closest friend, having spent some time the previous year with a camel caravan in Ethiopia. But Laila had told me that the Tubu women I'd be travelling with across the Ténéré would be likely to ride their camels for at least part of the way, and I'd never ridden a camel before. This, she said, I should put right here in Tidene.

She consulted Edoua, who toyed with his indigo veil while thinking for a minute before striding off into the pasture to return a while later leading a dark camel with a bullet wrapped in a leather pouch round its neck. Hanging below this amulet was what looked like a thin skein of wool.

'Oh yes,' said Laila, 'this will be a good one to practise on. He is red, and red camels are the most intelligent.' I hadn't realized that camels were colour-coded. 'Certainly,' Laila replied as if it was the most natural thing in the world. 'All Tuaregs know that white ones are the prettiest, the most elegant. And camels with different coloured patches like that one over there...' she pointed towards a couple of specimens pulling grass up by its roots and chomping it, one of which sported patches on its hide rather like a brown and white version of a Friesian cow, 'they are known to be the hardiest.'

My intelligent red camel was named Agadé and he stood there with his head held high looking superior, rubbing his jaws back and forth over his last blades of grass. I can't say he looked pleased to have had his dinner interrupted for my impromptu riding lesson.

Edoua tugged the rope tied to a ring set through Agadé's nose to make him sit, which he did with a world-weary sigh, folding his legs beneath him in a rather awkward fashion. Even sitting down, the camel was still as tall as I was.

After flinging a striped blanket across the camel's flank, Edoua picked up a saddle that had recently been removed from one of Agadé's colleagues. The wooden saddle, which sat snugly just in front of the camel's hump, had a high, narrow back inlaid with intricate leatherwork in red, sky blue and yellow. Its front, which jutted out over the camel's neck, looked like an extended arm with three thick fingers splayed at its apex. Once the saddle was secured with a rope beneath Agadé's belly, Edoua slung another blanket across the seat.

He turned to look me over as he chewed his wad of tobacco and said something while pointing to my feet.

'You need to remove your shoes,' said Laila.

I did so.

Edoua followed suit, flipping off his sandals and placing his gnarled toes on the calf of the camel's nearest front leg to show me how it was done. Holding Agadé's rope in one hand, he grabbed the base of the front of the saddle and in one fluid movement whipped his other leg over to sit comfortably atop the huge beast. Agadé continued masticating to himself, now supremely unconcerned.

Edoua eased his right foot into the skein of wool tied around the camel's lower neck and explained through Laila that this was the accelerator.

'You need to make like a stamping motion on its neck, but not as hard as stamping, more like a massage with your foot, to make him go. The harder you push with your foot, the faster he will go.'

Edoua dug his toes into the camel's neck and the animal unfolded his legs to stand. Edoua got him walking with another shimmy of his toes and showed how to steer with a simple pull on the rope to one side or the other. Before I knew it, Agadé was sitting down again and with consummate ease Edoua slipped out of the saddle.

He handed me the rope.

These things always look so easy when shown to you by an expert. I assumed that Edoua, who was fifty years old if he was a day, had been doing this for at least forty of those years, and possibly more. Later I was to see small children riding camels with the effortlessness of a seasoned expert. I, of course, was nothing of the kind.

Agadé made a loud snort when I placed my bare foot gingerly on his front calf and put my weight on it. I swung my other foot and managed to reach the seat of the saddle. With a quick shove from Edoua, I struggled into position.

'Good', said Laila with a winning smile.

Edoua grabbed my right foot and thrust it beneath the skein of wool on Agadé's neck.

'You can hold on to the bottom of this front bit,' Laila explained, tapping the base of the long arm-like protuberance at the front of the saddle. 'But don't hold the top, it is not strong enough. To make him stand, just dig your toes into his neck', she added.

Hanging on to the rein in my right hand and grabbing a hold on the front of the saddle with my left, I dug my toes into the rough fur. Agadé continued to chew the cud. Otherwise nothing else happened. I dug my toes in harder, giving my foot a thrust almost like a small kick. Still chewing, Agadé turned his head as if to take in the scenery. Otherwise, still nothing else happened. We'd reached a bit of an impasse.

Edoua took the rein from my hand and lifted it above Agadé's head. The camel got the message and proceeded to stand.

This sounds simple. I'd got myself seated on a camel and now the animal was standing up. Very straightforward, you might think. I'd seen the procedure more than a dozen times already since my arrival in the Aïr and naturally the rider had always looked totally poised. Admittedly, the camel usually seemed rather ungainly as it unfolded its legs and jerked itself up on to its knees in a puff of dust, but its Tuareg rider had always looked comfortable and unconcerned as he leant back and forward in one smooth, flowing movement while the camel gained height in a see-saw fashion.

Knowing that my turn would soon be coming, I had studied the process carefully. It appeared to be merely a question of shifting your balance forwards and backwards as the camel rose on its hind and front legs. But watching a demonstration and doing it yourself are worlds apart. Remembering when to lean forwards in the saddle and when to lean back had got muddled in my mind. To me it was an unfamiliar set of co-ordinated movements, like trying to remember which pedal is the brake and which the accelerator when you first sit in the driving seat of a car.

Agadé lurched forward on to his knees. I grabbed the saddle's protuberance in front of me to stop myself being flung forward and impaled on it.

'Not the top,' Laila shouted. 'The stick will break, hold it at the bottom.'

I shifted my grip and tried to lean back, but at that moment, the camel was raising itself on to its front knees and I should have been leaning in precisely the opposite direction. No sooner had I adjusted my balance a second time than Agadé was stretching his hind legs to their full extent and I was suddenly propelled forward again. This time I managed to grab a hold on the base of the saddle's front protuberance.

Laila was clapping. 'Great, that is really excellent. Now you are ready.' She was lying, but I loved her for it. I didn't know how I was still in the saddle, but I'd made it, and encouragement was just what I needed.

'Now go on, go for a walk.'

I dug my toes into Agadé's neck and to my amazement he moved off.

Walking was easy. Someone once told me that riding a camel could induce something akin to sea-sickness. It is said that in French colonial days men were seconded to the camel corps from the navy to combat this problem. Fortunately, I've never suffered from this condition so I can't comment. Agadé just seemed happy enough to wander back and forth as I got used to his rolling gait and the steady rhythmic foot massage I had to maintain on his neck to keep him moving. Steering was also simple since the camel was highly responsive to the slightest pull on his rein.

Things became slightly more challenging, however, when the two guys I'd shared the steam bath with in Tafédek leapt on to their camels and joined me for a trot. This required more rapid pressure to be exerted on Agadé's neck which wasn't difficult, although at the greater speed the need to give a brisk massage with my foot at the same time as steering was severely testing my co-ordination.

When the guys stepped things up another gear, into a sort of jogtrot, I started bouncing around in the saddle, which was decidedly uncomfortable. Leila shouted that I should hold on to the back of the saddle if I was afraid of falling. This was sound advice, since the prospect of plunging from this not inconsiderable height had indeed crossed my mind. It would have been like falling out of a large tree. I think both my balance and co-ordination are as good as the next man's, but holding on to the back of the saddle while continuing my foot action in front and keeping a firm grip on the rein, as half my thoughts were concentrating on the possible outcome of a Tuareg-style accident at work, became almost intolerable.

But at least it was taking my mind off the pain that was now rapidly developing in my buttocks. We continued the jogtrot for too long as far as I was concerned before finally trying to get the camels to run. To my immense relief, Agadé clearly wasn't very keen on running and I soon slowed him back down to a trot as the others dashed off into the distance in a cloud of dust. Camels aren't designed to move at speed. They look ludicrous when they try, their legs splaying out in all directions. Agadé was obviously aware of this and wasn't about to make himself look foolish. And I was certainly with him on that one.

When I finally dismounted and climbed stiffly out of the saddle, Laila gave me a hearty round of applause before looking curiously at the seat of my shorts.

'How are you feeling down there?' she asked me.

'Raw', I replied.

'I thought so,' she said, 'I think those are bloodstains.'

Late that afternoon, after I'd thanked Agadé and led him back to his beloved grass, I went for a stroll with Laila through the lush pastures of Tidene. It felt good to walk off the stiffness in my legs and, although part of me just wanted to rest, I certainly didn't feel like sitting down.

I had gained some appreciation of just how large Tidene was when we had first come upon it on arrival, but I hadn't realized how many people there were camped out in this verdant spot. Everywhere we walked I saw family groups camped beneath thorn trees, some having tied large rush mats in their branches for extra shade. Women were lighting camp fires and making ready soot-blackened pots for the evening meal as men with their backs to the sun quietly prayed on small carpets and rugs.

Towards one edge of the grasses, where low hills sprang up to give notice of the end of the pasture, a troop of camels and their riders were circling a small cluster of figures seated on the baked clay ground. Two other groups, mostly consisting of children, were sat nearby on rocky outcrops looking on as the camels paraded round and round. As we drew nearer, I could hear the faint sounds of singing and rhythmic drumming.

'It is their entertainment,' Laila told me as we approached and took up position to watch with the small boys perched on the rocks. 'The young men ride round the women trying to spot the best-looking ones.'

A light haze of dust was being drummed up from the desiccated surface as the camels continued their trot round the women in a tight circle. The boys we had joined, most dressed in traditional *boubous*, but some sporting dirty T-shirts and patched trousers, took little notice of us as we looked on. Over to our left, the other group of spectators were girls and young women, all dressed in dark tabards dotted with small mirrors that sparkled in the setting sun. Quick glances were shot in our direction between long periods spent gazing at the rhythmic spectacle before us.

'Tuaregs gather in places like this during the rainy season,' Laila told me, 'and the end of the rains is a time to celebrate.' September was the conclusion of the scant rains that fall in this part of the Sahara's fringes. As the dry winter set in, most of these nomads would move south, into the Sahel, the women to graze their goats, while the men would leave to ply the salt trade across the Ténéré.

The camels had paused in their circular routine and three girls from the group to our left sprang up and ran to join the tight cluster of women crouching in the dust.

'They will continue this until nightfall,' Laila went on. 'People are still arriving here because tomorrow there will be a big camel race.'

She looked at me and gave me her winning smile. I could tell what she was thinking. 'Would you like to?' she asked.

The answer was no, but somehow I didn't think it would be that easy to get out of.

It wasn't. The following morning, when I spoke to Edoua, it became clear that he had just assumed my practice session the previous day had been with the race in mind. I didn't like to disappoint him but, either way, I was pretty sure I'd do that. They used to say that it's not the winning that matters so much as the taking part, and most of me didn't really mind being old-fashioned for the day. The exception, as you would expect, was my behind.

Laila told me there would be another session of riding round the women that I could take part in as a warm-up and that's when I was reminded that my backside was still raw. But I managed to find a way of sitting on Agadé's saddle that involved leaning forward to put most of my weight on my thighs and, for a while, I forgot about my tender rear-end as I joined a gang of what must have been twenty or so riders trotting round and round a gaggle of young women huddled together beside a stunted bush in the middle of a clay plain.

The riders proceeded in their tight circle at a formal trot, holding their camels' heads up high on a short rein as the women sang their slightly doleful chants. Time was kept by one woman who banged half a hollow gourd with her flip-flop like a drum, her rhythm matching the strutting of the camels. Round and round we rode, within a few feet of the women, occasionally pulling away to avoid the small bush. I had drifted off to sleep the night before still mentally massaging Agadé's neck with my foot like a seasoned pro, so it didn't take me long to get back into the mood. After a couple of turns I had got my balance and I realized that I could do this without too much pain. I began to enjoy myself riding endlessly round to the mesmerizing beat. I decided that I was certainly better off than the supposedly honoured Tuareg females who had to pull their headscarves tightly over their faces to keep out the dust.

Riders fell out of line every now and again to rest or talk to onlookers and our progress was occasionally interrupted as one of our number abruptly bent low from his saddle and grabbed his chosen woman's headscarf and galloped off trailing the long piece of cotton in the wind. At these junctures, the done thing was to chase after the man with the scarf at high speed, but Agadé and I thought better of it and just ambled over to talk to Laila, who was watching.

As the sun rose higher in the sky, everyone retired to the shade of the trees and Laila and I settled down to what had become my favourite part of the Tuaregs' daily routine: lounging around waiting for it to get cooler. Laila sank a large gourdful of camel's milk and lay down on her mat to sleep, while I reclined to ponder my chances in the coming race. A small torpedo-shaped beetle was struggling across the sand where I lay. To the beetle, the sand grains must have seemed like boulders. It didn't take long for me to conclude that my race prospects were non-existent since I knew that Agadé didn't really like running, at which point I too stretched out on my front to sleep.

The sun was still burning at four o'clock but it was time to amble over to the starting point of the race. Since Laila was coming with me, I walked with her, leading Agadé by his rein, which had the added advantage of saving my buttocks from any pre-race distress. Camels and their riders were sauntering from all directions towards the spot in the lee of a ridge of rounded granite boulders. The finishing post of the race, which would be run over a roughly circular course of about three kilometres, was at the place where we'd been riding round the women that morning.

About thirty men and their camels were gathered at the starting point where I noted a preponderance of white, or pretty, animals over other colours. But Agadé being red and intelligent, I didn't think this would faze him. There was an air of expectancy among the riders as they made themselves ready for the big race, most looking introspective as they chewed on their tobacco. It was more than just honour that was at stake. A cash prize would be shared among the first three riders to pass the finishing post. Edoua, who I assumed was a little old to be still interested in racing his camel, stood nearby chatting to the man who I was told would start us off. I saluted my two friends from the steam bath at Tafédek who were busy tightening the ropes securing their saddles to their camels.

Before leaving for the finishing line, Edoua and Laila introduced me to some of the favourites, each of whom was quietly confident as he toyed with the stiff leather whip hooked around his wrist. I asked them all where they thought they would finish and every one said he would win, except a youngish man in a bright green *boubou* who told me he aimed to be in the first three. Surprisingly, all were politely dismissive of my chances.

The low esteem in which I was apparently held was not improved when the time came to mount Agadé. Kicking off my shoes, I stepped straight on to a long thorn lurking in the sand which sent me hopping around my mount in extreme pain as a ripple of mirth spread through my competitors. It was not a good start.

When I was finally up and in control of my camel, the starter stepped back and thirty camels inched forward in a ragged line jostling for position. All around me my fellow participants made final adjustments to their headdresses, pulling the veil part up over their noses, and I wedged my hat down tighter on my head. We all turned our heads to concentrate on the starter.

The man held up his hand and I tightened my grip on Agadé's rein. The starter's hand swooped down to smack on his thigh and we were off.

Cue pandemonium. One hundred and twenty long and gangly camels' legs shot off in all directions, propelling their riders forward in a great cloud of dust. Spurred on by his compatriots, Agadé kept pace with them for all of 50 metres, with me hanging on to the back of my saddle for dear life. In a blur of atmospheric dirt, whips were smacked on rumps and *boubous* trailed out behind in the turmoil. For the first minute or so, I surprised even myself by actually trying to keep up, despite the shots of serious pain that went flashing up my back like bolts of forked lightning every time my bottom bounced in the saddle. But as the other riders started to pull away, both Agadé and I came to our senses and he slowed to a gentle trot. We were left to eat their dust while we contemplated our predestined defeat.

Half an hour later, Agadé and I trotted across the finishing line and I put an extra effort into my foot massage to bring us in with a bit of dignity. I'd rather enjoyed our little outing through the stark boulders and wispy white grasses blowing in the evening breeze.

Hundreds of spectators had turned out to welcome the riders who were ambling about, many still on their mounts, enjoying the acclaim. Small boys were admiring the racing camels and a group of women in their spangled outfits were punctuating occasional outbreaks of song with eerie ululations.

I found Laila, who congratulated me on completing the course. Walking like John Wayne, I followed her over to meet the winner. It was the young man in the green *boubou* who had been modest about his desire to finish in the top three. He looked relaxed sitting sideways in his saddle, high above a small crowd of admirers, with one foot up on his camel's neck and the other dangling down over its flank.

After congratulating him on his victory, I asked how long he had been riding.

'Since I was twelve,' he said. He looked to be in his early twenties, which gave him at least ten years' head start on me.

'And how long was it before your bum got used to it?' I asked him, slapping my behind for emphasis, which was a mistake because it sent a shot of pain across my buttocks.

I could see the guy smiling behind the combination turban and veil that was still pulled up high over his nose.

'About five years', he told me.

I'd really never had a hope.

THREE

A lot of nonsense has been written in both the popular media and academic literature about the Sahara getting bigger. 'Desertification', the spread of desert-like conditions, has been touted for thirty-odd years as the Sahel's new horseman of the apocalypse. The Sahara, so the story goes, is slowly encroaching into the savannah grasslands, irrevocably engulfing the Sahel and pushing its inhabitants out. And the driving force behind this ecological disaster is the people themselves, irresponsibly abusing their resources and reaping the grim results. The Sahara's nomads, including the Tuareg and the Tubu, have come in for a lot of bad publicity in this respect. And the icon of this disaster story is the innocent sand dune advancing to swallow up productive agricultural land. It's a glossy image that oversimplifies a rather complicated situation.

In some places across West Africa there have been such problems, but it is not nearly so widespread as was once thought. A standard facet of the semi-arid climate on the Sahara's fringes is the recurrence of drought, and this natural phenomenon has certainly wrought havoc with people throughout the region. West Africa's terrible drought of the early 1970s put paid to the nomadic lifestyle for many, including Laila's family who lost all their camels and had little option but to settle down. They moved to Niamey, Niger's capital, where Laila now runs a small general store.

But droughts notwithstanding, the coming of the seasonal rains is what really dictates the size of the mighty Sahara. Every year, between about May and September, a broad band of air heavy with moisture pushes up across the savannah grasslands from the south and drops its load across the Sahel. With the coming of the rains, seeds of grasses and grassland flowers spring into action and within days the desiccated terrain is transformed into green pastures. Hence the Sahara expands and contracts each year with the rhythmic coming and going of the rains.

For the herders of Niger, the rainy season is a time of opportunity. Droves of livestock arrive from all directions to make the most of these northern pastures. In the area to the west and north of Agadez, these seasonal grasses have an added attraction. They are salty. Reduced in winter to licking blocks of salt carried across the Ténéré by the Tuaregs, sheep, goats, donkeys and cows, led inevitably by the haughty camels, are driven to this region during the rains to graze on grasses laced with their own vital minerals.

I'd been told that the annual migration of herders and their livestock to these rich seasonal pastures was a sight to behold, a time of celebration and festivities. So see them I was going to, for the next leg of my journey, a phase I also viewed as one of recuperation for my ailing backside before the full onslaught of my trek across the Ténéré with the notorious women of the Tubu.

Back in Agadez, Laila introduced me to a man who would act as my guide. Boubacar was perfectly qualified for the task. Brought up in a herding family, his life was still closely involved with Niger's pastoralists. Although, like Laila, Boubacar no longer herded animals himself, he ran a non-governmental organization that fought for pastoralists' rights. One of seventeen children, only six of whom had survived the ravages of childhood disease, Boubacar had been sent to a nomads' school when he was young. He had excelled and eventually found himself studying for a doctorate at a university in the USA. After a spell working throughout much of Africa for international aid bodies, he had returned home to set up his own grass-roots development organization.

As we drove west out of Agadez along a sealed road, Boubacar summed up the traditional economy of the West African pastoralist for me. 'Goats are their current account,' he said, 'the everyday spending money, while cattle are their savings.'

From the dusty streets of Agadez we had plunged straight into the savannah grasslands. After a brief stop at a military checkpoint we were now driving through a flat landscape dotted with acacia trees and small bushes of euphorbia with leathery green leaves the size of dinner plates.

'Donkeys have little importance,' Boubacar went on, 'they are small change.' We were passing a family group driving their goats and long-horned cows in the same direction that we were travelling. Several women, dressed in black, were walking alongside their small children who rode donkeys laden with cooking utensils and knobbly sticks of firewood.

'But at the top of every nomad's financial system are the camels,' Boubacar continued. 'They are the gold standard.' A man leading the family waved to us from the top of his golden camel as we sped past.

'All of their assets are in their animals. Few of these people deal in cash and so they are at a disadvantage in the modern world.' Boubacar explained that the government was proposing to sell parcels of land in this area we were now driving through, seasonal pastures that had been used by herders for generations, to farmers who would use them to grow crops.

'Traditionally these areas belong to the pastoralists. But these people do not hold title deeds, they do not have pieces of paper that say they own these pastures. The government owns this land, and if they sell it to the farmers, where will the herders graze their animals?

This is why the nomads must be brought into the cash economy. So that they can secure their age-old rights.'

We drove on, passing other groups of pastoralists with their animals. In places the grass was still lush and green, though elsewhere the pasture had begun to dry up, taking on the colour of straw. It looked tired and worn out as the rainy season was drawing to a close.

We stopped at a small stretch of open water beside the road, a salt flat that held water only during the rainy season. A string of these ephemeral lakes enabled herders to make their way northwards, watering their animals as they went. This one was surrounded by livestock. Goats and donkeys were milling around in the dust at the water's edge, as if awaiting permission to step forward and drink, while cows with glossy dark chocolate coats had already gone ahead and waded in up to their haunches to quench their thirst. A man wearing a round wicker hat decorated with red and black strips of leather and a red leather brim sat on a rock at the edge of the water. He had flipped off his sandals and was busy washing his feet while his women and children had set about replenishing supplies for their continuing journey. Some filled car-tyre inner tubes that had been cut in half and tied at either end to hold water. Others were using the more traditional goatskin that gently oozes water through its pores, in the same way that we sweat to maintain our body temperature, so keeping its contents beautifully cool throughout the heat of the day

This group were Wodaabi, Boubacar told me, his people. 'We Wodaabi are part of the Fulani mother tribe,' he explained, 'who are spread all across Africa from Senegal in the west to the borders of Ethiopia in the east. For us, the cow is the most important animal. We have a saying: "God created first the cow, then the woman, then the Fulani".'

He pointed to the cattle standing knee-deep in the water, their brown coats glistening in the mid-morning sun. 'You see how healthy those animals look. That is because of the salt contained here in this water and in these pastures. They call it the *cure salée*, or salt cure.

Nomads travel large distances, from all over Niger and even from northern Nigeria, for this *cure salée*.'

Our journey continued, stopping briefly in the sleepy town of Ingal for a quick lunch of greasy grilled goat and warm bread before heading towards a village named Teguidda-n-Tessoumt. The road had given way to a dirt track and the further north we travelled, the patchier and more parched the pasture became. Great dust devils loomed up in the afternoon heat to scurry briefly across the horizon before giving up the ghost and dying in the arid plain. We stopped every so often to stretch our legs, but as soon as our vehicle had come to a halt we were enveloped by the oppressive heat. Simply walking for a few minutes reduced me to a sweltering wreck, and the prospect of marching for days on end in these temperatures with the Tubu women was quickly losing its appeal.

Teguidda-n-Tessoumt was a haphazard collection of mud-brick dwellings whose reason for being lay in the saline well and mudflats behind them. For those herders who could make it this far north, these salty deposits represented a place of pilgrimage, a sort of animal version of Tafédek's steam bath. After gorging themselves on the saline grasses, here animals could lick the salt directly from the mud and rocks while the herders could buy blocks of salt to take back with them to southerly pastures as the rains retreated. Buying salt here at source meant the lowest prices, since herders did not have to pay someone else to transport them further south. Teguidda-n-Tessoumt was a smaller version of Bilma, the desert oasis from which the Tuareg carry salt across the Ténéré.

But as the ultimate goal of the *cure salée*, I found the village uninspiring. The place was tired and dishevelled. In another context, its sun-baked buildings, most without roofs, might have looked ethnically picturesque, but here they were just drab and neglected. I initially thought my impression might have been tainted by our long and tiring journey, but the following morning Teguidda-n-Tessoumt's effect was the same. It was a bleak and lacklustre place in unrelenting brown. The only dash of colour it could muster came in the form of two aged palm trees, but their fronds were so caked in brown dust that they too looked sad and miserable.

Moreover, the people also seemed weary and uninspired. True, they had to labour beneath a pitiless sun, filling an endless succession of shallow round depressions dug from the mud with salty water that slowly evaporated, leaving valuable salt blocks like the tops of giant field mushrooms. But I'd already seen plenty of people elsewhere who had to work in the same relentless heat and still maintained a sense of dignity and some enthusiasm.

And when they made the short walk home at the end of the day, to sit back and take their ease in their mud-brick abodes, the residents of Teguidda-n-Tessoumt relaxed in a vertical rubbish dump. In years to come, archaeologists might happen across the remains of the village's crumbling walls and marvel at the wealth of detritus stored in their fabric. There were jagged pieces of bone, fragments of forgotten plastic, ancient bottle tops, dirty rags and pieces of stick, all held fast in a matrix of sun-baked mud. Again, in another context I might have marvelled at the villagers' ingenuity in devising such an original method for disposing of their refuse, but here it just left the impression that no one could be bothered to pick out the rubbish from the muck.

Admittedly, it was just a mud village in a mudflat and no one came to Teguidda-n-Tessoumt for its good looks. But I didn't like the place. A less prepossessing community was hard to imagine.

After spending a day in the living rubbish dump of Teguidda-n-Tessoumt, we travelled back southwards, towards a spot where Boubacar knew his fellow Wodaabi traditionally gathered during the wet season to graze their livestock on the *cure salée* grasses. We turned off the dirt track after a couple of hours and bounced across the savannah until we started seeing livestock and the tell-tale smoke of campfires.

Since during the rains the itinerant Wodaabi tended to be less dispersed than in the dry season, gathering together to take advantage of the seasonal pastures, it was a time for feasts and social events, Boubacar told me. The grazing was good and the animals were fat. This was when the livestock tended to give birth, so the cows and goats had high milk yields. It was thus a time for celebration, and there was one particular ceremony, known as the *Gerewol*, that he was anxious for me to see. He reckoned that our chances of witnessing a *Gerewol* in this spot would be pretty good.

It took some negotiation before we found a place to stay, not because anyone was hostile to our presence but for precisely the opposite reason. Every man Boubacar spoke to immediately offered to put us up, but Boubacar was wary of causing offence by staying with the wrong family. He eventually took up the offer from an middle-aged Wodaabi man named Reeskua Durow who was clearly delighted with our decision.

Reeskua's camp was spread over a wide area of bush surrounded by his grazing cattle. A number of small calves attached to a rope were minding their own business in the wispy grass, tied there, Boubacar explained, to prevent them from constantly suckling their mothers, so leaving some milk for the family. Rush mats were spread out between the thorn bushes, and Reeskua's wife was busy beside a fire pounding millet in a large mortar with a giant pestle.

'Usually you would also see a fire for the cows,' Boubacar told me, 'so that they know where to gather at night, but not now because it is too dry at the end of the rainy season. The risk of the fire spreading is too great.'

Despite my protestations, our host insisted on lending Boubacar and me his family's beds, which he and his wife carried in pieces to a spot beside a thorn bush.

'This will be the guest bedroom', Boubacar announced with a broad smile.

The two double beds were superbly designed for nomadic life. Each consisted of four wooden stands with a broad base on which long trunks were balanced to make up the bed's frame. Across these struts, thinner slats were laid to form a sort of wooden mattress. The wood was hickory, strong but remarkably light, so ideal for the task. Several rush mats were spread over the wooden slats to finish the job.

Dusk has little meaning in this part of the world. Shadows lengthen and the sun's brightness weakens, but the moment between light and dark is barely discernible. There is no twilight to ease you across the transition from day to night in the African savannah, just a brief, final rose-tinted flicker of sunlight and then darkness blessed with the relative cool of night. As the stars began to make their appearance, Reeskua's wife brought a large half-gourd full of a porridge-like substance swimming in milk over to where Reeskua, Boubacar and I were sitting on the beds. Three wooden spoons were sticking out of our dinner and we tucked in. It was standard Wodaabi food, ground millet and milk, but in this case mixed with some shredded dates that I had seen Reeskua's wife stoning before the light had disappeared. The dates were a special supplement for their honoured guests, lending the otherwise tasteless porridge a welcome hint of sweetness.

When we had eaten our fill, there was still a substantial mound of porridge left sitting in its milky pool, enough for the rest of the family. As Boubacar explained, the head of the family and any guests always ate first but had to leave enough for the women and children so that everyone got their fair share.

A three-quarter moon had risen to bathe the scene in light, and as we relaxed after our meal a seemingly endless succession of men began arriving, all with long swords hanging at their waists and a selection of amulets dangling from their necks, each bidding good evening to Reeskua. They all brought mats which they spread on the ground around us to recline on. Further away, beyond the fire, I could see groups of women and children similarly gathering and chatting quietly in the moonlight. Otherwise, the only sounds were the restful crackle of the fire and the occasional moo from a cow. It was like a hushed party in the park after dark.

Some people made their own small fires and busied themselves with little metal teapots, and soon shots of strong, sweet tea in tiny glasses started arriving from all directions. As the evening wore on, people began to approach me for medical assistance. One man held his head in his hands, thumping his forehead with one of his fists, which I took to mean he had a headache. I dug two paracetamol out from my bag and handed them to him. I wanted to tell him to take the pills with a drink of water, but when I acted out the drinking process my pantomime just seemed to baffle him. He disappeared back into the shadows soon to return with another man who spoke some French. He was soon followed by a woman who asked through the French-speaker if I had a torch. She had a thorn in her finger which she proceeded to dig out with a needle in the narrow beam of light.

The following morning, I awoke as the sun was rising to see that Reeskua's wife had already got the fire going. Boubacar was also stirring and the first thing he did surprised me. He leaned over to look underneath our beds and announced with relief that our bags were still where we'd left them. 'There were so many people here last night, you never know,' he said, 'even though stealing is shameful for the Fulani.'

'But not for the Tubu', he went on as he carefully picked up his spectacles which he'd placed in one of his shoes overnight. I had told Boubacar of my coming rendezvous with the Tubu women.

He put on his glasses with both hands and looked at me with a half smile. 'Thievery is a tradition with the Tubu, you know. For them, stealing something would be a sign of courage.' It was all to do with the Tubu's excessive dowry demands, he explained, as he warned me to be extra careful with my possessions when I finally met them.

Receiving an impromptu lecture on cross-cultural property values wasn't really what I needed first thing in the morning, but I understood that Boubacar was only trying to help, even if his attitude towards the Tubu appeared to be somewhat one-sided. He had already confirmed Laila's story about their women keeping knives and in doing so had betrayed just a tinge of what I discerned as inter-ethnic rivalry. Of course, Boubacar's depiction of the Tubu as cut-throats and thieves might have been perfectly accurate, but for my own sanity I preferred to think otherwise.

But either way, I pushed such worries to the back of my mind as Boubacar and I pulled on our clothes behind the thorn bush wall of our guest bedroom. Boubacar told me that a major topic of conversation among the people who had gathered around us the previous night, all of whom had disappeared this morning, had been the *Gerewol*.

'There will be a *Gerewol* taking place today,' he said, 'over near the well.'

I hadn't seen a well as yet, but Boubacar assured me it wasn't far, just a few hundred metres away. 'And this *Gerewol* will be special,' he continued as he slipped on his shoes, 'because they have agreed that you can take part.'

Assuming that securing my participation had called for some neat diplomatic footwork on Boubacar's part, I thanked him, even though I wasn't entirely sure what to make of his pronouncement since I didn't know what a *Gerewol* was, other than some form of celebratory ceremony to mark the end of the rainy season.

'Perhaps you'd better tell me what's involved', I suggested tentatively as I pulled on my shirt.

'It is a ceremonial courtship dance,' he replied. 'Some have likened it to a beauty pageant.'

Visions of a Wodaabi version of Miss World flashed through my mind, which I didn't find stressful.

'What constitutes a beautiful woman in a Wodaabi's eyes?' I asked.

'Oh, you don't have to worry about that,' Boubacar replied. 'The women do the choosing. It's the men who have to make themselves beautiful.'

And so it was that I found myself taking part as a sort of special guest in a West African nomads' all-male beauty contest. Just a few minutes after we had finished dressing, a couple of young Wodaabi guys appeared and led me off to help me prepare.

The time it takes for women to beautify themselves prior to a night out in Britain is traditionally a source of considerable bewilderment to men at home. Despite the advent of the sharing, caring 'new man', the mysteries of a woman's wardrobe and her collection of cosmetics remain perplexing to many. How a British woman can possibly take one, two, maybe even three hours to get ready for a night out on the town is beyond them. Since I have two sisters and no brothers, I perhaps started out in life with a better inkling than many, but walking through the bush towards the well I soon realized that neither my sisters nor any girlfriend I have ever been involved with had anything on Wodaabi menfolk preparing for a *Gerewol*. When I asked Boubacar what time the ceremony was scheduled to begin, expecting a mid-morning kick-off, he told me it would get under way in the evening.

The well was situated on a small hillock surrounded by cows jostling for position in the mud. Their loud mooing was drowned out by an excruciating screeching sound made by the metal cable that brought the water bucket up from the depths. It must have been a deep well, because the two small donkeys whose job it was to pull up the bucket had to be walked, straining with the effort, a good hundred metres down the slight incline away from the well. A small boy was on duty to smack the donkeys' rumps with a large stick to keep them going.

My two new Wodaabi friends took me past the well to an area beneath a spreading thorn tree laid with rush mats. Sitting on the mats were about ten other guys, all with intense looks of concentration on their faces, peering into their hand mirrors. I was introduced and met by an interesting range of greetings. Some smiled as they welcomed me, while other guys just nodded hello, with no particular expression on their faces. One or two looked me up and down with barely concealed annoyance.

One of the disgruntled guys made a comment which generated a ripple of giggles from his mates. I looked at Boubacar for a translation. He was smiling.

'He says, "Never mind him, he's ugly anyway".' Boubacar paused and his smile was replaced by an expression of slight embarrassment. 'He thinks you look like a donkey.'

Even I found this funny.

Still looking at me, the guy shifted over, pushing one of his friends aside, and slapped the mat beside him for me to sit down. Since I wasn't a great threat, it appeared that he would tolerate my presence.

'It's a competition,' Boubacar told me, I think wanting to explain my mildly hostile reception. 'All these boys want to win. Every one of you is competing against each other.'

Tucking my legs beneath me, I bent down and joined my rivals as they continued preening themselves in their pocket mirrors. They were all good-looking young men, with long noses and high foreheads. One or two of them had a wide-eyed look of innocence about them, the large whites to their brown eyes making them seem pretty even to my mind. They all had perfect white teeth. I learned later that bright white teeth and eyes are essential to the Wodaabi ideals of beauty.

The chap opposite me, who wore a green *boubou* and black turban, was busy crushing a small piece of pale yellow substance on his flip-flop with the end of a hefty stick. When he'd reduced it to a yellow powder, everyone leant over to dab his index finger in the pile and began carefully smearing the stuff on his face. It was time to apply my foundation. The guy in green gestured for me to remove my glasses. Although I was reluctant to do this, since I wanted to be able to see what was going on around me, Boubacar said that only ugly people tried to hide their ugliness, so I concurred. I was getting into the swing of this.

'This first application will protect you against your enemies who want you to be ugly', he told me.

I set to, poking my finger into the light yellow powder and dabbing it on to my nose, mentally kicking myself for not packing a mirror. The guy in green gave me a quizzical look and pulled my finger away from my face. He stabbed his own finger into the yellow residue and touched it lightly on to my cheek, gently massaging the powder into my skin. The one who thought I looked like a donkey joined in on my other cheek. All of a sudden I had my very own make-up artists.

They took it in turns to do my face and pay attention to their own, our beautification continuing all morning. The protective light yellow foundation was followed by a brighter yellow powder. My face got a full covering of this, while others preferred a more discerning approach. The favourite seemed to be a vertical stripe running from the hairline straight down over the nose and finished with a big yellow dot made with the thumb on the chin. Some added similar dots to highlight their cheekbones. Every so often throughout the procedure, someone would hand me their mirror so that I could see what they were doing to me.

While the face powder was still being rubbed into my skin, one of the guys produced a cotton wrap from the depths of his shirt and unfolded it on the mat to reveal a tangled assortment of jewellery. There were rings, pendants, necklaces, bangles and bracelets in dark leather and silver. He selected a short string of leather inlaid with tiny white shells and gently took my wrist to tie it round. I felt like a talking, breathing life-sized Barbie doll.

Similar leather bracelets were secured around my ankles and a thong inlaid with silver filigree selected as my necklace. As we continued, the intense concentration with which the guys went about the business of dolling themselves up was occasionally interrupted as, apropos of nothing, they broke into song. It would start as a high-pitched cry and end as a chant that resonated from deep inside the chest. Boubacar described it as a sort of come-on mantra to the women. I tried to join in but my efforts reduced everyone around me to helpless laughter.

As the sun reached its height, and there appeared to be no natural pause in the proceedings, I took a break to rest from the worst of the midday heat. I returned from my power-nap a half-hour later to find jewellery still being handed round. Someone had produced a small vessel made of horn which contained kohl, and, using the blunt ends of thorns pulled from the tree they were sitting beneath, the guys had set about applying the black powder to the insides of their eyelids. Before I sat down, I was handed a long dark piece of cloth that turned out to be a purple tabard with a white rim. A long billowy number with lengthy slits up the sides, it was met with murmurs of appreciation when I pulled it on over my head. This was followed by a large piece of folded leather that I wasn't sure what to do with until a couple of the guys stood up to show me. It was a pair of camel-skin chaps, like the ones you see cowboys wearing in Hollywood Westerns.

I sat down to receive kohl round my eyelids and on my lips, designed to highlight the whiteness of my eyes and teeth, while someone tied another piece of jewellery round my forehead with long leather thongs encased in metal strips that dangled down over my ears to my shoulders.

A white turban was carefully wrapped around my head and an ostrich feather slipped into the top. It seemed that I was ready, so I stood up to present myself in all my finery.

The guy who had originally accused me of looking like a donkey cocked his head to one side. With his foundation and yellow stripes, pierced by large doleful eyes beneath his white turban, his demeanour was ghostly and waif-like as he gave me the once-over. I did a little twirl and he issued his verdict. Boubacar translated. '"Now maybe he doesn't look so bad",' he told me. 'And I think they are starting to be worried', Boubacar added.

But I wasn't quite there. The guy in green, who now sported a dramatic yellow stripe down his nose and an assortment of jangling bracelets on his slender wrists, gestured for me to sit once more. He produced a whitish chunk of what I took to be crumbly limestone from a pocket and began to pulverize it with a stick on his flip-flop. He pouted his lips to dribble a lengthy string of saliva down on to the powder and mixed the concoction into a paste with a long thorn. With delicate dabs of the thorn, he painted a line of white dots down the centre of my nose and a couple of roundels on my cheeks.

He passed over his pocket mirror. To me, I looked terrifying, but to a Wodaabi woman I was, apparently, a knock-out. Or at least, that was the idea.

The actual *Gerewol* ceremony lasted for only slightly shorter a time than the preparations. After a seemingly interminable wait for final adjustments and last-minute preening, my group of guys all trooped out into the late afternoon sun to gather in the clearing by the well. Behind us the donkeys were still performing the labours of Hercules to their own screeching accompaniment as the bucket rose slowly from the depths.

We were joined by literally dozens of other young men who appeared from every direction. Everyone was dressed up to the nines. Tabards and leather chaps seemed to be the order of the day, although some of the tabards were white and see-through, being full of tiny holes like an extra long string vest. Many contestants wore turbans like mine, adorned with delicate ostrich feathers, while others had gone for the conical wicker hat approach, some of these also sporting feathers in their rims. One or two had seemingly been unable to decide on their headgear because they wore both, a wicker hat perched precariously on top of their turban. I noticed that quite a number of guys also wore swords encased in long leather scabbards slung over their shoulders.

My group crowded together for a moment and then widened the huddle into a rough circle and began to sing. We took it in turns to stand in the middle of the group and perform a solo routine.

Boubacar, who had been conspicuously absent for most of the afternoon, appeared at my shoulder once more to explain that the songs
were like sentimental ballads sung to attract the ladies. But to my ears,
each one sounded more like a dirge than an exercise in crooning,
although I admit that they weren't helped by the donkey-generated
screeching in the background.

Nonetheless, they must have been working because ladies had
started to appear on the scene. Other than Reeskua's wife and a few
shadowy women the previous evening, I had not yet seen any
Wodaabi females, and I'd begun to take seriously Boubacar's explanation that it was the general lack of women in Wodaabi society that had
given rise to this whole gender-bending beauty routine.

But small groups of women dressed in black had begun to take
up position opposite our clusters of male crooners and, as they did so,
I detected an enhanced sense of earnestness come over our group.
Although our day-long cosmetics and dressing-up session had been
full of light-hearted banter, there had also been a palpable sense of
rivalry underlying it all. As the moment for the parade had got closer,
there had even been a couple of potentially nasty spats over mirrors
and face powder. This was, after all, a competition, and if you got it
right, I'd been told, the least you could expect was a night of some
passion. If lucky, you might even find your partner for life.

We broke from our huddle and wandered over towards the others
who were being assembled into a long line by a couple of older
Wodaabi men. Unwittingly, I got an inkling of what was coming next
when out of the corner of my eye I saw the guy who had likened me
to a donkey. I did a double-take, turned, stopped and watched him,
not believing what was clear for all to see. He was strutting across the
parched grass on tip-toe, slowly rolling his head from right to left. His
lips were splayed wide to show his teeth, which were tightly clenched,
and he was doing the strangest things with his eyes, rolling them up
into the top of his head and from side to side. Under any other circumstances, I'd have said he looked like a madman. As he walked, he was

slowly waving his arms up and down in front of him. For a moment I became convinced that he'd lost it. He'd seemed like quite a highly strung individual and I thought the long day of preparation had finally got to him. Until, that is, I glanced over towards the chorus line of guys that we were joining and saw that they were all at it.

For more than an hour we held our line, taking it in turns to show off our skills by quivering forward on tiptoe, eyes rolling and lips pulled back to reveal teeth clamped tightly in a fixed grin. Squatting on the ground opposite, the line of young women took mental notes against the Wodaabi benchmarks of beauty. We sang and we chanted, jewellery jangling, swaying back and forth to our own music, maintaining the wavy rhythm as the women looked on. Like so many out-of-work circus performers desperate to impress, we doggedly persevered with our facial gymnastics. It was a shimmering ballet punctuated by waving ostrich feathers, dancing strings of coloured beads and cowrie shells. I got so carried away that I forgot the screeching accompaniment from the donkeys behind us, or perhaps even they had paused in their interminable task to take in our extraordinary exhibition.

At strategic points in our performance, a young woman would be brought forward by one of the elder Wodaabi men and led along our line, so that she could view up close our flashing white teeth and eyeballs. Tentatively she would reach out and tap one of our number on the chest, smile bashfully, and retreat to her own camp. It was the moment that everyone in our chorus line had been waiting for.

When it happened to the guy who had compared me to a donkey he puffed up his chest with pride and smiled an even wider smile. When the next woman tapped me on the chest, I found it difficult to believe what was happening. I thought it must be a set-up as the young woman who had just touched me smiled shyly and turned to walk back towards her group. My donkey friend beamed at me and shook my hand. I caught sight of Boubacar who was looking on from the edge of the proceedings. He smiled and gave me a knowing wink.

Somehow, all this behaviour that to me was unconventional seemed strangely appropriate in the setting. I hoped that in some bizarre fashion the *Gerewol*'s gender reversal might have served as a fitting preparation for my imminent meeting with the Tubu.

FOUR

It was a long drive to meet the Tubu. It took two days. The distance wasn't that great, about 500 kilometres from where I'd taken part in the *Gerewol*, but there were no roads, so the going was rough. With my driver, Mohamed, I was travelling eastwards, away from the Aïr Massif, skirting the southern edge of the Ténéré Desert. My destination was a village called Termit, starting point for the date caravans.

The Land Cruiser bounced across endless desert plains, sometimes in the company of elf-like gazelles seemingly grateful for the opportunity to race. They would bound along beside us at high speed before veering off to disappear into the vast empty spaces. Stopping for food and rest in uninhabited oases that Mohamed found with intimidating ease, we were met by fearless small birds that hopped in and out between our legs in search of crumbs.

Grass, trees and bushes were in short supply between these pit-stops, except in a spot known as Gadoufawa where petrified logs lay scattered across the sands. Like giant sticks of flaky chocolate, reminiscent of the ones I like to stick in ice-cream cornets at home in the summer, they were remnants of a forgotten period when this area must have been much wetter. More than a metre long and super heavy now that they'd been turned to stone, these fossilized relics were the last witnesses to a change in climate thousands of years before.

Despite the fatigue brought on by the long journey and the sit-upon pain I still bore as a souvenir from my camel race, I was distracted for lengthy periods by the accomplice we had picked up in Agadez who had agreed to assist me in my dealings with the Tubu women. The difficulty I'd experienced in finding an English-speaking Tubu guide had brought home to me just how far I was venturing into the unknown. Only the most exhaustive enquiries had thrown up Sougui, a Tubu who worked in next-door Chad. He came from an eminent family, one of his uncles being a former president of Chad, and he had an old-fashioned yet timeless dignity about him. Like the Wodaabi guys I'd recently bared my teeth with, Sougui had a willowy, almost effeminate physique, but he was also a strikingly handsome man with a moustache and goatee beard. He was one of the few people I've met who could truly be described as having the demeanour of a nobleman.

Sougui hailed from the Tibesti Mountains in the north of Chad, volcanic soulmates of Niger's Aïr Massif. Tibesti was the ancestral home to all Tubu, he told me, but his personal knowledge of the area was poor, having spent most of his life abroad. After backing the wrong side in a coup in Chad in the early 1970s, his family had been forced to flee their homeland when Sougui was just three years old. He had grown up as a refugee, mostly in Algeria, but somewhere along the way he had picked up English. He had returned to his home country only a couple of years before, where, in a twist that I could-n't have fabricated, Sougui worked as a customs man.

Anxious to throw more light on these people who had been built up in my mind as fearsome characters, little more than brigands and cut-throats if Boubacar was to be believed, I asked Sougui how he would describe the Tubu character.

He raised his eyebrows and blew out his cheeks when I made my enquiry. 'This is a difficult question', he said. There was a long pause as our vehicle lurched slowly forward across a boulder-strewn patch of desert landscape.

'You need respect,' he said finally. 'Yes, Tubu people need respect. That is the most important thing to them.'

Before they were converted to Islam, there were traditionally three ways in which a Tubu could gain the necessary esteem, Sougui explained. One was to kidnap somebody from another tribe and take them to what is now Algeria to sell into slavery in exchange for a weapon. Another feat that would gain you respect was to drink alcohol, and the third, perhaps most daring act, was to kill someone.

'If you didn't do any of these things you were nothing,' he said simply, 'not considered.'

Later, resting beneath a solitary acacia tree as the sun went down at the end of our first day's driving, Sougui described to me how their courageous past had left the Tubu with exceptional powers of endurance and courage. He was sitting cross-legged making patterns with his fingers in the sand.

'They never show you what they are feeling. If a Tubu is hungry, you will never know it. If a Tubu is thirsty, you will never know it.'

I was reminded of a little story Laila had told me one day when we were walking through the streets of Agadez. We had passed the great mud minaret of the town's central mosque and found ourselves in the market. I had pointed to a woman squatting beside a blanket piled high with dates for sale, telling Laila of my quest to join a Tubu date caravan. The first thing she told me about the Tubu was an anecdote about their stamina.

'A Tubu can make a date last for three days,' she'd said. 'On day one, they nibble off the skin and suck it. On day two, they eat the flesh, and on day three they suck the stone.'

A scrawny bird, little more than a hatchling, had hopped on to Sougui's knee and was cocking its head to survey the scene for scraps from our dinner of canned lentils and tuna. We both watched as it dipped its head to peck at a speck of dirt on his *boubou* and then sprang away.

'The world of the Tubu woman is like the Ténéré,' Sougui continued. 'It is difficult to enter and impossible to fully know. They never show any emotion. If a Tubu woman loves you, even if she is ready to die for you, she will never show it.'

On the evening of the second day, exhausted after another long drive through the relentless heat, we stopped to camp in the embrace of an isolated sand dune that was crescent-shaped and as high as a two-storey house. Momentarily, a small desert fox was caught in the beam of our headlights, its eyes briefly shining before it turned to scamper away into the gathering darkness. We were within sight of the Termit mountains which sat wreathed in an ethereal mist on the near horizon. I wandered away from our dune on to a flat clay plain and lay down to hear the desert's silence. Fine white streaks of sand were strewn across the surface which had the texture of leather but sounded hollow when I tapped it with my knuckle. The scrape of my fingernail turned the clay to a fine powder. As the stars slowly appeared, a nearly full moon rose to cast its light like the sun peering through the haze after a volcanic eruption.

The following morning I spotted camel tracks across the clay plain leading towards the mountains. We followed them for a while before turning south along the rim of the hills to arrive around noon at the village of Termit.

The heat hit us with the force of a blast from a furnace when we opened the doors and climbed stiffly out of our vehicle. A gaggle of children ran up to greet us, followed by a succession of men who had learned that it is always better to amble in the high temperatures. Backed by a flat-topped, black volcanic plateau, the setting was dramatic. The village itself was less so. It consisted of an assortment of small shelters made from rush mats draped over stick frames that shimmered in the heat haze.

Termit was unimposing but, as far as Sougui and I were concerned, this was not its most significant drawback. For us, it presented a rather more pressing problem. The women's annual date caravan had left already.

About three days before, one of the old men told us as we sat in the shade of a thorn tree. I was slowly recovering from the immediate distress of the bad news.

'Do you think we can catch them up?' I wanted to know. I was thinking that our Land Cruiser could surely travel faster than a camel caravan.

The man turned to look at our vehicle parked beneath another tree nearby. He slowly shook his head. There were many difficult dunes to cross and he didn't think we'd be able to make it in a car.

Despondency welled over me once more. There was also another difficulty, in that I'd hired Mohamed to drive Sougui and me only this far, thinking we'd have no further need for him after Termit. I didn't know whether he'd even have the time to take us further, let alone enough fuel. Needless to say, Termit hardly ran to a petrol station.

Mohamed sat down beside us and fell into a hushed conversation with the old man, which he had to do through Sougui because Mohamed was a Tuareg and spoke no Tubu. They talked at some length, about the route the women were taking, as far as I understood. Sougui had sketched a rough map in the sand and they pored over it, pointing to spots marked with pellets of camel dung between the small sticks that represented Termit and Bilma, the ultimate destination. Other men from the village had gathered round to chip in with their views on the matter. Things did not look good, as Sougui pointed out to me the problematic stretches of dunes that he marked on his map with more twigs.

Our one hope, it appeared, lay in the oasis of Dibella, five or six days' walk from Termit. The men were sure their womenfolk would stop there for water. The question was, could we make it to Dibella before them, and so meet the women there?

Mohamed told me that he had the time and always carried extra fuel. He said that he thought the journey was possible by car. Although the old man stressed the difficulties that lay ahead, it was Mohamed, after all, who would be doing the driving and his quiet efficiency in getting us this far had impressed me. We would not follow the women's route exactly, he said, but there was a more roundabout way, parts of which he had driven before, that avoided the worst of the dunes.

He thought he could get us there in a couple of days if he drove for all the hours of daylight. We'd have to eat on the move, but he thought our chances of reaching Dibella before the women were good.

It was what some people call a 'no-brainer'. We left immediately.

The drive to Dibella was more difficult than the two days we had just completed. The grass finally faded away a couple of hours out of Termit and we were left with just the sky and a vast expanse of lemon yellow sand as we entered the Ténéré proper. But for the remainder of that first day the going was relatively straightforward. There were few dunes, just an endless succession of gently rolling sand hills, and having let down our tyres the better to grip the smooth surface, we made good progress.

The following day was more demanding. The sand became treacherous, one moment solid and unyielding, the next swallowing our vehicle up to its axles. I lost count of the number of times that Mohamed failed to extricate us from the arid mire by engaging his four-wheel drive and Sougui and I had to dig us out. We were equipped with sand ladders, rectangular metal strips punched with round holes that allow the tyres to grip when slipped under the wheels, but they became so hot in the midday sun that I burned my hands manipulating them.

But at the end of that day, Mohamed told us that he thought we were close to Dibella. Perhaps two or three more hours of driving in the morning, he said, and we'd be there. He had been navigating through the featureless terrain using the Global Positioning System affixed to his dashboard which bounced invisible waves off satellites to pinpoint our position. I asked him what he had done before GPS and he smiled. 'Tuareg Positioning System', he replied.

The dunes around Dibella were the largest and most troublesome we had encountered yet. As Sougui and I earned our keep by digging out the Land Cruiser for the umpteenth time, it struck me that although our vehicle had proved its worth in this treacherous topography, it still couldn't really compare to the traditional form of desert transport. This would never happen to a camel.

And finally, as Mohamed revved his engine and sped forward to scale the crest of yet another great dune, we saw Dibella. Two great black crags rose up on the skyline and a wide depression studded with palm trees was laid out before us in the sea of sand. It was epic.

For a brief moment, we forgot about our chase for the Tubu women as we pulled up at the small hole dug in Dibella's hard clay basin and sampled the water of the well. I tugged off my grubby T-shirt and plunged it into the shallow waters, less than a half-metre below the surface. It emerged cool and wonderful.

But the oasis was deserted. Mohamed drove us from one end of the depression to the other, past clumps of palm trees and the bleached bones of camels that had made it this far but no further. Birds twittered and we disturbed a jackal caught briefly out in the open before it shot into a tangled mass of fronds. But people there were none.

It seemed highly unlikely that we'd missed the Tubu caravan, having made it here from Termit in just a day and a half. But we couldn't know for sure. All we could do was wait.

That first night at Dibella was the coldest I'd yet experienced since arriving in Niger. I'd been used to sleeping beneath a single sheet but woke shivering in the small hours and had to pull on my jumper. It's not that it gets really cold in the Sahara in September, it's just the great contrast between day and night that makes it seem so. I'd set up my mini meteorological station before going to bed, thinking it would be a little something to help pass the time while waiting for the women, and when I checked it the following morning, I saw the night's low had been 23°C, or 73°F. That would have constituted a very satisfactory summer's day in Britain. But Dibella's high that day in the shade was 43°C (109°F). It was that 20°C tumble that had made it seem so chilly to me.

The women arrived just after we'd finished breakfast. Sougui had gone for a wander but came marching back to where I still sat beneath a palm tree, shouting for me to come and look. They were just a long line of specks on the crest of the furthest large dune, but they were coming towards us.

'Are you sure it's them?' I wondered.

'They are certainly women,' Sougui replied with his hand shielding his eyes. 'How many other female caravans can there be arriving here each day?'

He had already started walking out to greet them.

FIVE

Not all of them were women, despite being female. I counted eight human figures among the camels as Sougui and I strolled out towards the approaching caravan, but I was brought up with a start when I realized that one was a small girl who didn't look more than five or six years old. She was sprinting down the slipface of a large dune, her head uncovered to reveal a Mohican haircut and a cheeky smile. All the others wore headscarves, so were more difficult to assess immediately, but I could pick out two other junior figures walking side by side. Both of them looked to be about ten. As the gap between us narrowed, I could make out four older women, but the eighth and final member of the team, who was bringing up the rear riding one of the camels, was a young teenager.

The realization that half the caravan leading the camels, which numbered about two dozen, were children, prompted mixed emotions. My first reaction was one of relief, because I thought it must mean that their journey couldn't have been so harsh. But my elation soon turned to anxiety when the foolishness of that thought dawned on me. If this was the party we thought it was, these children had just walked for six days across a major world desert, in temperatures that had made me wilt while just sitting down. I'd measured the distance they'd covered from Termit to Dibella on my map. It was 275 kilometres as the crow flies, which probably meant they'd covered something like 350 kilometres up, down and around the soft sand dunes. They had passed the half-way mark on the trek to the oases around Bilma, but of course this was just the outward leg of their journey. They still had to walk back. These were seriously tough children.

They were indeed the party from Termit – Sougui had already established that much. He had fallen in line with the woman who led the foremost camel by its rope. When I approached her and said hello, she just nodded, barely reacting to my presence. Her face was partially covered by her headscarf, but I saw an old, leathery face with just two teeth. Behind her, the smallest girl, the one with the Mohican haircut, had joined the ten-year-olds and all three were studying me with a mixture of suspicion and confusion. I waved to them, and they looked startled before bursting into a fit of giggles.

Sougui and I lent a hand unloading the camels and tying their front feet together to stop them wandering too far. I asked him if he'd told the women who we were yet, and why we were here. After the unease I'd felt on realizing what these people were made of, I'd experienced a fresh wave of apprehension. This was the moment of truth. I'd been expecting – no, hoping – that these women would agree to us accompanying them on their journey, but their saying yes was by no means a foregone conclusion.

'I will ask them now', Sougui told me, and he launched into an explanation of our plans.

All eyes were turned on me. Their first reaction was probably not encouraging. Every one of the women burst out laughing.

The elderly one with the two teeth recovered her composure first. 'We have never taken a white man with us before,' she said. With hardly a glance in my direction, she said that she thought I was too weak. 'It is very hard', she added.

Sougui spoke some more and she replied again. The three children, still smirking, had gathered round to watch our exchange, though they still maintained a safe distance from me. 'She says that you will have to drink forty litres of water on the three-day walk to Bilma.'

I didn't think that this sounded difficult, assuming the camels could carry all that water. 'How much do you drink?' I asked the old woman.

Sougui translated. 'She says she has never measured it, but maybe ten litres over this period.'

This continued for a few minutes, but when it became clear to the old woman that she wasn't going to put me off, she just shrugged and said OK.

There's a lot of sand on planet Earth. It can be found in large quantities on the sea bed, at the bottom of lakes and rivers, in soils and on beaches. Tiny grains of fragmented rock, most of it made of quartz – the stuff we use to make glass – sand is everywhere. But of all the places that sand accumulates, none is more evocative or emblematic than a desert. When blown by the wind into the sleek form of a dune, it epitomizes the graceful beauty of a desert scene.

The Ténéré Desert is largely made up of sand. It comprises two great sand seas, or ergs, known as the Erg du Ténéré and the Grand Erg de Bilma, punctuated by volcanic outcrops like the black crags that overshadowed Dibella and the flat-topped ridge behind the village of Termit. The sand that sits in the Ténéré's ergs probably originally came from the foothills of Sougui's ancestral home, the Tibesti Mountains in Chad, along with material blown from the dried-out bed of Lake Chad, a body of water that at times in the past is thought to have been much larger than it is today. This vast volume of sand sits in the enormous depression that once held the larger Lake Chad, swept there by the prevailing winds that blow from the northeast and dominate the weather over this part of West Africa.

Just like the ocean has waves, the surface of sand seas are marked by dunes, and the dunes of the Ténéré are aligned by these north-easterly winds into elongated strings of linear forms that run from northeast to southwest. Since we were travelling almost due north towards the oasis of Bilma, we had to cross a succession of these longitudinal sand dunes.

They started almost as soon as we left Dibella the following morning. The women hadn't wanted to linger in the wide oasis because it offered little in the way of forage for their camels. There was a place with pasture, they said, a day's walk from Dibella.

They had paused to let their animals drink and to fill their goatskins with water before resting for the remainder of the day. The children were dispatched to collect supplies, and gathered a large pile of red dum nuts, the fruits of the palm trees. They showed me how to prepare them, smashing the hard nuts with a stone to remove the thin red skin and reveal a thick inner layer, the colour and texture of sawdust. It was very sweet to gnaw at. They collected what sticks of firewood they could find to supplement the camel dung they would gather along the way, and one of the women showed me how she made fire. This she did using a flint, a strip of rag that had been rubbed with some inflammable substance – the name of which was beyond Sougui's translation skills – and a handful of desiccated grass.

When she got the fire going, the teenager, who wore a large gold ring in her nose, began mixing a millet porridge in a soot-blackened metal pot for the evening meal. She and the smaller girls drew pictures of camels in the sand and showed me how they could count in French as their dinner bubbled away over the flames.

Before we ate, Sougui called me over to a spot beneath another palm tree and announced that he had something to give me. He grabbed his bag from the mat behind him and pulled out a sky-blue *boubou* and long mustard-coloured headscarf. I was relieved as well as grateful, because the woman with the two teeth had already told me how inappropriately dressed I was in my shorts, shirt and hat.

The dunes were both smooth and treacherous. A firm surface of sand would without warning give way to swallow my foot up to the ankle, turning a not unpleasant walk into a struggle against the elements. Sougui had insisted that we lead the caravan off, to show the women that we meant business. I hadn't realized it up to this point, but he was almost as nervous about our trek as I was. He confided in me that the women thought he was a city boy, and had little more confidence in his ability to make it all the way to Bilma than in mine. As we fought our way up towards the crest of the first big dune, the teenager, whose name was Dakou, looked at me and made what I could tell was a face-tious comment. Sougui smiled. 'She says she can't believe you're walk-ing', he told me.

The first hour was a hard slog, a tedious process through the gently rising dunes in which I'd take a step forward only to slip half a pace back in the soft sand. We had risen with the sun at about 5.30, aiming to leave by 7 o'clock, but it was nearly 9 by the time we had rounded up all the camels and loaded them. By now, as my watch ticked past 10 a.m., the sun had completed its benign early morning rise and was rapidly turning into a fiery orb. My forehead had started to sweat profusely beneath the folds of my turban. I was feeling weary and I didn't mind admitting it.

One of the string of camels I was leading had been set up with a wooden structure swathed in blankets, a saddle of sorts for me to ride on occasions just such as this. But although I felt very tired, like Sougui I was reluctant to show any signs of weakness, particularly so early in our trek. Except that when I turned to take in the rest of the caravan behind us, I saw that all the women had already mounted their camels. I didn't feel nearly so bad. If they were riding already, I thought to myself, why shouldn't I? Besides, I had already realized that trying to prove myself was an exercise in futility. My powers of endurance would never rival those of the Tubu. I was a mid-latitude man, not a macho man. I would be happy just to make it to Bilma in one piece.

I stopped my camels and pulled the one with the makeshift saddle to the ground. As I clambered aboard, a camel carrying one of the women and the smallest girl, Aiché, who wore her hair in a Mohican, ambled past. I'd expected them to laugh at me, but Aiché just gave me a beaming smile as she clung on to the waist of the woman in front.

Once up on my camel, I told Sougui what a relief it was to rest my legs. But he rejected the idea and trudged on. 'I don't want the women to think I can't do it', he said.

It wasn't until mid-afternoon that we reached the so-called pasture. It was just a few clumps of pallid scrawny grass dotted about a wide hollow in the lee of a protracted 50-metre dune ridge that snaked off into the distance. I was exhausted and my back was seriously uncomfortable. Riding the camel had been fine for my aching legs but I had paid the price behind. My buttocks had all but healed after my racing exploits with the Tuareg, but the Tubu saddle had if anything made a greater impact on my physique. The lack of support behind meant I had taken the strain of all the bumps and jerks of the walk on my back. Watching the women ride their mounts, the camel's effortless gait had not looked awkward, but my back didn't think so.

I helped the women set up their makeshift camp, a number of stout sticks dug into the sand and draped with blankets to provide some shade against the burning sun, before untying my bag from the camel and laying out the cotton drape I'd brought along as a mat-cum-towel. I sat down to rest my aching back. Seeing me doing this, the old woman with the two teeth held up her hands and bowed her head up and down, miming a praying motion. Then she burst out laughing. For a moment I didn't understand her joke, until I saw the similarity between my towel and a prayer mat. Like the Tuareg, the Tubu have a fairly relaxed attitude towards Islam, Sougui had told me, and I was yet to see any of the women praying. But I was pleased to be the butt of this joke because I took it as a small sign of acceptance into their party.

My interaction with the women would never have moved beyond this pantomime stage without Sougui there to translate, but it soon became clear that his presence was rather less helpful than I'd been expecting. At Dibella the previous night, Sougui and I had slept beneath a clump of palm trees on the other side of the oasis from where the women had set up camp, and I'd accepted this as a diplomatic distance. But now that we were all on the trek together, I had just assumed that we would join them at their camp. Not so. Sougui had carried his bag several hundred metres away from where I had laid out my towel next to the women's blankets.

I walked over to where he was reclining on the sand, wondering if I'd done something to make him sulk, and asked Sougui why he hadn't joined us. 'I cannot sleep near to the women,' he told me earnestly. 'I am a man who is not part of their family, so I cannot stay there.' He also said he wouldn't be able to eat with them. 'It is OK for you,' he told me, 'you are a foreigner, an outsider, but for me it is impossible.'

I tried to persuade him otherwise, but Sougui was uncompromising. It just wasn't the done thing in Tubu society. Which left me in a rather invidious position, split between my translator and mentor on the one hand and the Tubu women we were supposed to be with on the other. Not wanting to leave Sougui isolated or potentially embarrass the women with my presence – I was a man, after all, foreign or otherwise – I took my mat over to join him. In the days to come, his stance was to lead to some preposterous situations.

That night, I lay prostrate on my towel surrounded by hillocks of sand, lustrous in the light of the moon, marvelling at the hatchery of stars. My body felt heavy on the warm sand, attached to the Earth by some invisible force. I'd heard the Ténéré variously described as the land of fear, an uninhabited wasteland, and the place with no life. Boubacar had declared that the meaning of the word was simply 'nothing'. Mohamed, my driver, who had left us in Dibella when the women had arrived, had said the word meant 'empty'. But at the end of that first day of our journey, lying beneath the celestial glow, drifting off into a gentle slumber, the desert had a benign presence, a reassuring aura of security rather than jeopardy.

* * *

We were up with the sun again the next morning and on our way by 7 a.m. Walking was pleasant in the early morning, the sun not yet scorching, just leaving us to enjoy the desert's majestic scenery. It truly felt like being in an ocean of sand. Having left the emaciated 'pasture' behind, we walked for hours without passing a blade of grass, let alone a tree or bush. There was nothing to stimulate the senses but a landscape of dunes and sky. And the wind, for the most part little more than a breeze, but occasionally summoning the strength to send a spray of sandgrains bouncing across the ripples on the dunes.

As the sun continued its inexorable rise it became dreamlike and glaring, a blinding presence slowly eating into my stamina. The lead changed hands as one of us would pause to drink some water or untangle our procession of camels. As the old woman had said I would, I was drinking much more frequently than the others, and soon Sougui and I were bringing up the rear.

Three of the camels had been left to wander untied. They were young ones, Sougui told me, who refused to be fastened into a line. For the most part, these free spirits padded along beside the caravan, but when they strayed too far from our course it was the job of the two ten-year-olds, Hati and Binti, to fan out and usher them back into line. Sougui complained that his thigh was hurting, but he still refused to give in to the temptation of riding.

We stopped around midday and set up camp. The sand was firm and we had to dig deep to secure the sticks that were covered with blankets to give us some shade. Sougui helped, somewhat reluctantly, but when I slumped down with the women beneath the low-slung drapes, I got an inkling as to why. He refused to join us, saying he preferred to stand outside. He took up position a few paces away, wrapping his face in his headscarf against the sun's glare. The women took no notice of him, accepting his behaviour as normal. Despite my protestations, he refused to budge from his spot in the blazing sun.

Before we settled down to snooze, the woman with the two teeth told me she had been crossing the Ténéré each year to buy dates since she was a little girl like Aiché. She declared that this would be her last trip. The trek was too hard for an old woman like her, she said. When I asked why it was that only the Tubu women made this annual journey, she replied that it was an opportunity for her to visit relatives. A cousin of hers owned some date palms in Dirkou, one of the oases to the north of Bilma. This was where they would buy their supplies. I rephrased my question, wanting to know what the men did while they were away. They were tending the rest of their camels, she told me, as if this were explanation enough. Wearily, Sougui explained that the men had to be vigilant because animal theft was a constant threat and fights were not uncommon. Defending the herd was an exclusively male domain, involving codes of honour and cycles of revenge. It was not something the women could do.

It was mid-afternoon when we resumed our journey. Worn out from the morning's walk, I climbed into my camel's saddle straight away, but although his leg still hurt him, Sougui insisted he would continue on foot. We left the security of our makeshift camp to trudge back into the enormity of oblivion. And out of its nowhere, the Ténéré conjured a surreal moment. Three swallows appeared and swooped back and forth across our path, flicking their wings and gliding over our heads as if monitoring our progress as we plodded across the sands. For a minute or two, the monotony of our trek was relieved by this extraordinary sight. But their curiosity apparently sated, the swallows vanished, leaving me to wonder at this astonishing terrain as featureless as an ice cap or the open ocean.

We continued until after nightfall, stopping only because the moon was yet to rise and we could no longer see the dunes ahead of us. That night I slept more deeply than I remembered sleeping for a long, long time.

Sougui and I began the third day of our journey in high spirits. The women said that today we should make it to the oasis of Zoo Baba. It was a point they would normally have reached in two days and it was only then that I realized our energy-draining progress had been slower than their normal pace. Despite the fact that I'd been prepared for them to be blessed with remarkable endurance, their stamina still amazed me. While I had been guzzling water virtually non-stop since we'd left Dibella, I could count on the fingers of one hand the number of times I'd seen the women drinking. But I was less surprised by their fortitude than that of the children. Not once had I seen the girls complain.

Sougui's description of Tubu women as never showing any emotion had not entirely been borne out. Although for the most part they were impassive – not cold or aloof, but deadpan in the face of the desert's hardships – I had nonetheless tripped a sense of humour on occasion with my foreign behaviour. Perhaps unsurprisingly, I'd found the girls hardest to approach. While little Aiché, with her Mohican haircut, had been the first to surrender her reserve, laughing with delight when I introduced her to a game of catch with a pellet of camel dung, the others had tended to maintain their distance. Any attempt to engage the two ten-year-olds, Hati and Binti, in such friv-olous diversions was usually met with a dismissive wave of their hands as they strode off to sit with one of the women. Dakou was like teenagers the world over, happy to mock my efforts at camel riding when she felt like it, but usually indifferent to any comment I might make in an effort to engage her in conversation. She was even more expert than her sisters at the dismissive hand gesture.

Although we first saw Zoo Baba's rocky peaks at about 11 a.m., the oasis itself was a long time in materializing. Sougui reckoned we'd reach it within the hour, but to my mind he was being overconfident. I gave us another three.

I was nearly right because the final straits leading into Zoo Baba took us across some of the most difficult dunes yet. The previous day's terrain had largely been made up of flat, easy-going plains: vast corridors of sand hemmed in by strings of towering linear dunes that stretched off northeastwards into the void. But here the level sand plains had disappeared, to be replaced by chaos. We all had to dismount and lead our camels up and down an endless series of precipitous slipfaces. The angle of these slopes, the steepest part of any dune, are always set at between 30 and 35 degrees, depending on the size of the grains of sand. Descending a slipface is strenuous work. Your foot usually triggers a dry avalanche that swallows your leg, throwing you off balance in the cascade of sand. Camels know this and would prefer not to get involved, so we had to encourage and cajole our beasts into clambering down.

And each time we made these descents, we became engulfed once more by the world of sand, briefly losing sight of Zoo Baba's distant peaks before we were forced to scale the next, equally precipitous, dune, to regain the prospect of our destination.

Those final three hours before reaching Zoo Baba were the worst of our trip. The sun had reached its zenith and bore down on us from the heavens like a relentless tyrant intent on sapping our souls. Sougui and I were all in, and our camels, if such a thing were possible, seemed more weary still. For most of our journey, leading our charges was effortless as the camels adjusted their pace to ours, wandering along behind, their rope always loose in my hand. But now that they were tired and unwilling to traverse the treacherous slopes of the dunes, we had to pull hard on their ropes to keep them moving. To make matters worse, we had entered a territory infested with sandflies, perhaps a precursor of the oasis that beckoned. We struggled on through the sand, tugging our reluctant camels while swatting the biting insects from our hands and faces.

There may be some who would say that it was that final trudge through purgatory that made the vista of Zoo Baba's oasis so blissful when it finally came. They're probably right, but I think I'd have appreciated it anyway. Leaving the sand at long last to plod the remaining half hour to the well across stony ground, I was struck by a real sense of achievement.

It wasn't only me who felt the joy and relief of our arrival.

'The last two hours were the most terrible yet,' Sougui declared. 'They seemed like two years... of pain, and suffering and heat.'

Even Dakou deigned to smile at me as she arrived abreast of us. 'You're here,' she called, 'I've brought you to Zoo Baba.'

Unlike Dibella, there were people who lived in Zoo Baba. Six families to be precise, all of them Tubu. Their houses were made from desiccated palm fronds stuck vertically into the sand and held fast by cross sticks bound together with woven grasses to make walls. They stood proud among tall green palms and acacia trees, the latter in bloom, shedding bright yellow powdery balls of pollen on to the sands around them. Birds sang from the branches as goats wandered idly in and out of their dappled shade. After three days of relentless sand, it seemed like a sliver of paradise in the barren wilderness.

Not all of the rush walls in this wide oasis enclosed dwellings. Some stood without roofs, set apart from the houses on the edge of the sands. Chegou Abdullah, a tall man dressed in a snow-white *boubou* who had ambled over to greet us when we'd finished helping unload and water the camels, told Sougui and me that these were Zoo Baba's gardens. Intrigued, we gratefully took him up on his offer to show us what was inside after a much-needed rest.

He led us through a gap in the rushes into an oasis within the oasis. Neat patches of vibrant green foliage nestled in the sand. There were two sorts of melon, tomato plants and aubergines with small purple flowers, as well as a mass of something with tiny red fruit that was used to make soup. Mr Chegou bought his seeds in Bilma, he told us, a day's camel ride away. He fertilized the sand with crumbled camels' droppings. Over to one side of Mr Chegou's enclosure was a shallow well, the water visible less than 30 cm below the sands. For a short time after sowing, he said, he had to send his children into the enclosure in the early mornings to prevent the birds from eating the newly sown seeds. He explained, almost apologetically, that he had only recently planted the crops that lay before us, having been busy for much of the last month or two gathering Zoo Baba's small date harvest.

But although Mr Chegou was obviously entirely content with his lot in this isolated spot, for Sougui and me Zoo Baba also had its downsides. Flies buzzed around our heads constantly, even after the sun had gone down, which neither of us could understand. 'Can you imagine?' Sougui asked incredulously. 'The flies in Zoo Baba never sleep.'

The morning after our arrival, a more sinister drawback emerged. Sougui returned to his sleeping mat after washing his face to find a small sand-coloured snake curled up in the warmth of the sheet he had slept beneath. He called me over to examine it, but the creature had already taken fright and was slithering away towards an acacia bush. Sougui was looking disturbed.

'How are the Tubu with snakes, Sougui?' I asked him.

He paused, still shaken, staring at the receding culprit. 'There is no relationship between us,' he said simply. 'When we see, we have to kill.' But by the time he'd found a stick big enough to dispatch his unfriendly visitor, the snake had disappeared.

Anyway, it was time to leave for the final leg of our journey. Our route from Zoo Baba to Bilma started through the usual dunes but they were quickly joined by frequent jagged peaks that guided us all the way to our destination. The smooth plains of sand between the chains of dunes gave way in places to level tracts of bare rock littered with chunks of debris that looked not so much like pieces of stone as wrinkled chunks of rusting metal.

Across these areas, firm beneath the foot, the going was good, but crossing the chains of dunes still meant we had to coax the camels to do what their instincts told them not to. For the first time on our journey, the sun failed to shine. It remained locked inside a leaden sky as the wind took up the challenge and blew with increasing force, whipping the gritty tops off the dunes and into our faces. As I'd known before starting out, the Ténéré is renowned for its ferocious storms, and it finally seemed that the elements were going to deliver. This is the land of the Harmattan, part of the trade winds, a northeasterly that scoops vast quantities of desert grime from the area between where we were struggling to reach Bilma and the Tibesti highlands of northern Chad, and shovels it out to smother the skies over West Africa. Physical geographers, myself among them, have studied the region mostly using satellites, and declared this Bodélé Depression to be the largest source of desert dust on the planet. For thousands of kilometres, down as far as the Atlantic coasts of Ghana and Côte d'Ivoire, the atmosphere is filled with this grit from the Sahara.

Winter is the main Harmattan season, but its blast can be felt at any time of the year and it seemed that we were in luck. Throughout the day the gusts got steadily stronger, filling the air with sand, blurring the distinction between it and the ground. We stopped to camp on the edge of Bilma and Sougui and I ventured into town, leaving the women wrapped in their headscarves. They saw no reason to join us, they said, as they would be pushing on the following day, covering the last few kilometres to Dirkou.

But this was where I had to take my leave of the Tubu women and I wanted to find something to offer them as an expression of my gratitude. Bilma was a neat little town beside an extensive stand of palm trees, made up of sturdy mud-brick buildings, a market and even a couple of small general stores. Some of these constructions could boast electricity in the meagre light of the dust haze. Water from Bilma's well had been piped into the main square and children hovered around the standpipe filling their plastic containers. Sougui pointed out that a settlement with taps had to be considered as a serious town. But after spending the last few weeks far from solid dwellings and the trappings of a civilization closer to my own, I found its dusty streets claustrophobic and we quickly set about finding someone who would sell us a goat.

As Sougui and I made our way back to camp, me tugging my reluctant goat by one of its horns, I knew I was disappointed because my journey was over. For a brief moment, I'd crossed an invisible border into a forbidden world where the people were impassive and lived in houses of air. But now I'd returned to a more familiar place.

Sougui had bought a thank-you present too, and after I'd transferred custody of my goat to the women, he handed over a small bag of dates. Soon they would be acquiring much greater quantities of these fruits of the desert, but as far as I could tell the women seemed pleased with both tokens of our gratitude. Hati and Binti sampled the dates and looked as if they liked them too. After tying the goat to a camel saddle, Aiché joined them. She grinned as she grabbed a date and started to gnaw its sweet flesh. Then she took a handful and stretched out her arm to offer one to me.

That night the Harmattan gathered strength and blew with the force of a gale, blasting a constant stream of sand against my body. I wrapped my face in my headscarf against the stinging gusts, although sleep still seemed impossible with the roar of the wind. But at some stage I must have drifted off because when I awoke the wind had subsided and the sun was climbing into a milky, dust-laden sky. I was covered in sand. Somehow, despite my headscarf, it had still found its way into my eyes, nose and mouth. My teeth were gritty and it felt sore to open my eyes but slowly I sat up to look around.

Sougui was still prostrate, wrapped in his sheet and headscarf like a mummy prepared for burial. But behind him, the spot where the women had been was empty. They had gone already, leaving no trace, like snow on the desert's dusty face. It seemed like an appropriate way to end my trip across the Ténéré.

SWAMP
Papua

O N E

I hadn't been looking forward to swamp. From the beginning, I'd thought it would be the least hospitable of the four environments I'd be visiting. Like most people, I didn't perceive swamps as attractive. Try telling friends that you're intent on spending a month in a swamp and you'll quickly discover a certain consistency in their reactions. I was always met with looks of curiosity and disgust, a blend of suspicion and pity driven by the underlying question: why?

For this final leg of my adventures, I had travelled nearly half-way around the globe to New Guinea. The world's second-largest island, it is still an icon of remoteness thanks to its dense forests, towering mountain ranges and, of course, impenetrable swamps. Sitting in the libraries of Oxford, poring over maps and atlases, I'd been confronted by a region I knew little about. The island was surrounded by seas with unfamiliar names – Arafura, Ceram, Banda – a place sitting on the very edge of my mid-latitude consciousness. I had few ideas of what to expect, my mind throwing up just a vague impression of cannibalism among people caught in a Stone Age time warp. I quickly discovered that the island has a short recorded history. It provided scant material to distil into a few thin images.

Only in the early twentieth century did outsiders seriously begin to explore New Guinea's interior, slowly lifting its cloak of mystery to glimpse a world still living a prehistoric existence. It was the stuff of storybooks, a virgin land populated by birds of paradise and people armed with bows and arrows whose cultures centred on a ritual cycle of head-hunting. To the outside world, New Guinea was the epitome of beauty and the beast.

I had plumped for the Indonesian half of the island, formerly known as Irian Jaya but now dubbed Papua. Vast tracts of the southern parts of Papua are smothered by a permanent mire fed by torrential tropical rains, the runoff from the island's mountainous backbone, and the tides of the Arafura Sea that penetrate deep into the flat coastal plains. Nearly a third of Papua's land area is swamp, more than 125,000 square kilometres in total, comprising some of the most extensive and least disturbed waterlogged land in the whole Asia–Pacific region. It seemed like an appropriate place to end my mission to see how people survive in extreme environments.

As a physical geographer, I knew that bogs, swamps and marshes – usually referred to collectively as 'wetlands' – play an important role in the workings of our planet. They provide habitats for a very wide variety of plants and animals, and their status as temporary water stores helps to moderate river floods and protect coastlines from destructive erosion. They also act like giant water filters, trapping and recycling nutrients, so helping to maintain water quality and control pollution. While forests are often referred to as the lungs of the world, wetlands can be thought of as its kidneys.

But despite their benefits for humankind, these places still don't have an endearing reputation, and this is easily explained. Wetlands tend to be viewed as dangerous and disease-ridden because they often are. Standing water makes an ideal breeding ground for mosquitoes, bearers of such unpleasant and life-threatening diseases as dengue fever, malaria, viral encephalitis and filariasis. Besides these dangers, most people simply don't like the idea of a boggy transition zone between terra firma and the recognizably open water of lakes and seas. It's a difficult place in which to live a normal human existence; everyday activities such as walking, building houses and growing crops are hampered in this soggy netherworld that is neither one thing nor the other. The general dislike of swamps is further strengthened by images of monsters lurking in the primeval quagmire. The monsters might seem to be stretching it, but not by much if you consider that many tropical swamps are inhabited by crocodiles.

The ultimate aim of my journey to Papua was to make contact with a group of people, the Kombai, whose reaction to living in a swamp was to avoid it. They lived in tree-houses. But, initially, I thought I should confront head-on all the risks associated with these places, and I had arranged to join up with someone who knew about crocodiles, a man who had been wading the mosquito-ridden swamps of New Guinea on and off for more than twenty years. I met Jack Cox at a market stall in the town of Merauke, sitting astride a wooden bench dunking small doughnuts into a tall glass of milky coffee.

My first reaction was one of disappointment. He didn't look like a crocodile man. I'd had visions of a bronzed, barrel-chested loudmouth with rippling muscles toned from years of wrestling swamp monsters, probably peppered with a few jagged scars telling of uncomfortably close encounters. But although Jack was an inch short of six foot, he wasn't powerfully built and his complexion was decidedly pasty. His voice was deep and relaxed, with the hint of a Southern twang to his American accent. His manner was laid back, although he had an air of dogged self-assertion about him that made me think his approach to catching crocodiles would not be to overpower them physically in a face-to-face contest, so much as to wear them down with his grim determination.

We had arranged to meet in the market to get kitted up for our journey in search of crocs. The first thing I needed was a mosquito net, and we made our way along the rows of women selling sweet potatoes and onions in search of an appropriate outlet. I asked Jack just how bad I should expect the mosquitoes to be.

'Pretty bad,' he replied. 'They can cover your arms completely, so you can't see any of your skin and they have to queue up to take a bite out of you. You get so covered, you know, that if they had bigger wings it's almost as if they could lift you off the ground and carry you away.' He turned as we reached the end of a row of vegetable stalls and gave me an impish grin. 'Eating can be difficult too because they tend to fly into your mouth.'

We found a section of the market where they sold sarongs and other items of clothing. Near the front of one stall was a pile of mosquito nets. Jack looked them over and announced that they'd do the job. 'You need one with a fine mesh,' he explained. 'It's the real little mosquitoes you have to be careful of. They're the worst; they carry cerebral malaria. The downside is that you don't get any air passing through a net like this one, so it's like sleeping in a sauna.'

It seemed like a reasonable trade-off to me and I bought the net, asking Jack whether there was anything else we should be buying before our expedition into crocodile territory.

'Yeah, we need a rake.' He started to survey the market for a likely stall.

'A rake?' I asked. It wasn't the answer I'd been expecting. 'What do we need a rake for?'

'It's the most important piece of equipment for a croc hunt', Jack told me. He had started off through the crowd, heading towards an assortment of brightly coloured plastic buckets.

'If we find a big crocodile,' he said, 'and it doesn't like the idea of being caught, a rake gives it something interesting to ponder on. You shove a rake in its mouth to bite on and that gives you just enough time to get the hell out of Dodge.'

We'd arrived at the bucket stall. Among the hardware were machetes, knives, cooking pots and coils of rope. But there were no rakes. After talking to the stallholder, Jack forged on towards another hardware outlet and I followed, wondering if it might not be too late to pull out of what was looking like a decidedly rough and ready expedition.

The second hardware stall was also rakeless. I'd been surprised at how bustling a town Merauke was. Its wide, neat and clean streets were buzzing with motorcycles and sky blue taxis and, although it was February, some of the shopfronts still had their Christmas decorations up. It was a prosperous-looking place, endowed with an unusually large number of churches. Several of these boasted fairly dapper lawns, but I fancy that all had been manicured without the aid of a rake because it soon became clear that the Merauke market did not sell such an article.

Standing in front of our third hardware stall, Jack's face was thoughtful, tinged with disappointment. 'What about one of those?' I asked him, pointing to an assortment of wooden brooms. Jack grabbed one of the long handles and lifted it up for inspection. The broom, which had a vaguely home-made air about it, looked more than adequate as a sweeping instrument, but I was less convinced about its promise as an anti-crocodile device as Jack, clutching the handle in both hands, gave a couple of sharp thrusts towards an imaginary prehistoric reptile. The broom's unconvincing head didn't look to me as if it would do much to distract a large crocodile from clamping its jaws on an inviting piece of human flesh, but Jack was obviously less of the worrying type. 'OK,' he said slowly, 'I guess this'll do the job just as well.'

I deferred to his greater experience in these matters, but resolved at that moment always to stay well behind Jack on our expedition into the swamp. The stallholder, who had been observing Jack's pantomime with an expression of some bemusement on his face, made to show us how the broom was conventionally used. But Jack told him what we had in mind as he counted out the *rupiah* notes in payment. The stallholder nodded uneasily and then rapidly took great interest in something at the back of his stall.

* * *

Merauke was the first town of any consequence in Papua. Although the Dutch had long claimed sovereignty over the western part of New Guinea, following the Dutch East India Company's alliance with a nearby sultan in 1660, it wasn't until 1902 that they followed up with direct administrative control by establishing the port at Merauke. It was an embarrassed response to the fact that theoretically Dutch-controlled subjects – the fierce Marind-Anim – were regularly making sorties across the 141° east meridian to bring back trophy heads from British-administered subjects in the country we know today as Papua New Guinea. The Dutch had already noted the Marind-Anim's reputation as ferocious warriors, naming a couple of the rivers in south-east Papua in their honour: the Moordenaar (Murderer) and the Doodslager (Slaughterer). It was the Marind-Anim's penchant for human flesh that is supposed to have led to the colonization of the swampy area Jack and I were heading for. Groups that weren't as good at head-hunting as the Marind-Anim had fled from the mainland across a narrow strait to take up residence on two islands: Pulau Kimaam and its smaller neighbour Pulau Komoran.

If you look at a map of Papua, one of the first things that strikes you is the distinct lack of roads. The only modern form of transport that allows you to move any distance on this island is an aircraft, and the landscape is speckled with small airstrips. When I first saw these miniature red aeroplane symbols dotted across my map, the image I had of a largely wild and uncharted territory began to pale, but flying from Merauke to the airstrip that served the village of Kimaam the feeling of remoteness was quickly rekindled. The flight of 200 kilometres took us across a level, waterlogged landscape with few signs of human occupation. Small flocks of snow-white birds stretched their wings to soar across the vibrant green reedbeds, and the sun's glint from expanses of open water gave the impression that the swamp was saluting my arrival with a wink.

Our small plane touched down on Kimaam's grassy airstrip and trundled to a halt. I climbed out of the aircraft and into a cloud of mosquitoes. I was mentally prepared for this, Jack's comments having served as confirmation of an academic paper I'd read before leaving for Papua. The author of the paper, published in the journal *Tropical and Geographical Medicine* in 1959, had candidly stated that the island I had just landed on was reputed to be one of the worst mosquito-ridden areas of New Guinea. Dr Van Den Assem had identified no fewer than twenty-five different species on the island, adding that this number certainly didn't represent the complete local mosquito fauna. I had read his forensically detailed catalogue with mounting horror. There were descriptions of spotted ones and stripy ones, a species with brownish abdomen scales and another sporting yellow scales on its proboscis. The density of a cloud encountered in one location was described as 'astronomical', a comment I found particularly worrying given the complete lack of emotive language used elsewhere in the scientific paper.

With this foreword to Pulau Kimaam in mind, I had taken the necessary precautions of wearing a long-sleeved shirt and long trousers and had spent the last ten minutes of our flight carefully applying insect repellent to my hands and face. There are all sorts of repellents on the market, including several that smell of citrus and are touted as 'ecologically friendly', which has always struck me as a contradiction in terms because, if you wanted to be ecologically friendly, you wouldn't be wearing any repellent at all. Over the years I've tried most of the brands available, and have reached the conclusion that none of them is any good unless its active ingredient is Diethyl Toluamide, a chemical more commonly known as DEET.

DEET, which shouldn't be used on children, is flammable, and it's deleterious to a range of synthetic materials like nylon and plastic. I know the last danger to my cost, having on several occasions corroded the plastic parts of my spectacles. In other words, it's dangerous stuff, which is just what you want from an insect repellent. You can buy repellents made of DEET in varying proportions, from the mild 35 per cent strength to the maximum 100 per cent. Having read Dr Van Den

Assem's paper, I'd decided not to mess around. I had brought several tubes of 100 per cent DEET and I slapped it on all over.

Or at least, I thought I had. Within twenty seconds of landing, I'd been bitten on my eyelid. Foolishly, I'd forgotten to close my eyes and apply it there too. The next bite was on my lip, another area I had neglected to anoint.

The village was just a short walk from the airstrip along a muddy path that had been built up to snake its way through the marshy terrain. Jack and I were accompanied by a gang of small children and several men sporting bushy black beards, all of whom had come to see our plane fly in. Even these locals were regularly slapping mosquitoes on their legs and necks as they walked.

Kimaam, the village, must have been on slightly higher ground because it wasn't the collection of huts in a bog that I'd been expecting. It consisted of a smart little church and an assortment of wooden houses with corrugated iron roofs, linked by concrete walkways. An occasional bicycle plied up and down the thoroughfares, along with a single motorbike ridden by a man who never appeared to be going anywhere. I think he was simply driving back and forth to show off his shiny vehicle. Otherwise, the main means of transport was to be found down at the creek that wound its way through the centre of the village. Below a rickety wooden pier was tied an assortment of long wooden canoes, one or two with outboard motors.

Virtually all of the faces in Kimaam were Papuan, thick-set with tightly curled black hair. They were a contrast to those in Merauke, where every other person had been straight-haired and looked to have hailed originally from one of Indonesia's many other islands. I was told they were beneficiaries of the government's transmigration programme that has encouraged people from the country's more densely populated territories to up stakes and move to the remoter islands. It didn't surprise me that hardly any of them appeared to have opted to make their new homes on Pulau Kimaam. The few exceptions were to be found behind the counters of the village's shops and in the accommodation block that sat opposite the Roman Catholic church. Jack had ascertained that the church might be able to put us up, and a kindly nun led us across the way, beneath a spreading mango tree, to another church house where we could hang our mosquito nets over camp beds for the night.

That evening, after I'd lit mosquito coils in all four corners of our room, we tucked into a dinner of fish and rice provided by one of the nuns as Jack outlined our crocodile-hunting programme. New Guinea was home to both freshwater and saltwater crocodiles, he told me. The mangrove swamps that fringed most of the islands offshore were known to accommodate salties, but the scientific world was yet to discover what species inhabited the interior freshwater swamps. 'It would be really neat if we could find a freshy in the wild on one of these islands, because no one has ever done that before.'

Jack began his mission first thing the following morning, touring the village to interrogate anyone who knew anything about crocodiles in the area. He returned later that day with the hint of a smile on his face. 'Well then, young Nick, I think I've narrowed it down a little.' He took off his baseball cap and wiped his hand across his brow. 'Everyone seems to be pointing to Pulau Komoran, that's the smaller island down to the south of Kimaam. I think that's where we oughta go. But first I've got something I think you should see.'

He took me across the village, towards the creek. 'Before going on your first crocodile hunt, I think you should take a look at what we're after.'

We struck off the concrete path through a gap in the fence surrounding a low-slung house. A small dog jumped off the wooden veranda and approached to check us out, following us down the side of the building to the backyard where a youth was leaning against a shoulder-high wooden compound attached to the back of the house. Jack introduced us. 'This is Dominikus,' he said, 'and this is his crocodile pen.'

I shook Dominikus's hand and peered over the barrier. The bottom of the pen was a dark grey morass of mud and water studded with a large collection of small crocodiles laid out in a haphazard fashion. There must have been at least forty of the shiny grey juvenile crocs, though thankfully none was more than about a metre long. As is the way with crocodiles, they weren't actually doing anything. They were just lying, totally still, some half in and half out of the muddy water, others draped across their neighbours. I might have been looking at a photograph but for the pungent smell of excrement that wafted up from the pen.

'Dominikus caught all of these himself,' Jack was telling me, 'and rears them for their skins.' He was leaning against the top of the pen, examining the inanimate array of junior primeval monsters. 'They all look to be in pretty good condition too.' Jack pushed up the peak on his baseball cap and strained to peer closer at the fetid mire beneath us. 'They all look like salties to me,' he murmured, 'but let's take a closer look.'

At which point, Jack kicked off his flip-flops and clambered up the wooden fence. Before I could offer a word of warning, he had jumped into the pen and the inert tableau below us exploded as the juvenile crocs shifted with lightning speed towards the opposite end of the pen. A splatter of stinking mud appeared across my face.

'Want to join me?' Jack asked, as if he was inviting me for coffee and doughnuts.

I didn't think so. 'Isn't it rather dangerous?' I asked.

'No, not at all.' Jack crouched down on his haunches to survey the inhabitants of the pen. 'Don't worry,' he said, 'I'm not going to take any risks. I need all my fingers.'

But it wasn't his fingers that were of immediate concern to my mind. It was the potential fate of his toes that troubled me. I had big boots on, but I still wasn't about to join him. The only circumstances under which I could envisage me climbing into a pen full of crocodiles, albeit small ones, would be with complete and utter confidence in my mentor. Admittedly, Jack was calm and unruffled in the presence of these mini monsters, but this was still too early in our relationship for me to have total faith in his abilities. He was crouching barefoot, well within striking distance of several dozen carnivorous reptiles, and I'd just seen how fast they could move. I was also still trying to figure out in my mind whether the wooden broom we'd brought from Merauke was a reflection of inspired brilliance or the act of a madman.

'These little guys aren't about to cause any trouble', Jack said calmly.

Part of me could see his point. Now that the crocs had shifted to the opposite end of their pen, they were motionless once more. But there was another thing about Jack that I was still pondering. Ever since we'd arrived in Kimaam he'd been wandering around in his shorts and T-shirt, seemingly oblivious to the mosquito threat. I could see that he was being bitten, but only occasionally did he take evasive action with a slap on his arm, face or leg. Most of the time he just let the airborne persecutors land and suck away to their hearts' content. It seemed clear to me that Jack didn't experience pain in the same way that I did. For all I knew, the same might apply to his attitude towards danger. Until I'd fathomed just where Jack's thresholds lay, I wasn't about to place myself in any hazardous situations with him. While all these thoughts were flashing through my mind, Dominikus just looked on, with a slightly bored expression on his face.

'How do you actually go about catching one, Jack?' I asked from behind the safety of the wooden barrier.

'With little fellers like this you just pick 'em up', he replied, and he reached out a long arm towards the muddy puddle and grabbed one behind the head. Almost simultaneously, his other hand had grabbed hold of its tail. At the same time, all the crocs nearby made another explosive bid for safety, sending splashes of foul grey water in all directions.

Jack stood up with the crocodile firmly in his hands, and turned it over to look at its white belly. This wasn't something the croc appreciated and it tried to wriggle out of Jack's grip, opening its jaws to make a strange noise like a croaky bird. It sounded like *mo-ack*.

Jack had a firm hold on the creature, which was about a foot in length, and was concentrating on its upturned belly. 'Yup, it's a salty', he said presently. He could tell this by counting the rows of scales between its collar and its sex, he told me. 'Here,' he gestured, 'you hold him and I'll show you.'

After its protest at being turned over, the creature appeared to have come to terms with its captive state and had resumed the customary inert stance. I looked at Jack. 'Go on, you hold it tight here behind the head and it's not going to bite you. Take the tail in the other hand and you're in control. This croc's not going anywhere.'

As it was only a foot long, I took a very firm hold of its neck and put my other hand around its tail. The croc sat motionless in my hands. I flipped it over and Jack showed how to count its belly scales. It had thirty-two rows, which was well within the saltwater crocodile range. 'A salty has between twenty-nine and thirty-six rows,' Jack explained, 'while a freshy has twenty-four to twenty-eight.'

The croc in my hands still hadn't moved a muscle and I was growing in confidence. The fact that I had any confidence at all surprised me, since this was the closest I'd ever come to one of these swamp beasts. But, with it inanimate like this, I was able to admire its smooth scales. To my further surprise, I was also beginning to develop an admiration for the creature. It was almost cute.

But Jack had lost interest in my charge. He was surveying the pen once more. 'I think you ought to try a bigger one,' he was saying, 'and one or two of these guys look like they might just be freshies.' He had his eyes on one of the pen's larger crocs and was manoeuvring himself sideways, like a crab, towards it. 'What should I do with this one?' I wanted to know. 'Oh, just put it back', Jack said without looking up. I leant over the wooden barrier and released my croc head first back into the mud. It hit the ground with a gentle thump, moved a pace forward and sat there.

Jack was poised over his next target. It was a good metre long and appeared to be confident enough not to have joined its friends piled up at the opposite end of the pen to where Jack hovered. It was half submerged in the shallow stinky pond and had its beady eye on Jack. Suddenly, its mouth flashed open and it made a lunge towards Jack's bare foot. But its jaws snapped on thin air because Jack had neatly stepped sideways, simultaneously whipping his hand in to grab the croc's neck. The croc's tail made a vain effort to whisk round in a spray of grey mud, but Jack's other hand had already secured it and he lifted the writhing creature out of the sludge.

'There we go – now that wasn't difficult, was it?' I think the croc viewed the situation rather differently because it had its jaws open and was doing its croaky bird impression. '*Mo-ack, mo-ack*', it cried. 'Here, young Nick, you take it while I climb out of here and show you what's what.' Jack made to hand me the croc, but this time I wasn't so sure. This croc was obviously unhappy at being handled and looked significantly stronger than the first one. 'Perhaps Dominikus could hold it for now', I suggested.

Dominikus did as he was asked as Jack clambered out of the pen, eased his toes into his flip-flops and took hold of the crocodile once more. He crouched down with the croc, which was still croaking. The croc stopped writhing and became silent. 'Want to hold it now?' Jack asked.

I put my left hand round its neck and held it very tightly, my right hand taking hold of its other end at the base of its tail. The croc didn't move, but I sensed the pent-up strength in its physique. Its whole body was like one formidable muscle. Jack released his grip to leave me holding it. Nothing happened. The croc just lay in my hands, seemingly inert. I was holding it as tightly as I could, but I relaxed my grip slightly now that I recognized it had given up struggling. I turned it over so that Jack could count the rows of scales on its belly. There were twenty-seven. Jack looked at me. 'You know what that means, don't you?' He allowed himself a wry smile. 'This one's a freshy. That's excellent news.'

I was thinking exactly the same. Part of me was hoping that now we'd found a freshwater croc, we wouldn't have to bother with our expedition into the swamp. But I also knew that claiming a scientific finding was unlikely to be quite so simple. Dominikus said he had caught most of his crocodiles down in Pulau Komoran, but the fact remained that this one was in captivity, and it was always possible that this freshy had come from elsewhere. The only surefire way of confirming that there were freshwater crocodiles in the wild on one of these islands off New Guinea was to go out and catch one for ourselves and document it with photographs.

I put my thoughts to Jack and he nodded. 'That's right, but now that we've seen this boy,' he pointed at the croc still sitting quietly in my hands, 'I think our chances of finding one in the wild are pretty good. Now all we've got to do is get down to Pulau Komoran and find the best place to look.'

TWO

We hired one of the dugout canoes with an outboard motor to take us to Pulau Komoran. It took us down the creek from the village between steep mudbanks forested with mangrove trees and into the Muli channel, the strait separating Kimaam island from the mainland. Its waters were chocolate-brown but the briny spray sent up by the prow of our boat smelled of the sea.

The shorelines we sped past were an endless labyrinth of mangrove roots, like multi-limbed cartoon creatures tentatively stepping down to the water on their slinky legs. An eagle flew by with a silvery fish dangling from its talons, and the boatman pointed out bats hanging high in the trees. They looked like furry brown teddy bears suspended in the branches until the noise from our engine caused them to take flight, spreading their huge gossamer wings and waving as they disappeared beyond the treetops. Emerging from the Muli channel after several hours, we hugged the coast of Pulau Komoran to avoid the worst of the swell from the Arafura Sea before speeding up an inlet towards the village of Komoran. We were a couple of hundred metres inside the mouth of the inlet when the engine began to splutter. It coughed once or twice, then cut out completely and we slowed to a stop.

As the boatman opened the engine casing to peer inside, the first mosquitoes arrived. I buttoned the top of my shirt and prepared for action, rummaging through my bag for the insect repellent. Within minutes, I was surrounded. The first bite I received was on the end of my thumb; the next on my lower lip. The tube of 100 per cent DEET, in my opinion the most effective repellent known, was not known to the mosquitoes of Pulau Komoran. It was completely ineffectual. Despite constantly waving my arms around my head, I was very soon covered in bites. Even the boatman seemed to be bothered, slapping his neck as he struggled with the pipe that fed fuel to the engine. Jack, however, just sat there in his shorts and T-shirt, oblivious to it all.

While the boatman worked to fix the engine, we drifted towards the bank and its tangle of mangrove roots. As we did so, the mosquito cloud grew thicker. Jack announced that he wanted to get off to take a leak, so I grabbed an aerial root to steady the boat for him to disembark. Mangroves are coastal wetland forests. They are made up of salt-adapted evergreen trees, and are found in the intertidal zone of tropical and subtropical latitudes. Mangrove trees are therefore associated with ground that is both salty and muddy. Jack sank in up to his knees.

Mangroves are also associated with quite phenomenal numbers of mosquitoes, or at least they were here on Pulau Komoran. As Jack grappled his way through the knee-high morass, I was being eaten alive.

Jack disappeared into the undergrowth. Holding on to the root to stop us drifting away meant that I was reduced to waving just one hand about my head, while also using it to slap those mosquitoes I could see feasting on my root-holding hand. I didn't stand a chance. The mosquitoes were winning through sheer force of numbers. I felt like Gulliver in Lilliput, rendered helpless by the vast swarms of small biting insects.

When Jack re-emerged from the trees a few moments later, his legs and arms were literally covered in them. Even he had woken up to the scale of the mosquito problem by now. 'Will you look at that?' he said, sounding amazed. He was just standing there, perched on a mangrove root, looking at his legs. 'I've never seen so many mosquitoes in all my life.'

Interesting though this piece of information was, I wasn't really in the mood to discuss the situation. 'Get back in the boat, Jack, and let's get away from the bank', I suggested, trying my best to sound calm.

Once he was back on board, we grabbed paddles and took us back out into the middle of the inlet. The mosquitoes followed us. The boatman had closed the engine casing and was furiously tugging the ignition cord while smacking the back of his neck. I was nearing the point of apoplexy when the engine exploded into life and we moved off.

For the next ten minutes, I conducted a thorough search-and-destroy mission on any remaining mosquitoes that had hitched a lift with us. They were lined up on the inside of the canoe's hull like aeroplanes on an aircraft carrier, and perched in large numbers on every object below the level of the vessel's sides, protected there from the wind we generated as we gained speed.

Once the boarders had been dispatched, I took stock of my person. The creases in my trouserlegs held piles of small, waif-like corpses, and more tiny dead bodies littered my shirt. But these deceased specimens were definitely in the minority. Most of the mosquitoes had been, fed and left. I felt ravaged. The backs of my hands and my fingers were so covered in bites that when I clenched my fists it felt as if I was wearing gloves that were too small for me. I ran one hand over my neck and discovered that its topography had also been completely altered. It was just a jumble of lumps and bumps. It felt as if a few hundred grains of rice had been implanted beneath my skin. My face had been reshaped too. It must have been about three times its normal size. Like on my hands, its skin felt tight and unfamiliar. When I blinked, even my eyelids felt stiff and unwieldy. But the most curious thing about the whole experience was the fact that none of these bites actually itched that much. I guess that meant I was lucky.

An hour or so later, the mosquitoes returned when the boatman cut the engine so that we could glide in to the wooden jetty at the village of Komoran. But they were not the only welcoming party. The jetty was soon crowded with a throng of men wearing palm-frond headdresses, with white paint daubed on their faces. Some were brandishing wooden sticks adorned with white feathers, others bows and arrows. They looked agitated, gyrating up and down on the spot singing and waving their arms.

For a brief moment, I was unsure whether these people were here to greet us or repel us, but as soon as I clambered on to the jetty I was surrounded by fierce-looking men thrusting their hands towards me in greeting. Up close, I got a better look at their headdresses, most an eruption of fronds bursting out past their shoulders, others made of sticks that fitted over their skulls like the legs of a small chair. The sticks were decorated with feathers. The men were smiling and nodding while smacking the occasional mosquito on their bare torsos. It had taken Jack and me a couple of days to organize our boat in Kimaam and I could only think that someone had made the trip in the interim and told the villagers that we were on our way. Everyone looked pretty pleased to see us.

Jack and I were led down the jetty towards the village, where a horde of women and children were waiting. A woman dressed almost entirely in palm fronds – a tutu-like skirt, a long flowing necklace and a huge headdress – approached me, holding a garland of woven vines. It was studded with small grey and white seeds and suspended with leaves and feathers. She bade me welcome and hung the garland round my neck.

We were carried into the village by the throng, small children skipping along beside me holding my hands. The houses were wooden and raised up on stilts, their roofs neatly thatched in greying fronds. I was led to a house with a raised veranda fronting a wide open space where the crowd congregated to dance back and forth. Jack joined me on the veranda to watch. 'Some welcome,' he cried above the singing.

'One of the men just told me we're the first white people to visit this village for ten years.'

The singing and dancing continued for a half-hour, the villagers parading up and down in front of the veranda to the rhythm of drums. Then we were joined on the veranda by a man in a blue cap who raised his arms to silence the people and made an official announcement of welcome which Jack translated for me. As the crowd began to disperse, the man in the blue cap turned to me and said something. He was studying my face as he did so.

Jack did the honours again. 'He says, "The mosquitoes knew how to welcome you too".'

Warm though our welcome had been, the village of Komoran was just a staging post on our mission to find a freshwater crocodile somewhere in the island's swamps, and the following morning Jack and I set about enquiring after the best place to conduct our search. We were led straight to a man known in the village as King Crocodile, who showed us his collection of three hefty croc skulls. He set them out in a line on his veranda, which was blissfully free of mosquitoes thanks to the dense smoke coming from a fire burning coconut husks beneath. One skull was smaller than the others and had been smoked to a nicotine-yellow colour; the two larger examples were white, and Jack reckoned they had come from crocodiles four or five metres in length. King Crocodile also produced a full-length skin for us to look at. It took him and three of his mates to hold it up for Jack and me to inspect.

His collection was impressive – although I was concerned at the size of the specimens – but from the scientific point of view they were disappointing. None of them was from a freshy. Jack fell into a lengthy discussion with King Crocodile and his accomplices, the outcome of which was that we were advised to venture inland to an area of swamp known as Kowonep. There was a small patch of raised ground near the swamp where crocodile hunters from the village camped on such expeditions.

The tricky aspect of our prospective trip seemed to be the length of time it would take to get there. Everyone agreed that we'd have to leave the village at first light, because our journey would take us out to sea again and the timing of the tides was important. If we tried to motor up the right creek at low tide, we wouldn't make it past the mudbanks. But no one held the same opinion on how long it would take to reach Kowonep.

'The problem is that nobody's been there for a while,' Jack told me as we wandered back to the house we were staying in. 'They're not sure we'll make it with the outboard motor because the canoe is so big. There are always trees falling across the river, blocking the way. I guess we'll just have to go for it, and if we don't make it by nightfall we can sleep in the boat.'

We did make it to the dry patch of raised ground beside the Kowonep swamp in one day, but only just. We boarded our boat as the sun was getting up and the mosquitoes were getting airborne, bade farewell to the small crowd that had gathered to see us off, and sped away down Komoran's creek. The first hour or so before we reached the sea was a stop–start affair as the engine played up several times, but for me the inevitable mosquitoes that immediately hovered into view from the mangroves each time we came to a halt were not so much of a problem as they had been on our inward trip. This was because the previous evening Jack had presented me with a headnet. I wore it over my hat and it came with a drawstring to tighten round my neck. My immediate gratitude was tempered by the thought that he might have produced it rather earlier in our expedition, but nonetheless it went a long way towards preserving my sanity.

When we emerged from the creek out to sea, the air was fresh and mosquito-free and we sped along parallel to a sandy coastline lined with coconut palms before turning in towards the island once more and up a shallow channel lined by mudbanks. Seabirds were strutting across the mud, which stretched a good kilometre out from the shore-line. It was the presence of these broad coastal mudflats that for a long time had discouraged passing European explorers from venturing far into Pulau Komoran and its larger neighbour Pulau Kimaam. The southern and western sides of both islands are characterized by these expansive, gently sloping plains of mud accessible only through narrow channels by a small boat at high tide. Indeed, towards the west of Pulau Kimaam the sea bed slopes so gradually that seafarers coming from that side at low tide would run aground before sighting shore. And even when explorers did manage to venture into the coastline in rowing boats, all they found was more mud, swamp and unfriendly people fearful of head-hunting raids.

The first attempt to explore Pulau Kimaam was made in the 1620s by a Dutchman, but no one bothered trying again for another 200 years. It wasn't until the 1930s that outsiders really began to penetrate the interior of these islands.

The rivermouth we had entered was brown water flanked by grey mud topped with green foliage. A buzzard watched us pass from its perch high in a tree, and single snow-white egrets stood on the mudbanks like sentries guarding the entrance to a primeval swamp world. The mud was just a metre or two wide here, but it was excellent habitat for saltwater crocodiles, Jack told me. Almost as soon as he'd said it, I saw my first salty in the wild. It was about a metre long and shot out from the trees on my left to scuttle with surprising speed down the bank and disappear into the caramel water. In the next ten minutes we saw another half-dozen crocs doing the same thing. Most were juveniles, but the largest was about two metres in length.

Little by little, the river narrowed as we made our way inland, the trees gradually closing in, their roots splayed as if they were dipping their toes into the water. An electric-blue flash of wings signalled a kingfisher as it shot along the bank beneath the overhanging boughs. Partway up the river we were met by half a dozen men in small canoes who had set out from Komoran the previous day. They would accompany us to the Kowonep swamp, ready to take over from our larger vessel should it get stuck, to show us the way to the raised camp ground.

As we penetrated further into the interior of Pulau Komoran, we started to encounter submerged logs and fallen trees, their black branches sticking out of the water as if groping for air. The sunken trees began to slow our progress in the larger canoe, requiring the men who now accompanied us to wield their axes and lop off sturdy branches to allow us through. The temporary halts also heralded the arrival in force of mosquitoes eager for our blood. I still seemed to get bitten all over, despite my new headnet. On the first occasion that we stopped to chop at the obstacles, I sat up from my position slumped against a tarpaulin and soon found that I was now being bitten on my back, an area that previously had hardly been attacked. The reason for this was that the back of my shirt had become sodden with sweat where I'd been in contact with the tarpaulin. Stuck to my back, the shirt offered little protection against the bane of my existence in the swamp.

As we moved further upriver, I could see that the saltwater was giving way to fresh as slowly the mangrove trees faded from view to be replaced by other species with huge buttress roots. Lilies, almost as tall as a man, sprouted from the shallow water on the banks, though for the most part their flowers were long past their best, leaving seed heads as big as cricket balls. But the deeper we moved into the heart of the island, the more often our momentum was slowed by fallen trees. And my secret hope, that once we'd left the mangroves behind the mosquitoes might not be so bad, proved to be erroneous. At one point I wondered aloud whether the time had not come to abandon our large canoe and take to the smaller ones, but the men just smiled and continued swinging their axes.

As the day drew on, we rounded a bend in the river, now just a few metres wide, to be confronted by a sizeable trunk that had toppled neatly across the entire width of the watercourse. Not even the smaller canoes could squeeze under it. There was no alternative but to hack away at it with an axe, another forty minutes of back-breaking work for a few and mosquito hell for the rest of us.

Not far from this point, we came across another huge treefall, which again completely blocked our way. While the first man on the scene jumped nimbly out of his canoe carrying his axe, I looked at my wristwatch. It was five o'clock and the sun had already begun to fade beneath the trees. We had about another hour of light, and I was concerned that we might not reach the edge of the swamp before nightfall. I looked up from my watch towards Jack. He nodded, clearly thinking the same thing. I don't think either of us really wanted to spend the night in our boat with the mosquitoes.

A parley ensued between Jack, our boatman and most of the men from Komoran while the figure perched on the tree trunk continued to hack away at the offending article. While all this was going on, I just sat there watching the light fade and feeling useless. It was the closest I'd ever come to being literally up a certain well-known creek without a paddle.

After ten minutes of talking, Jack gave me the news. The area of swamp we were heading for and, more importantly, the piece of raised ground where we could camp, was not far away, perhaps another half-kilometre along the river. In one sense this sounded hopeful, but at the same time no one knew how many other fallen trees there might be along what remained of our course. If the previous half-kilometre was anything to go by, it could take us several more hours to get there.

'They say it's possible to walk,' said Jack doubtfully. 'We could leave the canoes here and come back for them in the morning.' I looked at the ground beyond the riverbank. I use the term 'ground' loosely because from what I could see it wasn't exactly terra firma. The mudflats had disappeared some hours before, along with the mangroves, and here the land was more waterlogged. But the sub-merged terrain was a tangle of tree roots which looked as if they might provide a relatively firm footing.

'How far is it?' I wondered. Thirty minutes came the reply. Three of the men from Komoran offered to show us the way. They too, it seemed, were not enamoured with the idea of sleeping in their canoes.

We climbed out of our boats, loaded up with bags, a few boxes of provisions and our tents and set off, leaving the rest of the men to continue forging their way by canoe.

The trees and their supporting roots soon petered out to leave a flooded landscape of reeds and small shrubs. The sun was setting rapidly and the men from Komoran raced ahead so that Jack and I were soon left bringing up the rear, wading through the calf-deep topography swatting mosquitoes as we went. A couple of times we had to call out for the men to slow down in the rapidly fading light for fear that we might get lost forever in this godforsaken wilderness. But half an hour later we were standing on a gravel ridge, mightily relieved that we'd found the spot where we could set up our tents and finally get away from the mosquitoes.

'How did you sleep?' Jack asked as I ducked out of my tent to nip through the rain and join him beneath a large orange tarpaulin that had been strung up on a series of stout poles cut from nearby trees. I hadn't slept particularly well, despite being exhausted by the previous day's journey, but at least I'd been able to shut my eyes alone, without the accompaniment of my flying insect friends. The problem was that they had left their calling cards all over my body, and the bites from these mosquitoes itched, unlike those I'd run into on the way to Komoran. As I'd lain in my tent scratching, my mind had drifted back to Dr Van Den Assem's scientific paper. It appeared that I'd encountered several of his twenty-five different species. Under other circumstances, my discovery that the bites from some itched while others didn't would have been interesting.

Fires were smoking at each end of the tarpaulin cover and it seemed that all the men we'd left to continue hacking their way along the river had joined us. They were huddled beneath the covering, smoking roll-up cigarettes and looking as jaded as I felt. 'They got in late last night', Jack said as he handed me a mug of steaming coffee. I sipped the hot liquid and listened to the pitter-patter of raindrops on our makeshift roof as I gazed through the heavy drizzle at the scene I hadn't been able to take in the previous evening. Our gravel ridge was roughly ten metres square beside a mass of tall reeds through which someone had recently punted a small canoe. Off to one side was a grove of sizeable trees, while in the other directions lay thick black mud that gave way to low ferns and undergrowth. It was hardly a breathtaking view. Last night it had been a murky swamp with mosquitoes, and this morning, in the daylight, it was swamp with rain. I felt as if I'd died and gone to purgatory.

Jack, as usual, was placid. 'Well, the mosquitoes don't bother me that much and you have to suffer a bit of hardship to explore one of the last great wilderness areas on the planet.' He was right, of course, but I wasn't in the mood. I could quite understand why no one had bothered to explore this island up to now.

We ventured out into the Kowonep swamp later that morning in one of the small canoes. It was a glassy expanse of open water that extended almost as far as the eye could see, dotted here and there with stretches of tough little reeds sprouting above its surface. The place was alive with birds, mostly geese, and the inevitable mosquitoes, though these were not so numerous because of the rain. There were no trees, but around the edges of the swamp, and on small raised clumps that popped up here and there, sprays of ferns grew to break up the monotony of the scene. These fern thickets were ideal places for crocodiles to lurk, looking for fish, Jack told me. But after an hour or so we were drenched and we hadn't seen one, and Jack decided that our best chance of finding them would be at night.

This sounded paradoxical to me, until it was explained that a night hunt would be conducted with a powerful torch looking for eyeshine. When a crocodile was spotted in the beam, it became mesmerized by the light, allowing us to sidle up and catch it. As the day played itself out, I moped about the camp, becoming increasingly nervous about the prospect of finally going out with Jack on a crocodile hunt, particularly now that it would be in the dark.

The rain had all but stopped by the time we set out at 5.30 p.m., just as the light was beginning to fade. Jack sat in the front of the canoe, with me behind, and one of the men from Komoran, Alex, at the rear with a paddle. All we took with us was Jack's torch, the wooden broom we'd bought in Merauke and a ball of twine to tie up our catch with. It didn't seem like enough equipment to me.

The first thing Jack did was brief Alex on how he wanted to conduct operations. Jack would sweep the surface of the water with his torch looking for the tell-tale red eye-shine of a crocodile. If he fixed one in his beam, he'd wave the torch vertically to indicate the direction, and Alex was to paddle towards it.

'And then what?' I asked as Alex propelled us into the swamp. 'You just catch it?'

'I do,' said Jack, 'or I thought maybe you'd like to.'

This, I thought, was an appropriately early cue for me to lay down a few ground rules of my own. I reminded Jack that whereas he had twenty years of experience in this game, I was just a beginner. In fact, the sum total of my crocodile know-how had been acquired by holding two docile juveniles at the pen in Kimaam. My only active involvement in this expedition had already been accomplished – I'd chosen the broom. Other than that, I saw my role as that of the observer, and nothing more. I had no intention of even trying to catch a croc in the wild, whatever Jack might have in mind. It was, after all, night-time and we were in the middle of a large crocodile-infested swamp on a small island off the coast of New Guinea, one of the most remote places on Earth. We were, therefore, a long way from the nearest hospital.

The tone I adopted to deliver this information was overly formal, an attempt, no doubt, to mask my anxiety at the thought of being on this hunt at all, but I thought it was necessary to make my feelings on the matter clear. Jack just chuckled. 'We'll see about that, young Nick, we'll see.' The 'young Nick' label was starting to irritate me, too.

The sun had all but disappeared below the horizon, casting a brief golden glow over Kowonep, as Alex paddled us further into the swamp. Now that we were free of the reeds, I found the balance of our canoe difficult to maintain. Its sides were high, but its draught was decidedly shallow, and the slightest movement tended to send the whole vessel lurching dangerously to one side. Given this instability, it wouldn't have been my craft of choice for a crocodile hunt.

While concentrating hard on not rocking the boat, my thoughts turned to the possible size of specimens we might encounter. It all depended on whether we came across salties or freshies, Jack told me. The saltwater or estuarine crocodile is the largest living crocodilian, he said. 'In fact, it's the largest reptile in the world. A mature male reaches a length of more than ten feet, but really big ones can grow to twice that length. If we come across a female, it could be up to fifteen feet long.' He was sweeping the beam of his powerful torch across the water in front of him. 'Freshies, on the other hand,' he added, 'tend to be shorter than that.'

To my way of thinking, this was another good reason for finding an elusive freshy, but even so it sounded distinctly possible that we'd come across a considerably larger croc than those I'd seen in the pen at Kimaam. I'd always known this, of course, but up until now I'd preferred not to think about it. Hearing Jack point it out in so down-to-earth a manner made my blood run cold. I asked myself what I was doing on this hare-brained expedition, and failed to come up with a rational explanation.

So I asked Jack how he could tell the difference, just from the eye-shine, between a big crocodile and a small one. 'Distance between the eyes', he murmured. He was obviously concentrating hard on the sweeping beam in front of him.

'What if we're side-on, and you only see one eye?'

'Approach with caution', he said.

We glided along for some time, accompanied only by the sound of frogs that resonated like castanets in the distance and the nearer buzz of mosquitoes and other flying insects. 'This really is great habitat for crocs,' Jack said as we approached a clump of ferns. 'These ferns are ideal for hatchlings.'

My spirits rose a little at the mention of baby crocs, but only briefly. 'I suppose if there are baby crocs here, there's a good chance that mummy croc might also be in the vicinity?'

'Maybe', was the only response I got from Jack.

'And what about daddy croc?' I wondered as I smacked a mosquito that had landed on the back of my hand.

'Also possible', said Jack. He continued sweeping the waterline beneath the overhanging ferns for several minutes before putting down his torch so that he could rub the back of his neck with both hands. 'I'm surprised we haven't seen any here,' he told me, 'but let's move on.' He asked Alex to move away from the clump of ferns and we glided off into the darkness.

A few moments later, Jack resumed his vigil with the torch. 'There's one,' he whispered calmly after a couple of minutes. I strained to see where the beam was trained on the water more than a dozen metres away, but couldn't spot a thing.

'Where?' I whispered.

'Right there at the end of the beam,' said Jack, who was bending low in the canoe, 'one bright red, beady crocodile eye.'

I still couldn't see anything at all in the darkness. 'You often can't see it unless you're low down and directly behind the beam,' said Jack. 'Let's get a bit closer.' And he waved the torch up and down a couple of times so that Alex knew where to take us.

As we moved off towards the crocodile, Jack whispered, 'Lost him.' He swept the torch in a tight arc across the water again to regain contact with the eye. 'I think he's gone.' Alex continued paddling towards where the torch was sweeping, but the crocodile had disappeared. 'It dived,' Jack told me. 'As long as you keep contact on its eyes, it just sits there mesmerized, but lose contact and it'll dive.'

We hung around the area for a while to see if the croc would resurface, but it didn't, and we moved off again. 'That's a shame, because it was a big one', Jack said. I couldn't tell whether he was being serious or just trying to scare me, but either way I wasn't that unhappy to have missed it. We'd been out on the water for a couple of hours or more by now and I was feeling stiff cooped up in the unsteady canoe. The minor thrill I'd felt at the prospect of finding a freshwater crocodile in the wild on an island off New Guinea had evaporated almost as soon as I'd set foot in our boat. The only good thing about the trip so far from my viewpoint was the fact that we'd made just a single sighting. That and the way my preoccupation with crocodiles had taken my mind off the constant high-pitched buzzing of the mosquitoes.

We paddled for some time before Jack made an effort to scare me again. I'd been trying to get him to admit that what we were doing was dangerous. He denied it, needless to say, but then he confessed that there was one situation that could be construed as risky. 'If we come across a daddy croc, he might mistake our canoe for competition. The underside of a canoe looks fairly similar to another crocodile, you see.' I thought I did, all too clearly. 'Now if that was the case,' Jack went on, 'and our croc felt like attacking, he'd have this boat over with one whip of his tail.'

This was just what I wanted to hear. I closed my eyes and shook my head, perhaps in the vain hope that this whole expedition would turn out to be a bad dream. But shaking my head was not a good idea, because it started the canoe rocking dangerously. I steadied the boat with my hands, and drew a deep breath. 'OK, Jack, if that did happen, and we ended up in the water, what should I do?'

Jack paused. 'Well,' he said, 'whatever you do, don't splash about, because that'll get him excited.' He was still sweeping the waterline with his torch. 'What you should do is dive under and swim away. Crocs rarely bite underwater and he's unlikely to follow you.'

I wanted to be absolutely clear on these tips. 'So don't splash, and dive, dive, dive.'

'That's right.'

I had noted that he'd said crocs *rarely* bite underwater and that it was *unlikely* to follow me, but I didn't pursue these points because the entire scenario was too horrible to imagine. I fell quiet, leaving Jack to continue scanning the water for swamp monsters while I digested this information.

This whole escapade had been preposterous from the start. If you chose to venture into a remote swamp in search of crocodiles, you might reasonably opt to do so with rather more equipment than a torch, a broom and a ball of twine. A gun might be handy, for a start. You might also do so in a vessel of solid construction. I was thinking of something made of thick metal, preferably a boat that was also nippy, with a large engine enabling a fast get-away in case of difficulties. But here I was in a cumbersome wooden canoe forever in danger of capsizing, a boat that a large male crocodile might rationally mistake as a competitor, a boat that could be flipped over and splintered with one whip of such a croc's giant tail.

I closed my eyes again, but didn't shake my head this time. The end was not difficult to imagine. Our aggressor would gobble us up with a few snaps of its jaws and use the boat's splinters as toothpicks. And the only thing we had to defend ourselves with was a home-made wooden broom.

Sadly for me, however, it would have been better to have had these thoughts before stepping into this canoe. As it was, I was stuck here and there wasn't much I could do about it other than suggest we might go home. So I did that.

Jack played his torch beam on his wristwatch. It was nearly nine o'clock and we'd been out for more than three hours. 'Let's keep going for a while yet,' he said, 'we've come a long way to look for this croc. It's too early to give up now.'

That, of course, was a matter of opinion, but for some reason I concurred, perhaps because I didn't want Jack to think he'd panicked me with his stories of aggressive males. Alex, meanwhile, kept paddling.

It was another long while before Jack spotted a second croc. It was off to our right, and this time I could just make out two glistening red dots at the end of his beam. We were all getting tired and Jack was determined not to lose this one, so he didn't wave his torch up and down but told Alex that he had one in his sights and asked him to take the canoe towards the spot. 'It's a small one,' Jack said, to my considerable relief. 'Just a baby.' He turned to me as we glided towards it. 'Want to look?'

Considering that it was a baby, I decided I did, and Jack passed me the torch, being careful not to lose the contact between beam and prey. I held it steady and crouched to look along the shaft of light. Two bright red eyeballs, like shiny little cherries, floated in the water in front of me. The croc didn't move, spellbound by the light. As we got closer, even I could see that it was a juvenile, not much bigger than the smaller one I'd handled in the pen at Kimaam.

'Want to catch it, young Nick?'

I very nearly said yes. It must have been the combination of tiredness and the release I'd felt on realizing that it was just a baby. It was a moment that would return to me later in my trip, in the small hours of the morning, causing me to snap open my eyes in a cold sweat.

'No thanks, Jack. You do it. I'll be happy just watching.'

We were almost upon the creature now and Jack whispered an instruction to Alex. We slipped up alongside the crocodile and Jack snatched at the water. His hand came up holding the unsuspecting crocodile by the neck. Jack had hardly even rocked the boat. It looked as easy as picking an apple off a tree.

When he had it firmly in both hands, he turned towards me and flipped the croc over on his knee. The creature gave a few more wriggles and then became calm as I held the torch on its belly and counted its rows of scales. There were twenty-five of them.

I couldn't remember which that meant it was, a salty or a freshy. I looked at Jack enquiringly. 'It's a freshy, no doubt about that,' he grinned. 'We just caught ourselves a freshwater crocodile.'

Despite all my fears, I was still able to summon a sense of achievement. I did feel good, having helped in a small way to nab the little beast.

'Good work, Jack.' I was genuinely pleased, as I think he was.
'Very good work. Does this mean we can go home now?'

THREE

'They call that place the "Warehouse of mosquitoes"', Father Niko told me with a knowing nod. I was in a canoe again, heading for a village named Jeobi. My accomplice was the local Catholic priest, a small man trussed up in a windcheater with a cotton scarf over his nose and mouth as protection against the mosquitoes. He didn't like them either so he was sympathetic when I recounted the story of my crocodile hunt with Jack. Mosquitoes were one of the hazards of Niko's job that he'd never really got used to.

Above the scarf, Father Niko wore dark glasses and a light blue sun hat. The outfit made him look like a member of the Tontons Macoutes, the organization of secret policemen whose rough justice became notorious in Haiti during the dictatorship of 'Papa Doc' Duvalier. It was an unfortunate image to have in my mind while talking to a man of the cloth.

I'd met Father Niko back in the church annexe in Kimaam where Jack and I had rested up on our return from Kowonep. Before leaving the swamp the morning after our crocodile hunt, Jack had once more counted the rows of belly scales on our croc, now bound up with twine, just to make sure, and photographed it from several different angles. He was going to report our finding to the World Conservation Union's crocodile specialist group.

When I'd explained to Father Niko my quest to see how people survived in the swamps of Papua, he'd suggested that I accompany him to Jeobi. Villages like Kimaam and Komoran were all very well, he'd told me but, strictly speaking, being located on rivers meant that they were on the edge of the swamp. Jeobi, on the other hand, was slap bang in the middle.

It was a six-hour trip west from Kimaam to Jeobi. The canoe that Father Niko and I were travelling in was rather larger than the one Jack and I had used on our hunt. It was also more heavily loaded. Both factors meant it was relatively stable. We had two boatmen to punt us, using long poles made from the stems of sago palm fronds. As we penetrated deeper into the island, away from Kimaam, the mangroves were thinning and the mosquitoes were becoming less of a problem. By the time we'd emerged from between the banks of the river, and entered a world of reeds, we'd left the trees and mosquitoes behind us and Father Niko pulled the scarf down from over his nose.

A narrow channel wound its way through the two-dimensional waterscape, making our punters' job difficult as they strained to manoeuvre the long canoe round tight bends in the sturdy reeds. Niko, visibly more relaxed now that he'd shed one layer of mosquito protection, was sprawled out with his back against one of the metal cases he'd brought along on the trip. I was feeling better too, glad to have the heat of the early morning sun warming my face. Niko had begun to tell me a little about the island that had been his home for the last few years (he was originally from Java). The large majority of the population of Pulau Kimaam, which he reckoned numbered about 13,000 people, was Christian, he said. 'There are sixty Muslims,' he went on, 'but no traditional religions left.' He delved into his pocket and pulled out a clove-flavoured cigarette. 'But in times of trouble,' he added as he fired it up, 'the people often turn back to their traditional beliefs.'

I'd been a bit wary of Father Niko when we'd first met, which was probably ignoble of me given the manner in which the church had accommodated me and Jack in Kimaam. But I'm not a religious person, and I was sceptical of how the messengers of God consider it their duty to scour the world for remote heathens and convert them to their faith. It struck me as all rather arrogant in a nineteenth-century sort of way. I thought I'd encountered a clear example of Christian conceit when I asked Niko to explain to me exactly what his job consisted of. 'I wander this island making people happy', he told me simply. But he said it with such innocent conviction that I couldn't in my heart of hearts accuse him of arrogance.

I'd warmed to Father Niko after that, although I continued to harbour doubts about some of the activities his Church was involved in. Why couldn't the God squad just leave people alone and let them get on with their lives in the way they have done for centuries? I still thought to myself. The catch in New Guinea was that the age-old lifestyle involved head-hunting and cannibalism.

Missionaries have been active in Papua for well over a century. They began arriving in droves as Dutch administrative control gradually took hold over the territory in the 1890s and early 1900s. The colonial administration recreated a division from home in decreeing that Protestants should work in the north and Catholics in the south, and evidence of this partition is still visible in Papua today. The majority of the many churches I'd seen on the streets of Merauke were Catholic, and the church in Kimaam, where Father Niko was based, was also of the Roman variety.

It was a priest who first ventured into the interior of Pulau Kimaam in the 1930s, visiting all the villages on the island. The gentleman in question, Father Thieman, later settled in the village of Kimaam and shortly afterwards a government officer was stationed there, eventually forming a separate government district for the island. Father Thieman and his successors were instrumental in bringing about an end to head-hunting on the island, which ceased some time in the 1960s. There is no doubt, even for a sceptic like me, that this was a positive development.

About half-way through our journey to Jeobi, it struck me that I hadn't seen a piece of dry land since we'd left Kimaam. The water and reeds continued until we were approaching the outskirts of the village, and large sago palms began to appear on the horizon. As we got nearer, the terrain that these palm trees inhabited materialized. They were perched on small islets, raised up just a few tens of centimetres above the waterline. Passing through these sago atolls, we came upon more islands planted with crops until we reached the village, which consisted of numerous small islands each with a house on. The high-ways and byways of Jeobi were made of water and the only means of transport between all these islands was canoe. We'd already passed several dug-outs on our way into the village, paddled and punted by people of all ages, from elderly women to small kids who couldn't have been more than four or five years old.

Father Niko had been right – Jeobi really was a village right in the middle of a swamp. It was an appealing little place, tranquil and picturesque with its glassy waterways and gently swaying palm trees. This in itself was remarkable enough, but the village became even more astonishing in my eyes when I learned that every one of these islands had been built by hand.

Exactly how this was accomplished, I was lucky enough to discover the following day when Niko announced that plans were afoot to construct a new island just off the one on which we had taken up residence. Niko and I had been adopted by a small family which lived in a long hut that appeared to have plenty of room for two more people. The hut had the usual palm frond roof, and walls constructed from sago palm poles like the ones our boatmen had used to punt us here. Inside, the floor was strewn with more fronds to sit on. The hut took up one end of an island dotted with coconut palms and banana trees and measuring some twenty-five metres long and less than ten wide.

Building one of these islands was a major operation, undertaken communally. First thing in the morning, Father Niko and I followed a couple of men and a few boys in their canoes out to the edge of the village to begin work. We had gone beyond the sago palms and cultivated islands to a huge area of marshy grasses, forging off the main channel that we'd followed on our journey into the village and along a straight waterway that had obviously been cut through the grass by the villagers. After a hundred metres or so, the waterway came to an abrupt halt. We were surrounded on three sides by the grasses and, to my surprise, the water they grew in looked to be only a few centimetres deep.

One of the boys, who was wearing a long pair of baggy red shorts, was the first to step out of his canoe on to the grass, soon followed by one of the men. Both of them were wielding machetes. Very gradually the grass they were standing on began to sink. It continued to do so until the boy was left with water up to his knees. I had thought that I'd become fairly well accustomed to the world of the swamp by now, but this sight I found extraordinary.

'Drift-grass,' Father Niko pronounced. 'They will cut some segments of it and float it into the village to build up the new island.'

The man and the boy had started scything the grass with their machetes. On the opposite side of the channel, the other man and a couple of other boys were doing the same. I still wasn't completely sure what I was looking at. 'So the grass is actually floating in some way?' I asked. 'Exactly', Niko replied, and he rapidly made a remark to the boy with the long red shorts. The boy sank his machete into the ominously dark water and began making a sawing motion along three sides of a small square. He bent down to lift what he'd cut. It was obviously very heavy, but what emerged was a sodden slab of peaty material a good forty centimetres thick. The grass was growing on its own enormous floating mat.

I looked out across the vast expanse of drift-grass before me, wide and flat and stretching away into the distance. Far from where I was standing in our canoe, two white birds took to the air and beat their wings to fly effortlessly across the skyline. I found it difficult to believe that the plain was not as I'd imagined. Far from being an inundated grassland with its roots anchored in firm ground, the entire landscape was adrift on a floating pad.

Niko and I stepped out of our canoe on to the drift-grass and I experienced the curious sensation of the ground sinking beneath me. The murky water came up to my calves, but walking just a few paces away from the canoe took me clear of the edge and on to a more stable part of the mat, which subsided to bring the water only up to the top of my boots.

Niko handed me a machete and we both set to, chopping the drift-grass. Once a sizeable area had been cleared, we needed to cut the mat. I saw how the others were doing it, by cutting around where they were standing but, as I came to the end of slicing a chunk of pad a few metres long by a metre wide, the whole thing sank to one side and I slipped off to find myself up to my chest in the swampwater. The others had neatly stepped aside, on to the main part of the drift-grass, to avoid succumbing to the same fate.

But it didn't matter because the only way of transporting the sections of mat we'd just cut into the village was to float them there. They were too heavy to pull by canoe so we had to push them all the way like human tugs. So everyone had to get right into the water. Everyone, that is, except Father Niko, who followed behind in the canoe offering words of encouragement and splashing us whenever he thought we weren't pushing hard enough. Perhaps it was his idea of spiritual guidance.

Back in the village a large number of men were also hard at work hacking away at a bed of reeds opposite the island Niko and I were staying on. The wads of drift-grass we'd brought were floated into position alongside other wads brought from the swamp in the preceding days. Together they formed a large platform about ten metres by ten. This, Niko told me, would form the base of the new island.

The two of us then joined in with our machetes on the reeds. I found that the reeds were anchored to the swamp bed, and that I could stand on their sizeable roots to gain a perch that was just stable enough to hold me as I swung my machete. The reeds had an almost woody consistency, with broad leaves sharp enough to slice my fingers if I wasn't careful. Once cut, the woody reeds were hauled through the water to be piled up on top of the drift-grass platform.

The platform had become a mass of these slashed reeds when the next phase of the operation got under way. This entailed more mats of drift-grass being floated on to the scene, where they were cut up into sections small enough to be lifted on to the main platform. Drift-grass mats began to appear from all directions, gently propelled towards the construction site by men walking along the swamp bed submerged up to their chests. All you could see of these drift-grass porters was their bearded heads, the tops of their shoulders glistening in the sun and their hands pushing the mats in front of them. I realized that the villagers must have been cutting the mats and floating them into the village for many days. I'd seen the floating sections, anchored with long stakes, positioned all along the network of waterways that linked up the islands of the village.

Beside the main platform, production lines of workers had assembled to continue the work. They consisted of a man slicing the arriving mats with his machete into chunks like giant pieces of sponge cake and pushing them through the murky water towards two or three others whose job it was to fling them on top of the reeds. Others stood nearby scooping up mud from the swamp bed to add to the accumulation. I plunged in to join one crew hauling the thick drift-grass chunks out of the water. It was back-breaking work. Saturated with swampwater, the chunks were very heavy indeed, and I was grateful after twenty minutes when the guy who was slicing the mats handed me the machete and we switched places.

For the first few hours, the level of the embryonic island continued to hover around the waterline as the sodden chunks of drift-grass we were piling on to the platform just pushed the platform deeper into the swamp. But eventually we'd piled up so many chunks that the submerged mats made contact with the bottom of the swamp and very slowly the island began to emerge above the level of the water. Back on throwing duty, I could see this happening. As the island gradually gained height, I was also keenly aware that the effort required to fling the saturated chunks of drift-grass was becoming progressively greater as we launched them up on to the emerging terrain.

I thought I might clamber out of the water on to the island for a rest, but extricating myself from a chest-high swamp on to a gigantic pile of mud was as difficult as you might think. Several men and boys were already in position on the mud heap, redistributing the chunks being thrown from the water on to the edges of the island to its centre. An elderly man with a greying beard, who was dressed only in his underpants, offered me his hand and I finally made it – only to sink up to my thighs in the oozing mud. Father Niko, who had managed the same challenging procedure a few minutes before, threw back his head and laughed out loud. He was reclining in the middle of the island in his mud-splattered T-shirt and slacks, laid out in a pose like a fashion model on a bed of sludge. It was difficult to imagine him looking any less like a priest.

'Little by little we are building this island,' he cried as I struggled across the mire on my belly to join him. 'There is another layer of reeds to come, they help to bind the mud together and improve the soil, and then more pieces of this drift-grass.' He paused to look at the feverish activity that was continuing all around us. 'Today it will reach perhaps a metre above the water, but overnight it will become lower as the water drains from the mud.' On all sides of the new island's square perimeter, rivulets of water draining from the chunks of drift-grass were already running back into the swamp. People had begun to wedge stout sago poles round the borders of the island to shore up its edges, so preventing them from slumping back into the water.

'Tomorrow we will build it up again, and so forth and so on for several days.'

I wanted to know how long it would be before someone could build a house on our newborn island. But this would not be for several years, Niko told me.

'First year, they will plant cassava here. Their roots will provide further help to bind the soil. After year one, more mud will be added, to build it up further. Then more crops will be planted: bananas and coconut trees. It is only after two or three years that they can construct a house and live on this island.'

I hadn't fully realized just how mammoth a communal task this was. And the only tool being used to raise this brand-new square of land from the waters of the swamp was the machete. Otherwise the entire operation was being conducted by hand.

Ever since my arrival in the swamps of New Guinea, my mind had been struggling to come to terms with the wetland conundrum. Did these places consist of murky water or sodden land? After a couple of weeks here, I still found it difficult to tell the difference. It seemed to be mainly a matter of opinion as to where one ended and the other began. Did the floating mats of drift-grass, for instance, constitute land or water? I couldn't decide.

One day in Jeobi I watched as a fish jumped out of the water and on to the island I was staying on. It flopped on to the ground in front of me and proceeded to cross the island, via a series of puddles in which it rested, pulling itself along by flapping its fins and flipping its tail. I took a photograph of the amphibious fish and looked it up on my return to England. It was a climbing perch that can spend up to six days out of water apparently, and is able to migrate long distances overland in search of better living conditions thanks to an accessory air-breathing organ to supplement its gills. For me, this fish was a step backwards. In my mind, the very existence of the climbing perch just served to further blur the distinction between land and water.

Other wetland mysteries were being resolved, however. When I first started my research into swamps, I found it difficult to imagine why anyone would actually choose to live in such a place. But the people of Jeobi had made such a choice, and their reason was compelling. Their ancestors had been driven here in desperation by the fierce Marind-Anim head-hunters.

Pulau Kimaam is 98 per cent swamp, a statistic that you might think would put a question mark over its status as an island, particularly since saltwater from the sea penetrates far inland. But it is an island because of its shape, which is roughly that of a giant saucer, higher round its rim than in the middle. The saucer is made of clay, which is impermeable to water, so when the monsoon rains arrive each year the saucer fills up to become one big soggy morass. The rainwater drains away into the sea only very slowly so that, by the end of the dry season, large parts of the island are more muddy than swampy – not a big difference, some might think, and I would be among them – but it never dries out completely before the rains come around again.

A crucial point in all this is that there are just a few slightly higher locations in this giant saucer of an island that are more or less permanently dry. Ever since the missionaries and the government authorities first came to Pulau Kimaam, they've been trying to get the people of Jeobi, and other similar villages, to move to higher land, reasoning, like me, that no one in their right mind could actually want to live in a swamp. In the 1970s, the Indonesian government decided, now that cannibalism was a thing of the past, that they would set about building a new village for Jeobi, a few paddling hours up the creek, on higher ground. They did so, and everyone was encouraged to abandon their homes and move to the new village. But within a few years, most of them had moved back. It turned out that the people of Jeobi really did want to live in a swamp.

They had good reasons for doing so. The soil in the new village was poor, and because it was high and dry it was too far from the swamp mud traditionally used to manure the fields. The new village was also a long way from the sago trees which thrive only in the water-logged parts of the island, and sago has long been the villagers' most important supplementary food. The fishing round the new village wasn't much good either.

All of this was explained to me one evening, a couple of days after our island-building exploits had come to an end. Father Niko and I were enjoying a dinner of fresh fish and yams with the family hosting us and a number of the men who'd been involved in constructing the new island. Bit by bit, the island had grown by day and shrunk by night until the announcement was made that the procedure was complete. It was now ready for its first crop of cassava to be planted. We'd celebrated our achievement at a mass held by Father Niko the following day, Sunday, when virtually the whole village crowded on to one of the islands to sing hymns and take the sacrament.

Niko and I had been on a little tour of some of the cultivated islands, on our way to dig up the yams we were eating that evening. We still had one of the men who'd punted us here from Kimaam to chauffeur us around, which was just as well because all the local canoes were fiendishly narrow and hence impossible to sit down in. I'd tried punting one myself but the inside of the dug-out was so constricted that my feet had to be placed one in front of the other, making balance very difficult to maintain. My attempts had met with obvious consequences, much to everybody's amusement.

On our excursion to excavate the yams, we'd passed a phenomenal display of agricultural diversity, from year-old cassava islands, via junior banana plants and coconut palms, to permanent crop islands boasting much larger coconut palms, sugar cane, yams with their vines trained up sago poles, sweet potatoes, mango trees, cashew nut trees, 'and so forth and so on', as Father Niko put it.

Gliding between the flourishing fruit and vegetable islands just served to confirm a thought that had been hovering in the back of my mind since my arrival in Jeobi – that this village was the most enjoyable and startling surprise I could ever have hoped for from my trip. I could quite understand why the villagers had rejected the brand-new government-built houses of new Jeobi to return here. The village they'd constructed themselves was picturesque and peaceful. When the early morning sunlight streamed through the palm trees, their dancing shadows playing across the slender canoes, the place took on a quality of enchantment that I'd rarely seen before. For a moment the palms would be reflected perfectly in the glassy surface of the waterways until a smiling child would glide silently past on her way to a grove of sun-dappled fruit trees.

I realized that my romantic impression of Jeobi was at least in part a starry-eyed reaction to the purgatory I'd been through with Jack in Kowonep, but it was all the better for that. And Jeobi had very few mosquitoes. As far as I was concerned, the village was a tropical Venice with coconut palms and dug-out canoes. But it was also more than that. It was the most unexpected of things: a little piece of paradise in a swamp.

FOUR

As I descended from the clouds over the mountains, the vast marshy plains of southern Papua were laid out before me as a lush carpet of green. Flying across the interior of New Guinea gave me a handle on the extent of this second-largest island in the world. I was making my way towards the climax of my journey into the swamp, to rendezvous with a group of people known as the Kombai, a clan whose reaction to being surrounded by bog was quite different to that of the people I'd recently left. While the villagers of Jeobi appeared to relish their amphibious existence, the Kombai took avoiding action. They evaded the sodden terrain by living in tree-houses.

For a few moments, a trick of the light lent a bluish haze to the landscape of the Asmat region below me, making it look like the sea, but this mock ocean soon evaporated in the morning sunshine to reveal a braided river weaving its course across the flat topography. The muddy channels criss-crossed between their sand banks, giving its wide swathe a marbled effect like fat through a long slab of meat. Beyond in all directions lay more rivers, thick tangled snakes of water meandering their way towards the coast. Narrower channels appeared as hairline cracks in the mantle of emerald trees. Every so often, as we neared our destination – an airstrip hacked from the jungle – a small clearing would emerge crowned by a towering tree-house.

My accomplice and guide on this final leg of my journey was another religious figure. I'd met John Cutts in Sentani, the small settlement servicing the airport at Jayapura, Papua's capital on the northern coast, and the numerous missionary organizations headquartered there. John was a veteran of Papua's missionary scene, having lived virtually all of his life in Indonesia's easternmost province. His American parents had been missionaries in the central highlands and John now ran his own foundation catering to the spiritual and development needs of tribal communities.

John was a youthful fifty-year-old, approachable, bouncy and full of energy. On our flight down to the airstrip at Yaniruma, I had broached the subject of missionaries as tactfully as I could. Just the word still struck me as old-fashioned, I told him, although my impression of the term was largely based on people like David Livingstone and similar characters of European origin who had trudged through the jungles of Africa in search of souls to save in the nineteenth century. The same process had not begun in earnest in New Guinea until the twentieth century, but they were still hard at it. On a large scale, too, judging by what I'd seen at Sentani, where the missionaries, most of them American seemingly, had a small airforce at their disposal.

Most of the missions operating in Papua today were, like his foundation, effectively development organizations with a religious flavour, John told me. He was, of course, well aware of the scrutiny under which evangelical missions found themselves while working in poorer countries, but the Church groups were much more sensitive to local customs than in times past. 'Even fundamentalist Protestants now allow local people to worship in their churches wearing the traditional penis gourds', he shouted above the noise of the small aircraft's engine.

John was also convinced that missionaries in Papua had often played a positive role in easing traditional peoples into the twenty-first century. 'Missionaries can bring medicines to remote communities, and they've often served as an important buffer between the government and the people.' Their numbers had also declined significantly in recent times, particularly after the late 1980s when the Indonesian government had decided to ask many of them to leave.

A missionary's life in the wilds of New Guinea was hard, frustrating and not infrequently dangerous, John went on. There were several stories of attempts to contact new tribes, even in the late twentieth century, ending in the discovery of missionaries' bodies riddled with arrows. The Kombai of this area we were approaching, like their neighbours the Korowai – groups that had been first contacted by outsiders only in 1980 – associated the arrival of people wearing clothes with the end of the universe, which in many ways it was, or at least the end of the universe as they knew it. In consequence, they weren't always exactly welcoming.

For this and other reasons, the Kombai weren't terribly interested in converting to Christianity by all accounts. When our plane landed at Yaniruma, the mission village established on the borders between their traditional territory and that of their neighbours the Korowai, John and I were met with a largely deserted settlement. A few people had gathered at the airstrip to watch us come in, but they were just the remnants of a population that for the most part had gone back to their traditional villages once the resident missionary had left town and not been replaced some years before. He had been a casualty of the government's decision to cull the numbers of foreign missionaries working in the province.

It wasn't an unusual situation in Papua, John told me as we wandered the overgrown paths of the abandoned village, the dilapidated wooden houses serving as a sorry reminder of the brief Western incursion. People from both the Kombai and the Korowai had come to the new village, attracted by the airstrip and perhaps the missionary. 'But two different peoples living together can cause tensions,' John said. 'They often trade accusations of witchcraft, so when the focus goes, people move back to where they came from.'

All the houses we passed were raised up about a metre above the ground surface, although it wasn't very marshy where we were walking. They were constructed from stout tree trunks and palm fronds, all now grey with age. It wasn't really a village in the tradition of the region: none of the abodes was a tree-house. But that wasn't a surprise. Yaniruma had been built in an attempt to lure the Kombai and Korowai out of the trees.

Twenty years was a short time when attempting to assimilate a Stone Age people into the ways of the outside world, John was telling me. 'During that period, the missionary who used to live here told me he made just two conversions, and one of those guys subsequently died.'

There being few people to speak of in Yaniruma, John and I had little choice but to venture into the thick rainforest surrounding the largely derelict settlement. After a night spent in one of the dilapidated houses, we headed off the following morning in the direction of the tree-houses we'd seen on the flight in, led by a small group of the people still living in Yaniruma who had agreed to act as our guides and porters.

John had spent the previous evening organizing the group and buying himself a bow and a set of lengthy arrows from one of the men. 'I might be able to pick up some dinner on the way', he said in answer to my questioning look. For me, this was the right response. I'd been concerned that maybe he thought some means of self-defence was going to be necessary.

I followed John into the bush. He was an incongruous sight in his shorts and pumps and brightly coloured T-shirt, carrying his bow and arrows over one shoulder and one of his bags over the other. He looked as if he was setting out to play a game of cowboys and Indians in the jungle.

But I soon discovered that John was a one-man culture clash. On the surface, he looked and spoke like a clean-cut American, but during the course of our walk into Kombai territory I realized that beneath the all-American exterior was a man completely at ease with the country we were trekking through.

The rough track we followed took us deep into the forest, where the roots of the trees were wrapped in brilliant green moss. Unlike the terrain on Pulau Kimaam, there was more mud underfoot than water, but the going was still tough and treacherous thanks to the numerous fallen trees and branches. We crossed a seemingly endless series of brooks and streams, usually by means of a fallen tree trunk that John and our guides tiptoed effortlessly along without breaking their stride. But many of these simple bridges were much trickier for me in my big boots. I soon learned to recognize when my inferior tightrope-walking skills were about to be put to the test because the ground became marshier and strewn with hundreds of pitcher plants, their bulbous cups brimming with rainwater. Our porters would pick these cups, empty them of their contents, and use them to scoop up water from the flowing streams to drink. The reason they didn't simply drain the rainwater became clear when I looked inside one of the cups to find its contents full of insects being digested by the carnivorous plant.

John would pause every now and again, to point out plants with edible parts, or creepers that might contain water. He borrowed a machete to chop down the tall, thin trunk of a nibun palm tree, cutting away its fronds and stripping the top of the trunk to reveal a tight wrap of white fronds that looked like a giant leek. It was crisp and refreshing to eat, with a delicate flavour not unlike that of a water chestnut. He tried three likely looking vines to drink from, but the first two turned out to be dry. You never could tell, he told me, since the presence or absence of water depended on many factors, such as the age of the vine and how recently it had rained. But when he struck the third with his machete, cool, fresh water gushed forth to quench my thirst.

And thirsty I was, because the atmosphere was thick with humidity that sapped my strength. My shirt had become drenched in sweat within an hour of the start of our march. It was hard going, but at least there were very few mosquitoes. Walking the forest trail, I soon felt like a giant wick, soaking up swamp water through my toes and feet and constantly perspiring it through my body and face into the muggy air. I was exhausted, and feeling the early signs of cramp in my legs, when we stopped beside a large brown river, I assumed for a late lunch.

We did eat something, but this was not the main reason for the break in proceedings. John was in a huddle with our porters and I could see that explanations were being made. He wandered over to me as I eased off my boots to massage my aching toes.

'This is as far as these guys will take us,' John told me as he squatted down on a fallen bough beside me and looked out over the fast-flowing river in front of us. 'These people are Korowai, and this river marks the end of their territory. Over there,' he pointed to the opposite bank, a good thirty metres away, 'is Kombai territory, and they won't take us across. It looks like we're on our own.'

I took it as a measure of my adaptation to the way things panned out in Papua, and the confidence I'd gained in John, having seen his intimate knowledge of the environment that surrounded us, that I wasn't too perturbed by this news. That and the fact that most of my concentration was taken up with my badly aching legs. Either way, our porters weren't going to be persuaded to cross the river, so there wasn't an awful lot I could do.

We paid them for their efforts and bade the porters farewell, John leading the way now, along a track that followed the riverbank. The porters had recommended that we continue in this direction because they knew of a house not far away where we could probably stay the night.

I became rather more perturbed when we turned up on the doorstep of the house we'd been directed towards. It was set back from the riverbank in a large area of felled trees that had been left lying all over the ground, making the approach to the long house difficult. The head of the house, who wore just a penis gourd and some bones through his nose, told us we couldn't come in. He stood at the entrance to his home looking us up and down. I could see several children in the shadows behind him, craning their necks for a look at their visitors. A small pig was rooting around in the dirt beside the man's feet. After some explanation from John, the man told us that we could pitch our tents outside. He certainly didn't seem overly friendly, which worried me at first, coming as it did after our porters had left us, but my sense of foreboding was eased when I tried to put myself in his position. If a couple of near-naked Papuan warriors carrying bows and arrows had turned up unannounced on my doorstep at home, I don't think my first reaction would be to invite them in for a cup of tea.

The night passed uneventfully, and John and I emerged the next morning to ask the man of the house how he might advise we cross the river. John had already told me he thought the best policy would be to construct a raft, but he thought it best to ask, just in case there might be a canoe lurking somewhere that we could borrow. There wasn't, but our host offered to help us build the raft.

He called together some of the other men who lived in the house and we all set off back into the forest in search of trees. It took all morning to build the raft and, soon after the necessary trees had been felled, John realized to our mutual distress that raft-building was not a regional speciality. To my mind, the lack of local skills in this department just underlined how little contact there must have been between the Korowai on this side of the bank and the Kombai on the other. We had broken into three parties to cut the necessary timber. John had taken me to find a couple of appropriate specimens that he said would float well, but when we reconvened at the riverbank, the other men had brought what John told me were ironwood trees. As the name suggested, this was heavy, dense wood. 'Not really the best for building a raft', John admitted.

And so it turned out, because after all the logs had been lashed together with rattan vines to make the raft, and John and I had clambered aboard, having first secured our bags on one end, the raft all but sank. But somehow, with the aid of an aerial ropeway, we managed to make it. The rattan rope had been taken across the river earlier by one of the Korowai men, who tied it to a tree and promptly swam back, with a definite look of relief on his face when he arrived. John and I clung on to the rope, moving hand over hand across the turbulent river, bringing our heavyweight vehicle along with our feet.

I scrambled up the steep bank as John untied our belongings and threw them up to me. Then he joined me and we waved goodbye to our Korowai helpers before turning to enter Kombai territory.

FIVE

It took us the rest of the day before we reached the tree-houses. Our Korowai helpers had told us that we might find someone to guide us if we followed the bank on the Kombai side to the right, because there were a couple of houses not far from where we'd crossed the river on our weighty raft. We did so, and the people we found were more amenable than their Korowai counterparts, eagerly agreeing to show us the way to a village of tree-houses several hours' walk away.

As we forged our way onwards through the swampy rainforest, John expressed surprise that he had been able to communicate with both these Kombai and the Korowai on the opposite bank. The two clans spoke different languages, neither of which John knew, but in both groups he'd found someone who spoke some form of Bahasa Indonesian. This was unusual for such a remote spot, he told me, but probably a function of their location on the river where traders must pass on occasion. The whole island of New Guinea is remarkable for its linguistic diversity. It has about 0.1 per cent of the world's population and yet contains 15 per cent of all known languages. In Papua, an incredible 250 different languages have been recorded, in addition to at least a similar number of dialects. This multiplicity of tongues is a testament to the territory's many hidden valleys and rugged, inaccessible terrain.

The landscape had changed subtly by the time we reached the small settlement of Kenalua, as gentle slopes started to hint at a third dimension to the flat topography. The village stood in a clearing strewn with felled trees, like the one where we'd spent the previous night. It emerged from the forest at the end of the rising trail which opened up to reveal a series of three tree-houses, each about ten metres high, rising up from an area otherwise dominated by a huge longhouse that must have been nearly a hundred metres in length. To see my first tree-houses up close was spectacular enough, but more impressive still was a fourth tree-house that towered behind the other three. It seemed to be a good thirty-five metres off the ground. Just looking at it was enough to give me vertigo.

Our reception on entering the village was unnerving. As John and I struggled across the jumble of huge tree trunks, I heard a cry and three men came running towards us brandishing bows and arrows. They fanned out into a half-circle with John and me at its centre, and stood firm before us, naked, fierce and agitated, shouting the odds. We stopped in our tracks, not sure how to respond. One of the men put a long arrow to his bow, pulled back the string and looked me straight in the eyes. All of a sudden, I was completely out of my depth. I was slightly in front of John and I had no idea what to do. Our porters, as far as I was aware, were some distance behind us. Involuntarily, I held out my arms, wanting to indicate that I bore no weapons. At the same time, I was desperately hoping that John had put down his bow and arrows.

My instinct was to step forward and offer my hand in friendship, but I stopped myself from doing this because for all I knew the gesture might mean something completely different to a Kombai. It was a stand-off and I'd run out of inspiration.

'Any ideas?' I whispered to John as he moved slowly up beside me. He had put down his bow and was quietly talking to the men before us in Bahasa Indonesian. Whether or not they understood what he was saying, I had no idea, but the tone was conciliatory. The man with the drawn bow let out another loud shout and fired his arrow down into the ground in front of him. To my immense relief, this seemed to break the ice and the three men confronting us visibly relaxed. John and I stepped forward to offer our hands and slowly each man shook them in turn.

Our porters arrived on the scene and explanations were made about why these two white men in clothes had turned up out of the blue to visit the village. To my further relief, the justification for our presence seemed to be acceptable. Half an hour later, John and I were happily installed in one of the smaller tree-houses chatting relatively amicably with our host, one of the three men who had initially confronted us on our arrival.

Fiambo wore nothing but a gourd over his penis, the tip of the gourd secured around his waist by a length of stout twine. Dangling from his left ear were half a dozen large hoops, bent quills from the huge cassowary bird which he said he hunted in the surrounding forest. Round his neck he wore two strings of small cowrie shells. His only other adornments were in his nose. These consisted of a polished white stone poked horizontally through the central divide and a couple of small claws, taken from the talons of a night hawk, which protruded straight through the bulbous flesh at the front of his nose to stick upward like tiny horns.

We were sat round a fire that smouldered on top of a pile of dirt ringed with stones at the male end of the tree-house. In addition to Fiambo, John, myself and one of the porters to translate, we'd been joined by Joel, Fiambo's young son who was perhaps seven years old, an elderly man with a grey beard whose nose decoration consisted of the bones from the wings of a flying fox that drooped down over his moustache like tentacles, and a younger man who wore a leaf wrapped neatly around the end of his penis and a large string of dogs' teeth around his neck. A black piglet, attached by a length of twine to one of the bamboo spars that made up the floor, was fast asleep at the feet of the elderly man. He was gently scratching it behind the ear as he listened to the conversation. At the other end of the tree-house, which was only about six metres square, was another fire, attended by a young woman in a grass skirt.

Access to Fiambo's abode had been by means of a thin but strong pole cut with notches for the feet. It hung vertically down from a narrow platform at the entrance to the tree-house. It had been necessary for me to bite my tongue before climbing it. The nauseous feeling that had come over me when I'd first seen the much higher tree-house had not been without reason. I don't like heights.

I'd been secretly delighted when I managed to shin up the pole without too much difficulty, but I didn't like the way the floor creaked ominously with every movement. The walls on two sides of the house were covered with palm fronds that had been flattened out to make solid partitions. The two ends, each opening on to narrow balconies, consisted of poles tied in a latticework. From my position next to the fire, I could look out at the village's tallest tree-house towering above the skyline like the nest of some giant bird.

I'd asked Fiambo, through John and our porter, why he lived up high in a tree-house. 'Our ancestors lived like this and we continue to do so', he replied straightforwardly. I'd heard a variety of practical reasons for the Kombai living above the ground, the desire to avoid the swamp being just one, although the position of this village on a hillock already meant they were well above the waterline. Others included being out of range of the mosquitoes and the benefit of cool breezes to leaven the heavy humidity, both advantages I'd already noticed in Fiambo's residence. But perhaps the most important motivation for living in a tree-house was the ease with which it could be defended, simply by hauling up the climbing pole. The Kombai, who do not practise head-hunting themselves, have traditionally been prey to raids from the neighbouring Citak, a head-hunting Asmat tribe.

I got John to put these suggestions to Fiambo, and he raised his eyebrows and nodded as the list was translated. 'Yes,' he said, 'what you say is right. This place is easy to defend. It's cooler and more airy up here and there are fewer mosquitoes.' He added that everyone enjoyed the views, too.

It's not every day that you get to meet a man from the Stone Age and my head was bursting with questions, but John and I were tired after our long walk and we didn't want to outstay our welcome so soon with too many prying enquiries. However, there was one last thing I wanted to ask before our first audience with Fiambo drew to a close. I had climbed to my feet and stepped out through the doorway in the lattice at the male end of the house, on to the platform so that I could properly take in the view of the tallest tree-house. Why was it so much higher than the others? I wondered.

I was told that it was a place for young men, those who had proved themselves to be good hunters. Perched on the narrow balcony, holding tightly to the frame of the opening I'd just stepped through, I was beginning to feel unwell again just looking at it. The fact that I was already ten metres off the ground, on the edge of a rickety platform, didn't help. Fiambo made the soaring structure sound like a young hunters' clubhouse, but he didn't explain why it was so high. I could only assume that it was a machismo thing.

John and I spent the best part of a week with the Kombai in Kenalua, initially sleeping in the cavernous longhouse with an assortment of dogs and domestic pigs before Fiambo suggested we come and stay in his tree-house. The invitation was a good sign, we both reckoned, since a degree of trust must have been reflected in his hospitality. Part of me had been quite content sleeping on firm ground, however, and didn't really fancy passing the nights in mid-air, but the downside of the longhouse was that it was infested with voracious cockroaches that had taken to eating the plastic parts of my spectacles – that and the difficulty of drifting off to slumberland with a horde of squealing pigs and howling dogs. The dogs were kept to assist in hunting and for their teeth, which were worth a great deal when strung on a string. Pigs were also reared for their value in institutionalized exchanges such as marriage, rather than for their meat, although they were occasionally killed as sacrifices to ancestral spirits and then eaten.

The longhouse had been built some months previously for a festival to which Kombai from villages all over the area had been invited. Such festivals, regular features of Kombai life, are designed to maintain good relations between fellow clan members. They are characterized by the mutual exchange of gifts, sacred rituals and dancing, all fuelled by copious amounts of food, particularly sago grubs.

The Kombai love these grubs, the larvae of the capricorn beetle, which to me are deeply unpleasant-looking: very fat, wriggling, white and semi-translucent with small, shiny brown heads. They can be found in the wild, where they infest rotting sago tree trunks, or can be specially raised by felling a sago palm and chopping it into pieces that are split and then wrapped in leaves, to prevent pigs from eating them. After that, the recipe is simple: leave for a couple of months and harvest.

As I'd seen in Jeobi, the sago tree thrives in the best swampy conditions, and a grove of the palms was located just down the hill from the village in a marshy area fed by a couple of streams. Fiambo took me down there one day to open up some nicely rotten trunks he'd prepared earlier. Two of his mates were already hard at it, peeling back the leaves they'd been wrapped in and splitting open the rotting trunks. A powerful smell of fermentation filled the air as the trunks were ripped apart and the three of them dug around in the decaying interior. The putrefied wood had the consistency of ready-made sawdust and was crawling with juicy white grubs.

The grubs are eaten raw or cooked, and when we all sat round a fire and Fiambo offered me the writhing mass of larvae on a leaf, I have to admit I couldn't face them. 'I usually prefer my meat cooked', I told him, so he flung a handful on to the embers of the fire while he and his friends munched away on the live specimens. When Fiambo started picking out the cooked ones from the ashes a few minutes later, they looked only slightly less unappetizing, their skins faintly deflated and leathery to look at. But I didn't think I could say no again, so I popped a small one into my mouth and sank my teeth into it. The skin burst, filling my mouth with a vaguely eggy flavour. It was very rich and not nearly as unpleasant as I'd feared it might be. In fact, I almost liked it, so I took another one.

The sago palm plays a prominent role in Kombai society, in everyday life as well as by providing the vital nibbles for the sago grub festivals. It's a tree with many uses. Its leaves are used to package food and folded to form the roofs of tree-houses, while the hard leaf stems are used to close tree-house walls. The women's skirts are made of the frayed fibres from the upper end of the trunk. Fresh marrow from the top of a mature tree or from very young palms is eaten raw and considered a special treat, but the mainstay of the Kombai diet lies in the trunk itself. I've come across people consuming many parts of a tree, its fruit, nuts, leaves and even the bark – cinnamon, for example. But never before had I heard of anyone eating the tree itself. Yet this is what the Kombai do.

Beyond where we sat around the fire chewing sago grubs, a group of women were hard at work on another sago tree. I'd watched earlier as Fiambo had chopped it down with his stone axe, cutting it into segments which were then prised open using a stick of very hard wood like a crowbar. Three women were standing in a row along a portion of trunk, each with a wooden tool wielded over the shoulder rather like a pick-axe, chiselling the pith inside it. They sang a rhythmic song as they did so. Every so often, another woman approached to fill a large string bag woven from fine vines with the pinky-orange fibres.

The bag was carried down towards one of the streams where a long contraption consisting of two connected wooden shafts was filled with the ruddy pith, dowsed with water from the stream and beaten with a large stick. Water laden with sago juice emerges at the bottom end of the shafts into a wooden bowl where the solids settle out, the water is discarded and you're left with soggy sago flour. This can either be wrapped in a leaf and stewed or moulded into lumps and grilled on the fire. It looked like jolly hard work to me, but nutritionists say that food extracted from the pith of the sago tree in this manner is a highly efficient way of obtaining starch, requiring fewer hours of labour than paddy rice, for example. We had been eating some of the grilled variety with our sago grubs. It didn't taste of much, a bit like eating burnt talcum powder.

While producing the sago flour appeared to be women's work, hunting was an exclusively male occupation. Fiambo took John and me out on a hunting trip along with Joel, his son, and a couple of the other guys. The first item on the agenda, Fiambo told us as we marched off towards the forest along a fallen tree trunk, was to see whether I could handle a bow and arrow. We found a spot among the trees where Fiambo propped up a leathery piece of wood to aim at and handed me the spare bow he'd brought along for me to use. It was long, almost as tall as I was when held upright, and the arrows, each with thin bamboo shafts about a metre long, came in three different varieties. There was a simple wooden point, used for small game like birds, and a rather more complex model with barbs. The latter was used against larger creatures, such as chameleons, and marsupials that sometimes had the wit, if shot with a non-barbed arrow, simply to pull it out and scamper away. As in Australia, less than 200 kilometres from New Guinea at the nearest point, the rainforests here contained no monkeys or apes. Instead there are marsupial tree kangaroos.

The most dangerous-looking arrow was reserved for really big game, like a wild pig or a cassowary. It came with a serious business end shaped like a half-funnel, designed to drain blood from the prey. Cassowaries, Fiambo told me, they could also catch by stringing a rattan rope across a likely trail just below head-height – roughly the same for a cassowary as for a person – which was designed to break their necks as they ran into it.

Firing these arrows was tricky, since, as John pointed out, they had no fleches, and were thus prone to career off in any direction. But after a few attempts, everyone was rather impressed with my efforts, and we set off in search of dinner.

We crept along through the undergrowth for some time with bows and arrows at the ready. Early in the proceedings, John stopped abruptly and pointed upwards towards a bird I couldn't see and let off his arrow, ineffectually as it turned out. I tried to follow suit, even though I still hadn't spotted what he was aiming at, but managed not to release the arrow with all my fingers at once and it clattered harmlessly to the forest floor. Fiambo and his son Joel, who were close by, saw this and howled with laughter, scuppering any chance of spotting another bird for a good ten minutes.

After half an hour, none of us had achieved any success, and our attention was turned to foraging for crickets. Joel turned out to be the best at this task, shinning up slender saplings to reach out and knock down dead palm frond cases where crickets were habitually found. As these cases were opened up, the crickets would leap out, to be caught deftly by hand. The potential danger associated with catching these small insects was also aptly displayed by Joel, who, on one occasion, started leaping up and down himself, much to the amusement of the others. A cricket had landed on the inside of his thigh and sunk its mandibles into his flesh. The little lad pulled the cricket off his leg with such force that the head was left hanging on to his thigh and had to be extracted separately.

Our hunting trip was not exactly a triumph of man over beast, and by the end of the afternoon we returned home with a couple of dozen crickets wrapped in a large leaf and some cup-shaped mushrooms that we'd found growing on a fallen log. Fiambo also carried a stretch of bark that he'd stripped from a sapling. It would be shredded to make very strong string, John told me. The food wasn't going to make us fat, but the crickets tasted remarkably good – uncannily similar to prawns in fact – when barbecued for a minute or two on the embers of the fire. We washed them down with slugs of water drunk from lengthy green bamboo stems.

That night, like every other night chez Fiambo, the last thing I saw before drifting off to sleep was the intimidating silhouette of the mother of all tree-houses etched against the night sky.

An annoyingly perverse division of my psyche had been telling me for days that I ought to at least try climbing up the damn thing. I've never thought of myself as a subscriber to the 'because it's there' school of thought with regard to conquering physical obstacles. But in retrospect, I can only now assume that I am, because there really wasn't any other rationale for doing so.

Late on the morning of our last day in Kenalua, John and I made our way down the slight incline from Fiambo's sensibly sized tree-house to the foot of the towering tree in question. Since rising with the sun as usual that morning, I had strolled out to the forest edge for some time alone, to contemplate my vertical assignment. I had also availed myself of the Kombai toilet facilities, but by the time I was standing at the foot of the rattan ladder that led up into the heavens, the palms of my hands were sweating and my stomach was churning alarmingly, as if it had independent confirmation that this was a very bad idea.

John, of course, hardly broke his stride to climb straight up the ladder right to the very top. I craned my neck to watch him disappear into the stratosphere, looking hopefully for signs that the ladder was defective in some way, so giving me an honourable let-out from the exercise. But no such luck.

I'd talked this operation over with John, and decided that I would attempt to scale this impossible height only if he could take a rope up top, tie it to the tree, and throw it down for me to secure round my waist. John would then take up the slack as I climbed, providing some security against a fall. Naturally, this meant John himself would have to climb the ladder without any safety devices, but he wasn't fazed by this. His confidence had just been borne out, making me feel a little bit like a weakling. I consoled myself with the thought that having been brought up here, John had probably been climbing trees like this one, though possibly not quite so high, since he was a child. Whatever the rights and wrongs of this, he was now up there, having secured the rope to the tree, and I was still standing below, most definitely not up there.

I looked again, up towards John, who was now sitting nonchalantly on the tiny platform far above my head. This tree-house was a good thirty-five metres high. That's at least a hundred feet off the ground. It was way too high for my liking.

Strange things go through your mind when you attempt the impossible. For anyone who might think that the word 'impossible' is overstating the matter, let me explain. I'm not exactly afraid of heights, it's just that I'd rather avoid them. My problem lies in that perverse part of my mind that not only enjoys being high in the sky without much to hold on to, but actually delights in telling the rest of me so. Not only that, but this contrary side to my personality, which normally lies dormant, becomes particularly rebellious when at altitude. The rebellion usually takes the form of suggesting that I throw myself off. So there we are. I'm not afraid of heights, but I'm terrified that I'll cast myself into the ether, just to see what it's like.

The first third of the ladder wasn't too bad. I'd checked the rope round my waist several times before leaving the ground, and now found that the rungs were made of stout sticks and the rattan holding them was steady and strong. I talked my way up, telling myself that this wasn't really that difficult an exercise and that the Kombai made the ascent on a regular basis, so the ladder must be safe. All I had to remember was to hold on to it and everything would be fine.

Then I reached a large stick that marked the point where the first length of ladder was joined to a second. I had to manoeuvre myself around it, which wasn't easy. 'Don't look down', I told myself, but this was stupid advice because I had to look down to see where to place my feet. 'OK then, only look at your feet,' I said. 'Just don't look at the ground.'

The next stretch of ladder, the middle third of the climb, took me higher off the ground, a statement of the obvious, but I said it anyway to prove to myself that I was still on my side. Under no circumstances was I going to try and fool myself about this.

I stopped, probably half-way up, and told myself that I'd done pretty well. 'Now, if you want to,' I said to myself, 'you can go back down.'

I hesitated, caught in two minds, which is not an advisable state to be in while standing half-way up a thirty-five-metre rattan rope ladder. I was mentally veering towards a descent when John called down from on high.

'How're you doing there? The view from up here is fantastic.'

I looked around. The view was rather good from where I was standing, too, but maybe it was better still from up top. I climbed another rung.

'You're going up,' I muttered. 'You're going to the top. Keep climbing. You're going up.' And my feet obeyed.

Two-thirds of the way up, the ascent became horrifying. Until this point, the ladder had been angled in towards the tree in the conventional manner, but its final third was vertical. I didn't like it. The treehouse suddenly seemed impossibly tall, but I knew that if I stopped now I'd be stuck, so I carried on.

The next step nearly launched me on an inadvertent attempt at unaided flight because the ladder swung violently and I just clung on, my back angled towards the ground. This was ridiculous and I was terrified.

'This ladder's going the wrong way!' I complained to John.

'It has to, to get over this branch and on to the platform here,' he cried. 'But keep coming, you're doing well. You're almost there.'

I moved up another rung, and then another. I hated every step. Why was I doing this? I asked myself, it's pointless. Much against my better judgement, I stood still for a moment, taking a well-earned breather, part of me reasoned. It was a serious mistake. My left leg started shaking involuntarily. I looked down, just as far as the trembling limb, and nearly laughed. But only nearly. I was too petrified to find it amusing, and even if I had laughed, I'd never have heard it above the alarm bells ringing in my head.

'My leg's shaking,' I told John, who had now ceased to be a speck far above the ground and had regained his status as a real person. I could see the coil of rope tied to the top of the tree trunk behind him, my lifeline against possible misadventure.

'Just keep coming,' he advised. 'You're almost there.' It was easy for him to say; rather less so for me to do.

'I suppose if I want to do a poo now,' I pondered aloud, partly rhetorically and partly to John, 'I'll just have to do it in my pants.' John didn't have an answer to that.

There were only a few rungs left. My leg wasn't about to stop shaking while on the rung where I stood, so I thought I'd try the next one. Implementing this strategy took my leg's mind off the shaking.

'You really have almost made it', John told me. He was right. If I'd stretched out my hand I could have touched his leg as it dangled down from the platform.

Somehow, I'll never know exactly how, I climbed the remaining rungs and eased myself across the narrow platform and into the tallest tree-house in the world. Inside, it looked just like Fiambo's, only higher.

From my position lying on my back on the floor, the only posture that felt even vaguely safe to my mind, I shook John's hand. 'Thanks', I told him.

Incredible though Kenalua's tallest tree-house was as a piece of engineering, I spent no more than ten minutes inside it and I hated every one of them. The view that John had raved about was virtually identical to the one I'd seen while standing only half-way up the ladder. There were trees everywhere, and below them, no doubt, lurked a lot of swamp.

As John and I made our way back through the rainforest towards the airstrip the next day, having said our goodbyes to Fiambo, Joel and all the other Kombai, I got to thinking about my sojourn in the swamp.

To my mind, as I'd suspected from the start, this had been the least hospitable of the four environments I'd visited on these trips.

Despite finding an unexpected slice of paradise in the village of Jeobi, I still shuddered at the thought of the phenomenal swarms of mosquitoes I'd encountered with Jack, and the serious concerns I'd felt when paddling through Kowonep in search of crocodiles. But the biggest surprise of all lay in the reaction to my ascent of Kenalua's tallest tree-house. I had already begun to blank it out, consigning much of the experience to my memory's out-tray. But just as my recollections were fading, I compared my bid for the Kombai heavens to the earlier terrors I'd faced and decided that I'd rather spend a month in an unstable canoe with the crocs and mosquitoes than ever try to climb a ladder up to a thirty-five-metre-high tree-house again.

It was fitting that the dizzy heights of the Kombai's living quarters had wrapped up my year of investigation into how life is lived in four extreme environments. Each community I'd encountered had adapted to terrains that I still saw as difficult, but which to them were just what it was like where they lived. If you're born and brought up in the swamps of New Guinea you think nothing of nipping up and down from your tree-house every day, just as an Inuit jumps into a kayak as soon as he can walk, a Tubu woman regards a thousand-kilometre return journey across a sand sea as completely normal, and a Biaka can discern the tracks of a duiker where I see just a carpet of dead leaves.

And what, I thought to myself, would any of these remote communities make of the life that I was returning to? After baulking at a thirty-five-metre-high tree-house, I was about to hop aboard an aircraft that would take to the air without any visible means of support and rise to an inconceivable ten thousand metres above the surface of the planet. This giant mechanical bird would whisk me half way across the globe, back to the libraries of Oxford where I'd sit in my little world, surrounded by books, pondering the options for my next journey. And which world would an Inuit, Biaka, Tubu or Kombai prefer? I think I knew the answer to that.

Index